Subject to Famine

"In the districts above the Ghats
the rainfall is precarious and
the area is often subject to famine."

—*an anonymous Indian civil servant*

Subject to Famine

*Food Crises and Economic Change
in Western India, 1860-1920*

Michelle Burge McAlpin

Princeton University Press
Princeton, New Jersey

Publication of this book has been aided by a grant from
the Paul Mellon Fund of Princeton University Press

This book has been composed in Linotron Primer

Clothbound editions of Princeton University Press books
are printed on acid-free paper, and binding materials are
chosen for strength and durability

Printed in the United States of America by
Princeton University Press, Princeton, New Jersey

for
S. B. M.

Contents

List of Tables

List of Maps

List of Figures

Acknowledgments

As I was writing my dissertation on railroads and cultivation patterns in nineteenth-century India, it slowly became clear to me that existing studies of famines left many questions unanswered. At the same time, my work in the records left by the British Raj made it plain to me that materials existed to write a very different kind of study of famines and that such a study could be very useful to our understanding of the economic history of India. In attempting to write that different kind of study, I have accumulated many debts.

Alan Heston graciously shared with me his machine-readable data on the agricultural statistics of Bombay Presidency from 1885 through 1920. Jackie Sherman processed data for 1855 through 1884 and merged it with Professor Heston's data. Scott Matthews offered us occasional but vital assistance with data processing. Tufts University supplied computer time.

Collection of raw data from the files of the India Office Library and Records was made possible by two grants from the ACLS-SSRC Joint Committee on South Asia. Such data collection was made easier and quicker by the assistance of the staff of the IOL, especially Dr. Richard Bingle.

Once I had processed my data enough to be ready to talk about it, many groups were kind enough to listen to me and to offer suggestions. I want to thank the participants of the Cliometrics meetings in Madison in 1976; the workshop on Impact of Risk and Uncertainty on Economic and Social Processes in South Asia, held in Philadelphia, November 1977; the Harvard Economic History Workshop; the University of Washington Economic History Group; the Delhi School of Economics; the Columbia South Asia Seminar; and the MIT-Boston University Faculty Seminar on South Asia.

Donald Attwood, Robert Frykenberg, and Carl M. Stevens were kind enough to read a draft of the entire manuscript and offer suggestions. Dharma Kumar was unfailing in her support and criticism. Catharine R. Stimpson read the manuscript for both content and style, and she should not be blamed for my continued use of the passive voice.

The University of Pennsylvania South Asia Program and the University of Washington South Asia Center both provided me with office space and colleagues at different stages of my work—Pennsylvania when it was still in early stages and Washington as I wrote the final draft.

Marian Bollen of the University of Washington and Loretta Opes of Tufts University typed significant portions of the manuscript with efficiency and good cheer. Pat Callahan provided support in a variety of ways. Carmella Ciampa did the numerous maps and graphs that this kind of economic history requires. Dean Nancy Milburn used the Dean's discretionary fund to partially defray the expenses of final preparation of such a data-intensive manuscript.

My greatest debt is to Morris David Morris, who offered encouragement and criticism at every stage of this project.

Glossary

The spellings of transliterated words follow those in H. H. Wilson, *A Glossary of Judicial and Revenue Terms*, 2nd ed. (Delhi: Munshiram Manoharlal Oriental Publishers and Booksellers, 1968), except that diacritics have been omitted in order to simplify the appearance of the printed page. Words that are used only once in the text and that are explained where they occur are not included in this glossary.

bajra	spiked millet
balutedar	a village servant or a village officer
banjaras	itinerant cattle drovers who transported bulk goods (e.g., grain, cotton)
bigha	a pre-British land measure of varying sizes, usually less than one acre
budki	a hole or pit dug by the side of a stream to collect water for irrigation
chali	land that pays full revenue, and is cultivated by permanent residents of the village
chali ryot	the holder of *chali* land, a full member of the village
fasli	the harvest year; in Bombay, the *fasli* was the Christian year minus 590—i.e., A.D. 1818 = *fasli* 1228
inam	a grant of land at reduced tax rates, or a grant of the right to collect the land tax from some land
inamdar	the holder of an *inam*
jowar	a tall millet; sorghum
katguta	land held at a fixed rate of revenue, usually less than the ordinary rate
kaul	usually, the right to cultivate some land without paying taxes for the first several years; used by pre-British governments to repopulate deserted villages and to settle new lands
khandmakta	land leased at a reduced rate
kharif	the rainy-season or autumn crop, planted during or just after the onset of the monsoon
kulkarni	the village accountant
kunbi	a peasant
malkuri	a revenue official in charge of part of a *taluka*
mamlatdar	a revenue official in charge of a *taluka*

maund	a measure of weight, usually 82 pounds in Bombay Presidency
miras	inherited property or rights, especially land which is held by hereditary right
mirasdar	the holder of *miras* land; a full member of the village
musub	shallow red soil
patel	the village headman
rabi	the cold-season crop, sown as the monsoon retreats
regur	deep black soil
ryot	peasant, cultivator
taluka	part of a district
takavi	concessionary loans from the government for agriculturists
uparis	non-permanent cultivators in a village, usually having fewer rights than *chali ryots* or *mirasdars*
watan	the hereditary office, property, and privileges of a *balutedar*

Subject to Famine

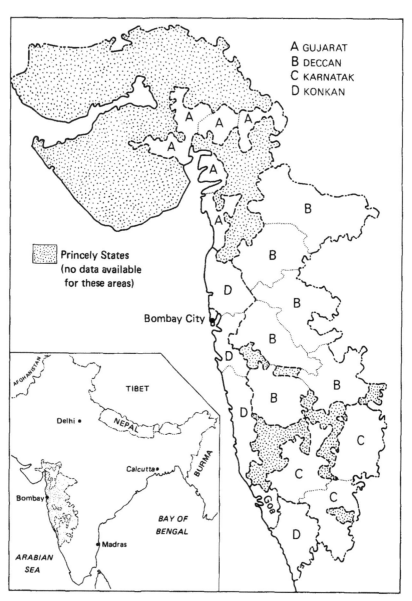

Geographical Regions of Bombay Presidency

Introduction

In the closing years of the nineteenth century, wide areas of India were wracked by famine. So severe were these famines that between 1891 and 1901 population increased by only a little over three million, while the previous decade had witnessed a population increase of almost 25 million. In Bombay Presidency the population actually declined between 1891 and 1901. The magnitude of the loss of lives is horrible to contemplate.

These famines were, and have remained, a touchstone both for anti-imperialist rhetoric and for interpretations of the economic history of the nineteenth century. In the preface to the first edition of his *Economic History of India in the Victorian Age*, R. C. Dutt contrasted the splendor of Queen Victoria's Diamond Jubilee with the 1896-1897 and 1899-1900 famines. Dutt wrote:

> Amidst signs of progress and prosperity from all parts of the Empire, India alone presented a scene of poverty and distress. A famine, the most intense and the most widely extended yet known, desolated the country in 1897. The most populous portion of the Empire had not shared its prosperity.... The Famine was not over until 1898. There was a pause in 1899. A fresh famine broke out in 1900 over a larger area, and continued for a longer period. The terrible calamity lasted for three years and millions of men perished. Tens of thousands were still in relief camps when the Delhi Darbar was held in January 1903.[1]

In the text of his still very influential book, Dutt provided a lengthy analysis of the changes in the Indian economy that flowed from British rule and led to famine.

In the years since Dutt's work appeared, his analysis has not been subjected to serious examination by scholars who work on India. In part this reflects the general lack of studies of the economic history of Indian famines, but it also reflects the sympathy with which most writers have viewed Dutt's strongly anti-colonialist views. For instance, in his major history of the administration of famine relief, B. M. Bhatia essentially took Dutt's analysis of the causes of

---

[1] Romesh Dutt, *The Economic History of India*, vol. 2, *In the Victorian Age* (first Indian edition, with a critical introduction by Prof. D. R. Gadgil, Delhi: Publications Division, Ministry of Information and Broadcasting, Government of India, 1960), p. v. (Originally published in 1904.)

famines in the late nineteenth century as given and worked from there.[2]

This book is a challenge to Dutt's analysis of the causes of famines (and the impatient reader is invited to turn immediately to Chapter 7 for the details of both Dutt's views and my challenges to them). But because there is a whole economic history of India implicit in Dutt's arguments, and because we know, still, so little about the general pattern of food crises and famines in nineteenth-century India, the book must also do much more.

Food crises and famines were widespread in the pre-modern world, and they are, distressingly, not unfamiliar in our own time. It will be useful to examine the best of the literature on such events to see how the Indian pattern may be similar or different, and to see how information gained from a study of nineteenth-century Indian food crises may contribute to a general understanding of the subject. This exercise is undertaken in Chapter 1.

It is a commonplace that the quality of the agricultural season in South Asia is a function of the monsoon, but there is little literature that relates fluctuations in the harvest to year-to-year variations in the monsoon. Similarly, farmers who live in areas where drought is a frequent occurrence are known to have developed strategies for limiting the disastrous effects of droughts. We urgently need to think more about these adaptations, especially if our increasing ability to intervene in times of drought is to permit us to mitigate rather than complicate or worsen the crises. Chapter 2 focuses on these two important and related issues—the degree of instability to which agriculture was subject and the mechanisms by which the populations of drought-prone areas sought to protect themselves.

When variations of rainfall exceed the ability of agriculturists to adapt, and when the society in which they live is unable or unwilling to provide them with alternate ways to survive (i.e., food or jobs at which to earn wages to trade for food), the number of deaths mounts. Chapter 3 asks two questions: (1) Who dies in a famine and how is the shape of the population different after a famine? (2) In specific Indian famines, how much did death rates rise?

Dutt's argument about the negative impact of British rule was based heavily on the effects he attributed to systems of land taxes the British developed for areas other than Bengal. This makes it necessary to examine the structure of the land tax system in Bombay

[2] B. M. Bhatia, *Famines in India 1860-1965: A Study in Some Aspects of the Economic History of India*, 2nd ed. (New York: Asia Publishing House, 1967).

Presidency, the levels of taxes collected, and the impact of the system on the various members of rural society. Chapter 4 undertakes these tasks.

While Chapter 4 focuses on the Bombay Survey and Settlement system and its immediate effects, Chapter 5 takes a broader look at changes in the economic environment. Changing cultivation patterns, evolving patterns of trade in foodgrains and pulses, and new opportunities in the nonagricultural sector are all examined.

Drawing together the information on fluctuations in output from Chapter 1, on changing mortality in famines from Chapter 3, and on economic changes from Chapter 5, Chapter 6 closely examines the period around the turn of the century to determine if the ability of the system to cope with harvest shortfalls had altered significantly.

The seventh and final chapter of the book presents Dutt's analysis of the causes of the famines at the end of the nineteenth century and confronts that analysis with data drawn from the earlier chapters, especially Chapter 4. Chapter 7 also contains an attempt at a new synthesis for the Indian economic history of the nineteenth and early twentieth centuries.

Because there are so few good quantitative studies of regions and their sub-units, no attempt was made to do this study at the all-India level. Instead, I have chosen to focus on Bombay Presidency and its constituent parts. There are several justifications for so doing. First, Bombay Presidency contained within itself areas that often had droughts, food crises, and famines, and also areas that were secure from such disasters. Second, the nature of the land revenue settlement in Bombay Presidency generated unusually good data on cultivation patterns and on a set of other relevant variables. Third, Dutt regarded the land tax system of Bombay Presidency as the worst of the alternatives to the Permanent Settlement of Bengal. If it is possible to contradict his analysis with data drawn from Bombay, the force of the challenge is greater than if data from some more (in Dutt's view) benign system are used.

1. Food Crises and Famines

"True famine is shortage of total food so extreme and protracted as to result in widespread persisting hunger, notable emaciation in many of the affected population, and a considerable elevation of community death rate attributable at least in part to deaths from starvation."[1] When we observe a society which has experienced true famines, three major questions present themselves. First, what caused the shortage of food? Second, if the society has had a number of famines, how have the people and the government attempted to prevent food shortages that might become famines? Third, has the society changed over time so that famines have become more or less common? In particular, has the society moved from a state in which it experienced true famine to one "when in consequence of the failure of the harvest over a large area the price of food is raised and the usual employment of labour for wages is diminished in such a degree that the poorer classes will perish from starvation unless Government intervene with measures of relief"?[2]

These three questions are explored in this chapter. The first section discusses briefly a variety of historical causes of food shortage. The second gives some examples of the kinds of systems that have evolved to mitigate the effects of weather-induced shortfalls in harvest. The third section discusses the evolution in western Europe from periods of true famine to later times of food crises. A final section suggests how the study of western India in the nineteenth and early twentieth centuries can help to shed further light on all these questions.

I. Causes of Food Shortages

An initial shortfall in food can have its origins either in a natural calamity or in the actions of men and governments.[3] A plant disease

---

[1] M. K. Bennett, "Famine," in *International Encyclopedia of the Social Sciences*, vol. 5, ed. David L. Sills ([New York:] Macmillan & Free Press, 1968), pp. 322-326.

[2] Bombay Presidency, *Famine Relief Code*, 1885, p. 1.

[3] Cornelius Walford attempted to catalogue all the famines of the world through

may begin the deadly pattern, as the potato blight did the great Irish Famine of the 1840s.[4] An insect pest can consume the growing grain and prepare the way for famine, as in Russia in the 1740s and again in 1822.[5] Excessive rains can prevent the maturation of crops, as in the Great European Famine that began in 1315.[6] Government policy can contribute to shortfalls, as when the tsar's government continued to meet export quotas in spite of droughts in 1891 and 1892.[7] The depletion of the countryside's stores to meet the needs of an army or a bureaucracy, alone or in combination with some natural catastrophe, can make a region ripe for famine, as in the Honan Province of China in 1943 and 1944[8] and in Bengal in 1943.[9] Or, as was the case in the food crises with which this book is concerned, the failure of the rains may be the first link in the chain that can lead to famine.

There is an essential difference between shortages initiated by the weather and all others, in that weather-induced shortfalls are, in the statistical sense, predictable. The weather patterns that cause crop failures occur as part of a normal, if variable, weather pattern. There are, to be sure, extraordinary weather-related crises, of which the cold summer of 1816 is perhaps the best example. Temperatures in the north Atlantic region (and perhaps others, for which records are not available) were lower than at any other period on record. But they occurred, not as part of the region's usual weather fluctuations, but because of unusually heavy atmospheric dust levels caused by the eruption of the volcano Tomboro in what is now

---

1878. He also attempted to fix their causes. Very few of the famines he listed have been studied in enough detail to make their origins clear, nor did he cover all parts of the world equally well. It is, nonetheless, probably the most extensive list of its kind. "The Famines of the World: Past and Present," *Journal of the Royal Statistical Society* 41 (September 1878):433-526; 42 (March 1879):79-265.

[4] Cecil Woodham-Smith, *The Great Hunger: Ireland 1845-49* (New York: Harper and Row, 1962).

[5] Arcadius Kahan, "National Calamities and Their Effect Upon the Food Supply in Russia (an Introduction to a Catalogue)," *Jahrbucher für Geschichte Ost-europas* Neue Folge 16 (September 1968):353-377.

[6] H. S. Lucas, "The Great European Famine of 1315, 1316, and 1317," *Speculum* 5 (October 1930):343-377.

[7] Richard G. Robbins, Jr., *Famine in Russia, 1891-1892: The Imperial Government Responds to a Crisis* (New York: Columbia University Press, 1975).

[8] Theodore H. White and Annalee Jacoby, *Thunder Out of China* (New York: William Sloane, 1946).

[9] A. K. Sen, "Starvation and Exchange Entitlements: A General Approach and Its Application to the Great Bengal Famine," *Cambridge Journal of Economics* 1 (March 1977):33-59.

Indonesia.[10] The cold weather caused widespread harvest failures in Europe, but these failures should probably be distinguished from the more common fluctuations in output that characterized medieval agriculture. The cold summer of 1816 was an extraordinary event; the harvest fluctuations of the medieval period were not. Because variations in the harvest have been *expected*, societies and their constituent parts have devised sets of actions that can reduce the variability or that can provide insurance.[11] Most of the steps that might be taken to reduce fluctuations are expensive, however, and poor societies have been able to afford fewer of them than rich societies.

II. Reduction of Risk and the Creation of Insurance

One of the easiest and most common ways of coping with variable weather has been to choose crops that can tolerate a range of conditions and still produce some harvest.[12] Reductions of variability (and perhaps increases in yields as well) have at some points in the past been achieved by control over water supplies to mitigate the effects of too much or too little rain.[13] In pre-modern times, selection of weather-resistant seeds and control of irrigation were generally the only means available to lessen the effects of the weather on the harvest.

In the last two centuries, fluctuations in food availability in the

[10] John D. Post, *The Last Great Subsistence Crisis in the Western World* (Baltimore: Johns Hopkins Press, 1977), chap. 1.

[11] I use "expected" here in the statistical sense, rather than in its everyday meaning. Therefore, this sentence should not be taken to mean that any particular harvest fluctuation is expected (we expect the harvest to be bad in 1641, good in 1645, etc.) but rather that fluctuations are expected (some of the years between 1641 and 1645 will be bad, some good).

[12] In England, early-ripening barley made it possible to get a crop even when a wet spring delayed sowing from March to May. Joan Thirsk, ed., *The Agrarian History of England and Wales*, Vol. IV:1500-1640 (Cambridge: Cambridge University Press, 1967), p. 170. In China, the importation of early-ripening rice made it possible to grow rice over a wider area and to replant after floods. Ping-ti Ho, "Early Ripening Rice in Chinese History," *Economic History Review* (series 2) 9 (no. 2, 1956):200-218; Mark Elvin, *The Pattern of the Chinese Past* (Stanford: Stanford University Press, 1973), pp. 121-124.

[13] For China, see Elvin, *Pattern of the Chinese Past*, pp. 124-128. For South India, see David Ludden, "Ecological Zones and the Cultural Economy of Irrigation in Southern Tamilnadu," *South Asia* (NS) 1 (March 1978):1-13, and "Patronage and Irrigation in Tamil Nadu: A Long Term View," *Indian Economic and Social History Review* 16 (July-September 1979):347-365.

western world have diminished as agricultural revolutions have both raised average yields and reduced the variance of yields (or at least the probability of disastrously bad harvests). In the nineteenth century the cold wet clays of the English Midlands were finally conquered by laying drainage fields.[14] In arid regions, deeper wells, higher dams, mechanical water pumps, and new technologies such as trickle irrigation have improved irrigation capabilities. Scientific breeding of seeds has improved the speed with which new varieties appear and has widened the range of weather conditions to which plants can be deliberately tailored.[15] But all of these methods of reducing the harm that weather can do required the presence of an industrializing sector. Even the drainage of England's clay soils could not proceed until the 1840s, when a cheap clay tile was produced.[16] These methods were not available to pre-modern societies, where humans and animals provided most of the power and where technical knowledge was not generally advanced enough to rapidly manipulate genetic codes.

In the absence of the ability to reduce overall fluctuations in harvests except by choice of varieties and control of water, a number of societies evolved more or less elaborate farming practices and social patterns to reduce risk and ensure survival. For instance, along the ecological frontier at the southern edge of the Sahara, the Tuareg, a pastoral nomadic people, had a social and economic system that enabled them to exploit the resources of the desert when they were plentiful (i.e., when the rainfall was good) and to retreat southward into regions of sedentary agriculture when drought reduced the desert's ability to support life.[17] Using their superior military power to establish command over resources, the Tuareg had incorporated captives, poor nomads, and sedentary agriculturists

[14] E. L. Jones, *The Development of English Agriculture 1815-1873* (London: Macmillan, 1968), p. 15.

[15] S. H. Wittwer, "Food Production: Technology and the Resource Base," in *Food: Politics, Economics, Nutrition, and Research,* ed. Philip H. Abelson (Washington, D.C.: American Association for the Advancement of Science, 1975), pp. 85-90.

[16] Jones, *Development of English Agriculture,* p. 15.

[17] This account of the Tuareg is drawn from the excellent work of Stephen Baier and Paul E. Lovejoy. See Stephen Baier and Paul E. Lovejoy, "The Tuareg of the Central Sudan: Gradations of Servility at the Desert Edge (Niger and Nigeria)," in *Slavery in Africa,* eds. Suzanne Miers and Igor Kopytoff (Madison: University of Wisconsin Press, 1977), pp. 391-411; and Stephen Baier, "Economic History and Economic Development: Drought and the Sahelian Economies of Niger," *African Economic History* 1 (No. 1, 1976): 1-16, and "Long-Term Structural Change in the Economy of Central Niger," in *West African Cultural Dynamics,* eds. B. I. Swarz and R. E. Dummet (The Hague: Mouton, 1980), pp. 587-602.

into a hierarchy whose levels determined rights and obligations through the cycle of drought and recovery. At the top of the pyramid were clans of the Tuareg nobility, who managed large numbers of dependents engaged in a variety of occupations. They settled some of their slaves on estates where they cultivated the millet the nomads needed to supplement the milk from their herds. Other dependents were entrusted with animals with which they also led nomadic lives. Still others engaged in trade with peoples farther south using the capital of their Tuareg masters. The entire system was held together by fictive kin relationships, very limited burdens of servility (in good times), and the ultimate threat of Tuareg military power.

When a drought began in the Sahel, the Tuareg nobility, with their herds and immediate families and slaves, retreated south to the estates on which their dependents were settled, claiming lodging, grain, and grazing land from them. Tuareg masters also called in the animals they had entrusted to other dependents. The loose control the Tuareg nobles maintained over their dependents facilitated the shift south when drought struck. In the variable climate of the Sahel they had developed a

> system of priority of access to resources maintained by the stratification of status. The distinctions between different kinds of dependents—which had little importance in prosperous times— came into play in periods of scarcity, when they provided a pattern for sloughing off excess populations. The social pattern offered a clearly delineated blueprint of the order of precedence from nobles down to [the lowest slaves].[18]

When the weather improved, the Tuareg nobles went back to the desert with their herds and as many dependents as the reduced herds could support.

The Tuareg controlled the region from at least the seventeenth century until the great drought of 1911-1913. By that time the actions of French colonial administrators had destroyed the military supremacy of the Tuareg nobility, in part by requisitioning increasing numbers of camels. As the Tuareg and their dependents fled south from the drought, a significant amount of permanent sedentarization took place. While some Tuareg returned to the desert after the drought ended, the desert-side economy did not regain its former levels. In addition, the Tuareg progressively lost control both of the desert-edge grazing (to Fulbe cattle herders) and of their

---

[18] Baier and Lovejoy, "The Tuareg," p. 404.

refuge areas.[19] Coupled with over-grazing on available lands and deep wells that altered grazing and migration patterns, these erosions of their economic resources left the Tuareg with very few options and helped to make their sufferings particularly acute in the Sahel drought of 1968-1974.[20]

The system of the Tuareg handled risk in two ways. First, by diversifying both their economic activities and the locations of these activities, they reduced the chance that a drought would leave them without enough resources to survive and resume their life in the desert. Second, the Tuareg used their military might to redistribute risk away from themselves and onto their dependents. When a drought occurred, it was not just that they had invested in sedentary agriculture that saved the Tuareg, but that they could enforce the primacy of their claims to the resources of that agriculture.

In an environment where much less diversification was possible and where military power lay elsewhere, European peasants had a smaller, different set of options available than the Tuareg nobles. While the open-field pattern of European agriculture has been subject to very many explanations, recent studies that focus on its risk-reducing properties appear persuasive. Plot-scattering in open fields was desirable because of the variation in soil types, drainage patterns, and microclimates (i.e., the south-facing side of a hill vs. the north-facing side). The diversity of plots within a single family's holding has been explained two ways. McCloskey has argued that the variability of each family's harvest was reduced over what it would have been had they held a single consolidated plot. In a dry year the high land with rapid drainage and good exposure to the sun yields a smaller crop and the low-lying land a larger crop. In a wet year, the advantages are reversed. A farmer who held *only* high, well-drained land or *only* low, damp land would see his total harvest vary with the weather. But by holding a scattered set of plots the farmer reduced the variance of his total harvest even while the variability of the yield from each plot remained unchanged.

Furthermore, because the plots of a scattered holding were ready to be worked at different times, a farmer could maximize the use of his own labor and that of his full-time farm servants and minimize

---

[19] Baier, "Change in Central Niger," pp. 593-596.

[20] John C. Caldwell, *The Sahelian Drought and Its Demographic Implications* (Washington, D.C.: Overseas Liaison Committee, American Council on Education, 1975).

the use of casual hired labor.[21] The use of own labor served to maximize productivity because of the observed tendency of laborers to work harder when the returns are for themselves.[22] The minimization of use of casual hired labor had another benefit to farmers. A few regularly employed laborers could easily be supervised by a farmer who was in the field among them. His own work pace and standards would set theirs. A larger number of laborers used over a shorter time would have had much higher supervision costs, if the same level of work could have been obtained at all.

Fenoaltea has further argued that, while open-field agriculture minimized each family's normal need for casual agricultural labor, it did not completely smooth the flow of consumption from year to year. To move towards that end, storage of foodgrains in excess of the current year's needs was also undertaken by those with resources to do so. This form of self-insurance is an attractive one only where there is a significant chance that the price of marketed supplies of grain will rise enough to overcome the high costs of storage. If situations are anticipated where there may be no grain available at any price, storage of grain in excess of the current year's requirements is certainly desirable. While only the top fifty percent of the population might be able to afford any storage as insurance, there is evidence that they did seek this form of insurance.[23]

Whether we accept the argument that holdings of scattered plots within open fields were intended to minimize the variations of harvests from year to year or the alternative that scattering maximized output by permitting maximum use of own labor while *storage* of grain provided insurance, the importance of weather-induced risk in shaping the actions of medieval agriculturists is clear. The role of risk reduction in the eventual enclosure of open fields is less obvious. In both cases it seems possible that the system was overdetermined or had joint products: Scattering both reduced the variation of each family's harvest *and* minimized use of casual hired labor; and consolidation occurred when risk could be reduced by

[21] Donald N. McCloskey, "English Open Fields as Behavior Towards Risk," in *Research in Economic History*, vol. 1, ed. Paul Uselding (Greenwich, Conn.: JAI Press, 1976), pp. 143-152.

[22] Stefano Fenoaltea, "Risk, Transaction Costs, and the Organization of Medieval Agriculture," *Explorations in Economic History* 13 (April 1976):143-144; "Fenoaltea on Open Fields: A Reply," *Explorations in Economic History* 14 (October 1977): 408.

[23] Fenoaltea, "Medieval Agriculture," pp. 137-141; "A Reply," p. 407.

new techniques and communal control impeded the adoption of those new techniques.[24]

Studies like those of the Tuareg and of open-field agriculture in Europe are rare. It may be that the development of elaborate systems to provide insurance against harvest instability is itself rather rare. Certainly the phenomenon of variable harvests and the threat that they will bring death and starvation have been more common than studies of systems of insurance at the village level or below.

On the other hand, attempts by the state to devise methods of insurance have been, if not widely studied, at least widely noted. In pre-modern societies the most widespread state action to limit fluctuations in consumption appears to have been the storage of grain in some form of "ever-nomal" granaries. In China, a system of granaries was designed to supplement the insurance provided by other methods, especially elaborate water-control systems.[25] While the granary system may have been more elaborate on paper than it was in reality, it called for the establishment and maintenance of three types of granaries to both stabilize prices and provide emergency relief. Imperial granaries were located in each province and district, administered by local officials under imperial rules and regulations. These granaries, often serving urban areas, were to be filled with grain purchased at harvest and contributed by wealthy members of society. They provided relief by selling grain at "normal" prices (i.e., below prevailing prices in times of scarcity) and by giving

[24] McCloskey has argued that the main function of plot-scattering was the reduction of year-to-year harvest variation and that peasants sacrificed about ten percent of potential income to achieve this insurance. Fenoaltea has argued that the main function of scattered plots was to permit optimal scheduling of work using family labor and that in a period of population pressure on land, villages would not have sacrificed income to achieve stability for families' *shares* of the total harvest. If consolidated holdings actually had higher average yields, Fenoaltea argues, then villages would have consolidated holdings and redistributed food with interest-free loans each year. But no brief summary can do justice to the richness and elegance of the debate between Fenoaltea and McCloskey. Full citations to the debate are provided in the bibliography.

[25] Hsiao cites an early twentieth-century work that lists twelve measures for coping with famines, including construction of water works to avert crop failures, public works employment in famine-stricken regions, encouragement of grain trade, and a variety of "relief" measures. A number of these latter measures (giving grain to the destitute, selling grain at reduced prices, and grain loans) were dependent on the existence of stored stocks of grain. Hsiao himself has provided the best discussion in English of the granary system in the nineteenth century, as well as a brief history of the system, and the following paragraphs rely on him. Kung Chuan Hsiao, *Rural China: Imperial Control in the Nineteenth Century* (Seattle: University of Washington Press, 1960), pp. 144-183, 549-552, 605.

loans at no interest or by waiving interest where crop losses exceeded 30 percent. The imperial granary system was supplemented by charitable and community granaries in the countryside. Charitable granaries drew their grain stocks from wealthy people seeking imperial rewards, and the grain was given away to those who needed it. Community granaries of the countryside seem to have been intended as a decentralized supplement to imperial granaries. The intended source of their stocks is not entirely clear, but one imperial edict stated that "the original intention is to make the people accumulate a reserve by themselves, so that urgent needs of the people may be met by their own resources and provisions."[26] However, contributions to the community granaries could be rewarded in the same fashion as those to charitable granaries.

The granary system worked best when a strong imperial government could compel compliance with its edicts, and it deteriorated as imperial control did. Even in areas where the desire of local officials to maintain the granaries in their districts was above reproach, their limited command over resources made the task difficult. In the poorer provinces, grain reserves could be accumulated only at the cost of current consumption, and this was obviously very difficult. Insufficient as the system of granaries may have been to relieve distress caused by crop failures, it was probably the best alternative in a large country nearly lacking in means of transport for bulk commodities. Unfortunately, no very thorough studies of the degree of insurance provided by the system are available in English.

By the nineteenth century, Russia also had a system of government-mandated grain storage to smooth fluctuations in consumption. Expanding on an earlier program of grain stores for tiding government-owned serfs over harvest failures, the tsarist government in 1834 required the maintenance of grain stocks throughout Russia.[27] The intent was to collect grain from peasants over a number of years so as to maintain a storage reserve equal to 200 kilograms of grain per adult male. However, the poverty of the peasants from whom the grain was collected, the frequency of harvest failures, and the inefficiency of the bureaucratic establishment prevented the achievement of the desired reserve, although some grain was stored in public granaries. With some of the lowest yield-to-seed ratios in Europe and with agriculture expanding south and

[26] Quoted in Hsiao, *Rural China*, p. 151.
[27] All details of Russian programs are drawn from Kahan, "Natural Calamities in Russia," unless otherwise noted.

east into more drought-prone regions, the nineteenth century in Russia was marked by repeated harvest shortfalls and a recurrent lack of resources to meet them.

In both Russia and China the ability of the state to limit the effects of harvest failures was sharply constrained by the lack of cheap transport for bulk commodities. Even after the construction of the Grand Canal to move grain from southern China to supply the administration and army around Peking, transport was still at least one-third of the cost of rice in the north. Away from major water routes, transport was even more expensive, doubling the cost of rice for a relatively short overland journey.[28] Russia had similar problems with lack of transport, although the geography and climate yielded a different set of specifics: Rivers that could provide transport were frozen much of the year, spring thaws turned roads in the black-earth country to quagmires, heavy snows blocked land transport in winter.[29] Because of the difficulties and cost of shifting grain among regions, encouragement of storage within a region was an economical alternative. But in both states the small role of the government in the economy—the small percentage its collections and expenditures had in the total—limited the leverage it could exert to prevent or relieve famines. When famine was the result of massive shortfalls in grain production, even the redirection of all government resources to the relief of shortages could barely reduce the suffering.

III. The Evolution from Famine to Food Crisis

The removal of the constraints of both limited transport capacity and small relative government size, supplemented by some increases in productivity, had an important role in the elimination of subsistence crises in western Europe. During the eighteenth century the combination of new staple crops like potatoes and maize increased the productivity of agriculture, as did changes in rotations and other improvements in farming practices.[30] These increases in

---

[28] Lack of transport for bulk commodities rendered relief of famine in four northern provinces of China almost impossible when drought occurred in 1877. Ping-ti Ho, *Studies on the Population of China, 1368-1953* (Cambridge: Harvard University Press, 1959), pp. 231-233.

[29] Robbins, *Famine in Russia*, pp. 56, 61-62, 72.

[30] Langer has argued that higher yields from potatoes and maize were important in permitting the growth of European populations before major improvements in agricultural practice occurred. William Langer, "American Foods and Europe's Population Growth 1750-1850," *Journal of Social History* 8 (Winter 1975):51-60.

output were sufficient to remove the sting from many of the fluctuations in harvest caused by the weather.

While the "cold summer" of 1816 and its attendant harvest failures occurred very late in the evolution of European states and transport networks, an examination of the success with which various regimes dealt with that severe scarcity can illustrate the most important differences between the medieval and early modern situations. By 1816 long-distance shipping and colonization had made available better external sources of food. For all or almost all areas of Europe, increased imports from the United States and the Russian empire did much to alleviate the shortfalls in Europe's own harvest. Imports from Russia were facilitated by a shift of trade from Baltic ports to Odessa in the ice-free Black Sea.[31]

With the availability of imported grain and flour, the "primary task of European governments was to compensate for the grain deficit and thus to keep food prices within reach of the poorest segment of the population."[32] Not all governments encouraged imports with equal degrees of vigor or success. The more developed states, either through private commercial channels or under government auspices, imported enough food to avert more than modest rises in mortality.[33] Britain, France, and the German states generally succeeded in keeping food within the reach of the poor and in limiting mortality. But less developed states, including the Hapsburg Empire, Ireland, and the rural areas of Italy, all "experienced the familiar sequence of famine and mortality characteristic of the old regime."[34]

The problems of the less-developed regions in securing food were only one aspect of the ultimate problem of relief to the poorer sections of society. Means had also to be devised to distribute the grain or bread. In some areas, imports on private or government account kept market prices within reach of most of the populace. In Britain, where an established system of public poor relief minimized the administrative problems, expenditures on poor relief rose 46 percent between 1815 and 1818. Even so, cities and towns found they needed to open soup kitchens and increase general relief. Some cities also

---

[31] All of the discussion of the food crisis of 1816-17 relies heavily upon Post, *Last Great Subsistence Crisis*. For his views on American and Russian food supplies, see p. 55.

[32] Post, *Last Great Subsistence Crisis*, p. 53.

[33] Post, *Last Great Subsistence Crisis*, pp. 110-122.

[34] Post, *Last Great Subsistence Crisis*, p. 60.

sought to use public works to put money into the hands of the poor.[35] In most of the rest of northwest Europe a combination of public and private charity prevailed. In the Hapsburg empire the "extensive survival of the manorial system and feudal relationships in the empire . . . insulated some peasants against the extreme distress experienced elsewhere."[36] The monarchy exhorted the big landowners to remember their obligations to the poorer strata of society in times of crisis. Post attributed differences in mortality among European states to the effectiveness of their welfare efforts and implicitly linked the effectiveness of their welfare efforts to their degree of development.[37]

The very development of transport and increase in the power of the state that enabled governments and private agencies to mitigate the worst consequences of crop failures introduced a set of conflicts that matured along with the transport and the state. So long as transport networks were poor, crop failures tended to be severe where they occurred but to leave other regions quite unaffected. Relief supplies, if they could be gotten, had to come into the region by water transport. Adjacent land areas, their own harvests effectively safeguarded by the high cost of overland transport, might see increased numbers of beggars or vagabonds from the famine-afflicted region, but they did not typically see merchants proposing to buy up some portion of their harvest at high prices. In the event that such merchants did appear, the local authorities were commonly willing to limit or forbid exports. From the sixteenth century on, as food prices rose and improved roads lowered transport costs, overland transport of grain became more feasible. The improved and expanded market networks made it ever less likely that a single region would starve because of the failure of its own harvest. At the same time, these growing markets meant that the shortfall of grain in one region could raise prices in others where the harvest was normal or abundant. Those who depended on purchases in local grain markets for some or all of their daily bread resisted these tendencies. At the corporate level, market rules proliferated that guaranteed retail purchasers first claim on supplies of grain and other comestibles. At the popular level, poorer people dependent on the market for food sometimes took actions to forcibly prevent the export of local foodstuffs.

[35] Post, *Last Great Subsistence Crisis*, pp. 63-64.
[36] John D. Post, "Famine, Mortality, and Epidemic Disease in the Process of Modernization," *Economic History Review* (series 2) 39 (February 1976):24.
[37] Post, *Last Great Subsistence Crisis*, p. 67.

The growth of the state and its dependents (the army, the bureaucracy, and frequently the towns themselves) placed further pressures on the old ways of allocating the harvest. The state needed to gain control of surplus grain to guarantee food to its dependents at reasonable prices. The old rules and customs that divided the emerging state into numerous grain markets were viewed as impediments to the state's need for control. But as the state gained power at the expense of the localities, internal markets widened and prices in different regions tended to converge to reflect high demand anywhere in the system. To the extent that the state was based in cities, the need to guarantee low food prices was a particularly pressing one. The populace tended to attribute rises in prices to hoarding by bakers, millers, and traders, and if actions by the authorities did not quickly lower prices to "just" levels, food riots could occur. Particularly when such riots occurred or threatened in capital cities, they could not but be a threat to the continued power of the rulers.[38]

After 1830, both food riots and blockages of export of grain generally vanished from western Europe. Rising incomes, increased imports of foodstuffs, and the shift of power away from rural areas (or some accommodation with rural interests) all contributed to their end. But for the period that they had existed, food riots and blockages represented a new food picture for western Europe. No longer did absolute shortages of food threaten massive malnutrition and death. Instead, high prices and low incomes, perhaps coupled with significant amounts of unemployment, threatened the ability of the poorer sections of the population to consume their usual diet. With blockages and food riots, these sections of the population were making clear their belief that they had a right to certain amounts of food at certain prices. They sought to resist the pull of market forces drawing grain from one region where it was cheap to another where it was dear. European states coped with their discontents either by regulation of markets to keep prices low, or by some form of relief designed to raise their incomes.

We can trace three stages in the evolution of European food supplies from medieval to modern times. In the first of these, subsistence agriculture and self-insurance, either by individuals or localities, predominated. High transport costs and political disorder

[38] Discussion of the forces underlying food riots is drawn from Charles Tilly, "Food Supply and Public Order in Modern Europe," in *The Formation of National States in Western Europe*, ed. Charles Tilly (Princeton: Princeton University Press, 1975), pp. 380-455.

prevented the movement of grain overland for any considerable distance. When crop failures exceeded the insurance available locally, true famine occurred and people died of malnutrition and the diseases attendant upon it. In the second, improvements in transport and political order facilitated the movement of grain, at least in years of some crop shortages, among regions. This had two effects: famine and rises in mortality were reduced, but regions with good harvests faced higher prices for marketed food. Because of the inelastic demand for food, even modest reductions of marketed food supplies can cause large increases in price, and it was these increases (or the perceived threats thereof) that stimulated the food riots and blockages of exports that characterized this stage. In the third stage, further declines in transport costs, new crops and improved farming techniques, and the availability of new sources of supply from the United States and southern Russia completed the process of mitigation of local crop failures begun in the second stage and simultaneously limited the rises in prices in regions with good harvests. The diversification of sources of food supplies generated other problems for farmers, but that is a story of the problems of plenty, not scarcity.

IV. The Usefulness of Studying India

This brief survey of food crises highlights several themes that need attention if we are to increase our understanding of such crises in either the past or the present. First, we need to take greater cognizance of the relationship between weather and crop failures, not as a year-to-year pattern of cause and effect, but rather as an environment of predictable variation. When we do so, it is then possible to view a major portion of food crises not as isolated manifestations of the wrath of whatever gods may be, but as part of a pattern of yield variability. This leads naturally to a second theme, that of attempts by various units of society to generate insurance against crop failures and generally to provide smoother streams of consumption than production. The creation of insurance requires both real resources and some institutions of a more or less formal type (see the foregoing examples of the Tuareg and open-field agriculture), and we need to examine the total costs of insurance to the society. The third theme that emerges is the changing nature of what we call food crises as modernization of the economy and the state takes place. It is a commonplace to say that true famine (absolute unavailability of food) has been replaced by lack of purchasing power for some sections of the population. But research on the transformation of food crises has been as limited as the observation that it occurred has been widespread.

India presents an unusually good opportunity for the study of all these problems (and many others as well). When British rule became a fact in western India in the early part of the nineteenth century, a society of settled agriculturists with a fairly low level of technology acquired a set of rulers, a very thin layer to be sure, who set about keeping records of revenues, crops, rainfall, births, deaths, epidemics, and famines (among other series). These data permit us to reconstruct patterns of crop failure and famine, as well as their demographic consequences. The voluminous reports of early British civil servants also permit us to explore the forms of insurance that farmers in Western India sought to create. And last, but perhaps most important, we have the information to trace the evolution of food crises in western India from "true famine" to "lack of purchasing power" and to observe the roles of general economic changes and administrative relief efforts in the curtailment of mortality from crop failures.

2. *The Famine Phenomenon: Insecurity and Adaptation*

Much of India is covered with rather good soil; almost all of India has warm temperatures and long growing seasons. All that is needed, for much of India, to make soil and sun productive is water. But for great tracts of the subcontinent that derive almost all of the moisture needed for agriculture from the monsoon rains, the supply of water is uncertain. In some regions, like Bengal, while drought can be a threat, the greatest danger is that the monsoon will bring floods and cyclones. But for a much wider area the danger is that the rains will be scanty or poorly timed. Seeds may fail to germinate if there is too long a break in the rains. Seedlings may wither and die. The supply of grass and other fodder for livestock may shrivel if the rains do not come. The village supply of drinking water can grow scarce and foul. If the immediately preceding years have been ones of good rains and good harvests, there may be enough grain stored in the village to avert starvation. But if the several previous harvests have been poor, supplies of grain will be low, and villagers will face hunger and starvation. A famine will begin.

Now, in the last quarter of the twentieth century, the sequence from inadequate or badly timed rainfall is unlikely to proceed beyond the destruction of crops. Expansion of transport networks, of alternate economic opportunities, and of government relief efforts have sharply diminished, if not entirely eliminated, the probability that agriculturists and their cattle will face starvation. But this chapter is concerned with the period before these changes occurred. For centuries a significant portion of Indian agriculturists have lived in drought-prone areas. With the exception of the southwest coast and small parts of the southeast coast, no part of the subcontinent escaped experiencing some degree of famine during the nineteenth century. This chapter attempts to answer two basic questions about one region, the Bombay Presidency, where drought was particularly common: How can the variability of agricultural seasons be measured? What adaptations and insurance mechanisms did the agriculturists of this region use to cope with that variability?[1]

[1] The precise geographical coverage and level of aggregation of the analysis will

I. The Monsoon and the Agricultural Year

Most of the Indian subcontinent receives nearly all of its yearly rainfall during the summer monsoon.[2] Fueled by the sun's heat, a great circulation of air determines the goodness of the agricultural year in India. As the tilt of the earth with respect to the sun changes through the course of the seasons, this great circulation moves farther north in summer and back to the south in winter. It is in summer, when the northern edge of the pattern lies close to the Himalayas, that winds blow across the Arabian Sea and the Bay of Bengal.[3] By the last week in May these moisture-laden winds bring the monsoon rains to Sri Lanka (see Map 2.1). By the first of June the rains have advanced into the southernmost parts of peninsular India. Over the next ten days the rains move to Bombay. By June 15 the monsoon will cover all of Gujarat. Along the west coast the rains are heavy, as the sharp rise of the Western Ghats traps much of the moisture in the winds. To the east of the Ghats rainfall diminishes quickly for some distance inland and then begins to increase again as more moisture enters the area from the portion of the monsoon coming in from the Bay of Bengal (see Map 2.2).[4]

Once the rains have begun over western India, the fields prepared during the hot weather can be sown with *kharif* crops. These include jowar, bajra, and cotton, as well as some less important grains,

vary from chapter to chapter because of the nature of the available data and because certain questions asked are relevant to some but not all parts of the Bombay Presidency. As the frontispiece map shows, the Presidency consisted of four geographical regions—Gujarat, Deccan, Karnatak, and Konkan. Each of these regions (frequently called *divisions* in British records) was made up of several districts, for a total of eighteen districts in the Presidency. Each district, in turn, contained several *talukas* and each *taluka* consisted of 50 to 300 villages. There are some data series available for each of these levels. In general, the smaller the unit (i.e., village as opposed to *taluka, taluka* as opposed to district) the more fragmentary, inconsistent, and inaccessible are the surviving series. The construction of uniform data for, say, the district level is not possible because not enough *taluka*-level data survive to produce reasonable district-level figures. For those variables where district-level data are available, it is possible to produce series for regions or divisions. Confronted with these problems, I have tried to work at a consistent level within each chapter and to work at the most disaggregated level possible with the given data sources and a reasonable economy of time and space. Maps are provided to assist the reader in locating the specific geographical areas being discussed in each chapter.

[2] O.H.K. Spate, *India and Pakistan, A General and Regional Geography*, 2nd ed. (London: Methuen, 1957), chap. 2.

[3] Reid A. Bryson and Thomas J. Murray, *Climates of Hunger* (Madison: University of Wisconsin Press, 1977), pp. 101-103.

[4] P. K. Das, *The Monsoon*, 2nd ed. (New York: St. Martins, 1972), chap. 2.

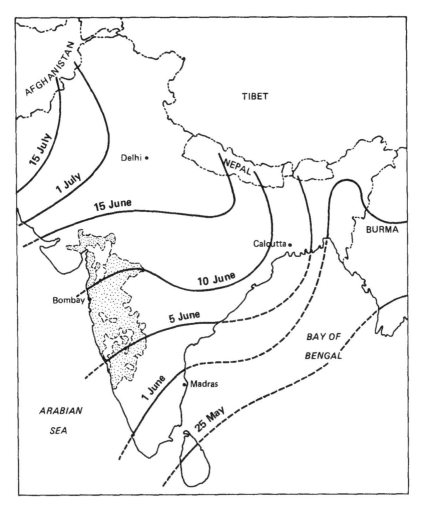

MAP 2.1 Advance of the Monsoon

SOURCE: Das, *The Monsoon*, p. 12.

pulses, and oilseeds, The better the early rains are, the more crops
will be sown on lands that can grow either *kharif* or *rabi* (cold
weather) crops. When the monsoon is "good," showers will continue
in the region through July, August, and September. As the monsoon
retreats (the shifting of the great circulation of air back to its more
southerly location), most of western India receives additional rainfall
between September 15 and October 15 or November 1 (see Map
2.3). In the expectation of these rains, fields are prepared for the

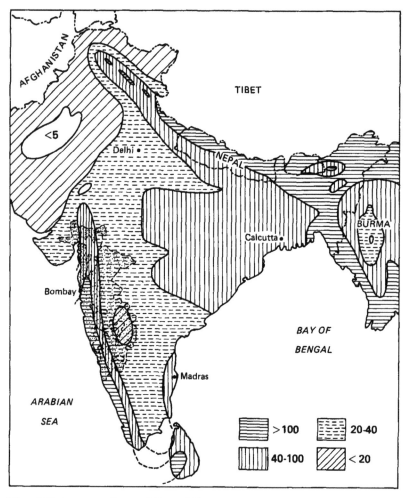

MAP 2.2 Average Annual Rainfall

SOURCE: Spate, *India and Pakistan*, p. 51.

rabi crops, including wheat, jowar, pulses, and oilseeds. The rains of the retreating monsoon are less certain than those of June and July, and the yield from *rabi* crops is correspondingly more variable. The balance between *kharif* and *rabi* plantings in a given area is determined by soils and rainfall patterns.

The determination of the agricultural calendar by the monsoon can be seen in the sowing dates for jowar. In a southern district of

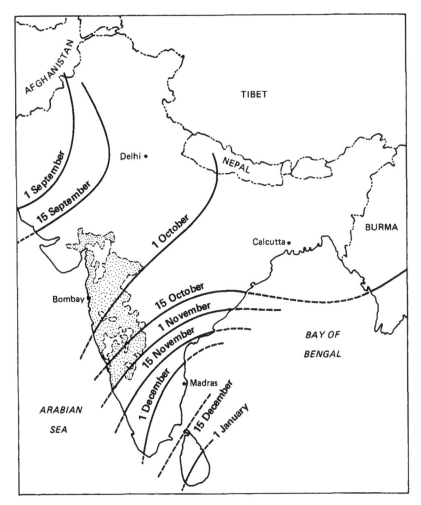

MAP 2.3 Retreat of the Monsoon

SOURCE: Das, *The Monsoon*, p. 15.

the Presidency, like Bijapur, sowing for the *kharif* crop begins in the first week of June and continues through the first week of July. In a district in the middle of the Presidency, like Ahmednagar, sowing begins in the last week of June and continues through the middle of July. At the northern extremity of the Presidency, in the district of Ahmedabad, sowing of jowar does not start until almost the middle of July, and it continues until the first week of August.

In all of these districts there is a second period during or just before the retreating monsoon passes through them when the *rabi* crops are sown.[5]

When this pattern of circulation is altered, the monsoon rains "fail" or are "scanty." Due to the failure of the entire circulation of air (governed by the intertropical discontinuity) to shift as far north as its normal location, the monsoon does not advance all the way into Rajasthan, Sind, and Punjab.[6] The southwest monsoon winds blow with less force and less moisture is carried across the Ghats to be dropped on the dry districts of the Deccan and Karnatak. Since the southern districts of Gujarat lie open to the sea (rather than shielded behind the Ghats), they are not always affected as severely as the Deccan and Karnatak. But northern parts of Gujarat may be affected by the general failure of the monsoon to advance into Rajasthan and Sind.

When the monsoon deviates from its normal pattern, agricultural operations are disrupted. If the early rains do not occur, agricultural operations for the *kharif* crops may not even begin. Little or nothing will be sown. If the early rains occur, sowing will take place, but germination may be limited by lack of continuing showers. If germination occurs, seedlings may not survive an extended break in the rains. As the crops grow, later breaks in the rain or scanty falls limit the number and size of maturing plants. Many of these problems can occur even in a year with near-normal amounts of rainfall if it falls at the wrong times. On the other hand, a quite good yield can result if all of a less-than-normal amount of rainfall comes at exactly the right times.

Deviations of the monsoon from its normal pattern have been common. While the data exist for some regions to analyze rainfall day by day (as H. H. Mann did for four districts in Bombay Presidency),[7] it will be enough here to indicate the year-to-year variation in total precipitation to which districts could be subject. Figure 2.1 shows fluctuation in rainfall for one district in each of the Presidency's divisions. Table 2.1 summarizes rainfall data for seventeen districts.

Of the four divisions of Bombay Presidency, only three—Gujarat,

[5] Bombay Presidency, Department of Land Revenue and Agriculture, *Dates of Sowing and Harvesting Important Crops in the Bombay Presidency* (Bombay: Government Central Press, 1904).

[6] Bryson and Murray, *Climates of Hunger*, pp. 104-106.

[7] H. H. Mann, *Rainfall and Famine: A Study of Rainfall in the Bombay Deccan, 1865-1938* (Bombay: Indian Society of Agricultural Economics, 1955).

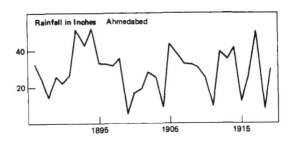

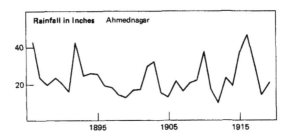

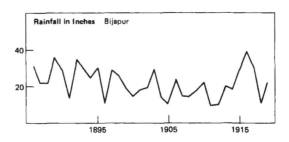

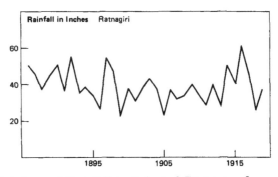

FIGURE 2.1 Annual Rainfall in Selected Districts of
Bombay Presidency, 1869-1920

SOURCE: Appendix A, Table A-1.

the Deccan, and the Karnatak—have had weather-related famines. In the thirteen districts of these divisions for which data are given in Table 2.1, the average rainfall of two districts is below 25 inches per year. Four more have average rainfall between 25 and 30 inches; three districts receive 30 to 35 inches; one has average rainfall between 35 and 40 inches; the remaining three districts get more

TABLE 2.1. Summary Statistics on Rainfall

Division and Station	(1) Years Covered	(2) Average Rainfall (inches)	(3) Standard Deviation (inches)	(4) Coefficient of Variation (percent)	(5) Range (inches)
Gujarat					
Ahmedabad Observatory	1869-1945	30.56	11.76	38	4.84-78.64
Kaira	1858-1945	32.04	12.65	39	6.05-68.70
Broach	1878-1945	36.97	13.48	36	9.61-69.99
Surat Observatory	1877-1945	42.38	14.41	34	14.29-84.61
Deccan					
Khandesh (Erandol)	1879-1945	28.69	8.34	29	12.26-52.49
Nasik	1866-1945	28.84	9.07	31	14.57-60.62
Ahmednagar	1869-1945	24.41	8.67	36	8.46-44.62
Poona	1875-1945	27.95	8.26	30	12.37-47.42
Sholapur Observatory	1877-1944	27.75	9.28	33	12.81-68.13
Satara	1860-1945	40.86	9.42	23	17.27-68.38
Karnatak					
Belgaum Observatory	1856-1945	50.28	9.97	20	28.74-86.88
Bijapur	1878-1945	22.33	7.65	34	9.58-39.03
Dharwar	1878-1945	31.89	7.71	24	20.17-48.33
Konkan					
Kolaba (Alibag)	1878-1945	84.33	20.38	24	28.37-145.02
Thana (Bassein)	1878-1945	77.66	20.06	26	30.76-130.28
Ratnagiri Observatory	1877-1945	101.65	22.54	22	56.19-165.53
Kanara Observatory	1880-1938	118.79	23.67	20	72.33-184.39

SOURCE Calculated from Appendix A, Table A-1.

than 40 inches of rain annually. In contrast, the four districts of the Konkan division all have average annual rainfall greater than 75 inches. When we look at the variability of rainfall from year to year, we find that the average coefficient of variation (standard deviation as a percentage of the mean) for the Gujarat districts is 37 percent; for the Deccan districts, 30 percent; for the Karnatak, 26 percent; and for the Konkan, 23 percent. The relationship of these fluctuations in rainfall to those in crop yields will be discussed below.

II. The Variability of Agricultural Output

Because a main purpose of this monograph is to examine the consequences of crop failures, it is clearly necessary to have some measure of year-to-year fluctuations in agricultural output. The ideal series would be one for total output of foodgrains and pulses in tons per year. No such series exists nor, I will argue, should attempts be made to construct it. If we consider the components of such a series, the problems will become clear.

A series on total output would have to be made up (for the period before the interpretation of aerial photographs became a science) as the product of total acreage planted and average yield per acre. Serious errors in either of these parts will be transmitted to the final product. For Bombay Presidency, the cadastral survey (discussed in Chapter 4) resulted in the creation of village records of size of fields that could be used by village-level officials to report on the acreage planted with different crops in their villages. For administrative purposes, villages were grouped into *talukas* and *talukas* into districts. The acreage statistics were summed over villages into *taluka*-level reports and then over *talukas* to district reports. Generally speaking, the reports on acreages planted for all those Bombay districts where the cadastral survey had been completed are considered quite reliable.[8] One component of a series on output is therefore available.

Existing figures on yields per acre for major crops grown in Bombay Presidency are made up from two components. The first of these is the *standard yield*. This yield was fixed, and revised from time to time, by the revenue and agricultural authorities and was in-

---

[8] The acreage statistics have not been so widely commented upon as the yield statistics, in part, I suspect, because most people who work in the area do consider Bombay Presidency's acreage figures to be good. This assumption of goodness rests largely upon our knowledge of how they were collected rather than on any independent checks. For further information, see Appendix D.

tended to represent an average or normal yield. To obtain yield per acre figures for a specific year, the standard yield was multiplied by a *condition factor* that, in theory, gave the relationship of that year's crop to the standard. The product of the standard yield and the condition factor was called the *revenue yield*, although for most of the period this figure had no regular relationship to how rigorously land taxes were collected.

The standard yields are the least reliable of these figures. Initially, in the 1880s, they were fixed at levels that were too high, if we judge them by the more reliable yield figures of the 1940s and 1950s. The episodic revisions to which they were subject generally lowered them with the intent of bringing them closer to actual yields and *not* with the intent of reflecting real declines in yields per acre. The result is that the series of revenue yields derived from standard yields has a spurious downward trend for some crops.[9]

We have little more information about how condition factors were generated than we have about how standard yields were derived. Village-level officials were supposed to examine the crops in their area and report on them, assigning the current crop a valuation in annas (an anna is one-sixteenth of a rupee). Agricultural land was also sometimes classed in annas, and this system of classifying crops may have predated the British administration. However nicely village officials may have judged year-to-year fluctuations in crops, there is no certainty (nor was there any in the nineteenth century) about their standard.[10] Would a crop valued at sixteen annas have been the best crop to be expected? Or would it have been an average crop? There is evidence that it was neither, i.e., crops are occasionally valued at eighteen or twenty annas, but the average of all valuations is far below sixteen annas. There is also no certainty that valuations are linear, i.e., that an eight-anna crop was one-half the yield of a sixteen-anna crop. Given these problems, it is not possible using historical standard yield and condition factor data to construct a series of total outputs of food grains and pulses in which any confidence can be placed.

But perhaps the addition of some contemporary data could enable us to construct a reliable output series. Alan Heston has argued that by using data on (1) yields generated by crop-cutting experiments

[9] Alan Heston, "Official Yields Per Acre in India, 1886-1947: Some Questions of Interpretation," *Indian Economic and Social History Review* 10 (December 1973):303-332, and "A Further Critique of Historical Yields per Acre in India," *Indian Economic and Social History Review* 15 (April-June 1978):187-210.

[10] Heston, "Official Yields," pp. 313-320, and "Further Critique," pp. 194, 199.

conducted in the 1940s and 1950s as the standard yields, (2) fluctuations shown in the condition factors, and (3) acreage statistics, generation of a reasonably good series on output is possible.[11] While this methodology is the best available, the resulting output series still rests on a questionable assumption: that there was no change in yields, either upwards or downwards, over a period of 60 years. There is about as much evidence for this assumption as there is for assuming either an increase or a decline in yields, but that merely reflects the early stages of our research into the subject rather than any special support for Heston's assumption. So even if we make use of contemporary data to fix the level of average yields, construction of a series on quantity of output still requires enormous faith. And it yields a series that for historical work may be spuriously precise.

If available series on agricultural output are rejected, what alternatives can be devised? It is well to keep in mind that Heston was attempting to measure the *value* of output for all of agriculture, while my primary purpose is to have a measure of the *fluctuations* of food production from year to year. This simplifies the task. One important element in any measure of food production must be the acreage on which food crops are grown—statistics that are both available for most of the Presidency and quite reliable. The second element needed is some indicator of the *variations* in yield per acre, even if the absolute levels of yields seem impossible to ascertain with any high degree of confidence. There are two obvious candidates for such an indicator: condition factors and annual rainfall. The problems with condition factors have already been discussed, but it is not clear that these problems militate against their use as measures of year-to-year changes, provided that we take care how we use them.

There are also problems in the use of annual rainfall as an indicator of fluctuations. While it is a commonplace that the quality of the harvest in South Asia is a function of the quality of the monsoon, the relationship has defied estimation with historical data. The most serious study of the relationship is H. H. Mann's work on rainfall and famine. Noting that while total rainfall was certainly important in determining how good the crops would be, Mann argued that a better predictor of the quality of the harvest could be derived by using a measure he labelled "effective" rainfall. By this he meant "the *maximum* portion of the rain which could under the

---

[11] Heston, "Further Critique," p. 209.

most favorable conditions be useful for sowing or for growing crops in the famine areas of the Deccan."[12] To arrive at this figure he sought to eliminate from the total rainfall that which was clearly useless for agriculture, such as falls outside the growing seasons, scattered showers at the onset of the rains that were inadequate to permit sowing, rainfall in excess of two inches per day, and other isolated falls not likely to be useful. Mann also considered the rainfall by various dates in the growing season in his attempts to find a way to predict the "goodness" of the season. The measure of the goodness of the season Mann used was constructed by taking the acreage planted with staple crops (generally jowar, bajra, wheat, cotton, and rice), multiplying this figure by "the relative yield of these crops," and converting all figures to a percentage of the best year on record.[13] While his efforts were heroic, his results were disappointing (as he was the first to admit). The linear relationship between effective rainfall and the goodness of the season was low for the four districts Mann investigated, and he tried no other specifications.[14]

The lack of success Mann met with may have been due to his data (his measure of goodness, which appears to include standard yields, is particularly suspect) or to the linear specification which he used. While we could vary the form of the relationship, we would need a relationship between rainfall and output estimated from very high-quality data before we could discard the information we have on fluctuations—namely, condition factors. Such a relationship may become available at some time, either from contemporary work or from as yet unexplored unofficial sources on yields in the nineteenth century.

But even if the statistical problems of data and specification could be overcome, it appears that Mann's approach is flawed. There is a conceptual reason for hesitating to use rainfall as an indicator of food production. If, as I will argue later in this chapter, farmers choose the varieties of crops they plant (drought-resistant vs. not-so-resistant), the mix of crops they plant (more bajra, less jowar, etc.), and the planting times to try to reduce fluctuations in food production, their very success will decrease the power of variations in rainfall to explain variations in output. The more options farmers

---

[12] Mann, *Rainfall and Famine*, p. 8.

[13] Mann, *Rainfall and Famine*, p. 30. It is not clear from Mann's statement whether his measure of relative yields is the revenue yield or the condition factor. I suspect that it is the former.

[14] Mann, *Rainfall and Famine*, p. 34. The highest correlation for the whole season's rainfall and the "goodness" of the year was $r = 0.482$ for Bijapur.

have available to them to adapt to different rainfall regimes, the lower should be the correlation between rainfall (either its total amount or its distribution) and output. Extremes of rainfall (either low or high) that lie outside any ability to adapt may still be highly correlated with output of food, but there will be a middle range in which adaptation to the timing and amount of rainfall will limit variation in crop production.

To develop an indicator of fluctuations in food production, then, we are left with reasonably high-quality acreage statistics for most of the districts of Bombay Presidency and with a set of condition factors which we will assume are relatively good indicators of year-to-year changes in output per acre. As noted above, the standard against which anna valuations of crops were determined was never ascertained in the official statistics. However, from 1886-1887 to 1896-1897, it was *assumed* that the average was sixteen annas, and standard yields were translated into revenue yields on this basis. That is, if a district was reported to have a twelve-anna crop, the revenue yield would be taken as 75 percent of the standard yield. In 1897, dissatisfaction with this system and with standard yield values led to (1) downward revision of standard yields and (2) a new assumption that the average anna valuation was twelve instead of sixteen. Subsequent to 1897, then, if a district reported a twelve-anna crop, the revenue yield would be taken as 100 percent of the standard yield.[15] While these changes help to make the series of revenue yields completely unusable, there is no reason to assume that reported anna valuations of crops are not comparable throughout the period. That is, while we may not know what the village official had in mind by his anna valuations, it is reasonable to assume that his standard was consistent from year to year. If we grant this, the condition factors can be used to produce a consistent series from 1886-1887 onwards if we translate them into percents by setting twelve annas equal to 100 percent. Because the season can be poor in one district and not in another, we will construct a separate indicator for each district. Even though railroads eventually succeeded in making transfer of grain into an area of local harvest failure routine, local failures still need to be considered because of the lack of work for agricultural laborers and the consequent lack of income to buy food that necessarily accompanied a failure of the rains.

[15] Heston, "Official Yields," pp. 318-319.

Construction of the Indicator

There are three steps in the construction of this indicator of annual crop fluctuations. First, I have prepared, for each district for each year, a *weighted condition factor* for jowar, bajra, wheat, and rice. These four crops were used because only for them were both acreages and condition factors always available.[16] The condition factor was reweighted for each year because changes in the timing or extent of rainfall may have been met with shifts in land among grain and pulse crops. The weight assigned to each crop in a given year was determined by adding up the acreage planted with the four crops and taking the proportion of this total acreage occupied by each crop.[17] Second, to account for the change in acreage planted that can occur in response to variations in the rains, the weighted condition factor has been multiplied by the total acreage planted with foodgrains and pulses. It would, of course, have been preferable to have condition factors for more grain and pulse crops enter into the weighted condition factor, but in the absence of long series of condition factors for crops other than jowar, bajra, wheat and rice, this is not possible. A second best solution is to extend the weighted condition factor for these four crops to all of the land planted with foodgrains and pulses. Multiplication of the weighted condition factor by the total acreage planted with foodgrains and pulses yields a series (or a set of series—one for each district) that we might call "effective acreage harvested" if we were confident that twelve annas actually represented an average crop. Lacking such confidence, and because the series contain very large numbers and are very difficult

[16] Even these figures are consistently available for only thirteen of the eighteen districts of Bombay Presidency. A series for Panch Mahals could not be prepared because the major crop was maize, for which no condition factor was available. This is the most serious omission because Panch Mahals was very definitely a district where distress from crop failures could and did occur. Series were not prepared for the Konkan districts of Thana, Kolaba, Ratnagiri, and Kanara for two reasons. First, as noted above, they are all coastal districts receiving very heavy rainfall (75 to 120 inches annually) and growing primarily rice; they have never been reported as liable to famine. Second, with the partial exception of Thana, their acreage statistics are much less reliable than those of the rest of the Presidency, due to the difficulties encountered (and the length of time required) in completing the cadastral survey.

[17] It would be more usual to use quantity weights to construct our weighted condition factors. Unfortunately, to construct quantity weights (i.e., according to the share of each grain crop in the total output of grain) would require us to use figures for the "standard" or "normal" yields of crops. The standard or normal yield, of course, is precisely what we do not know. Therefore, acreages planted with each grain crop have been used to construct the weighted condition factor.

to scan, each series has been converted into an index. To do so, each value in the series was divided by the mean value of that series and multiplied by 100 (the latter merely to eliminate decimal points). The resulting series is an *index of the quality of the agricultural season*, or IQAS.

An example, reproduced in Table 2.2, may make this clearer. For Belgaum in 1894-1895, the areas planted with rice, wheat, jowar, and bajra are listed in column 1. Column 2 shows the proportion each was of the total acreage planted with these four crops. The condition factors are given in annas in column 3 and as percents on the basis of 12 annas = 100 in column 4. The weighted condition factor for the year (the sum of the products of columns 2 and 4) is 79.72, which is rounded to 80; and multiplying this by the area planted with all foodgrains and pulses (1,410 thousand acres) yields a figure of 112,800. This figure is divided by the average of all such figures for Belgaum from 1886-1887 to 1919-1920, which was 95,700, and is then multiplied by 100, to give an IQAS of 118 for 1894-1895. This process was carried out for thirteen districts of Bombay Presidency for the period 1886-1887 through 1919-1920. A summary of the results is presented in Table 2.3.

Before proceeding to discuss these results, let me make clear some

TABLE 2.2. Sample Calculation of a Weighted Condition Factor and IQAS, Belgaum 1894-1895

Crop	(1) Area Planted		(3) Condition Factor	(4)
	Thousand Acres	As a Proportion of Total of 4 Crops	Annas	Percent
Rice	111	0.11	9	75
Wheat	114	0.11	9	75
Jowar	601	0.59	10	83
Bajra	194	0.19	9	75
Total	1,020			
All foodgrains and pulses	1,410			

$$WCF = \sum_{i=1}^{4} p_i CF_i = 80$$

$$IQAS = \frac{1,410 \times WCF}{95,700} (100) = \frac{112,800(100)}{95,700} = 118$$

SOURCE: See text.

TABLE 2.3. The Variability of Agricultural Seasons, 1886-1887 to 1919-1920

Division and District	Mean Weighted Condition Factor	Coefficient of Variation of WCF	Standard Deviation of IQAS
Gujarat			
Ahmedabad	70	32	47
Kaira	72	35	44
Broach	74	28	38
Surat	82	23	30
Deccan			
Khandesh	83	27	30
Nasik	78	31	35
Ahmednagar	66	36	40
Poona	71	36	43
Sholapur	66	32	37
Satara	72	25	31
Karnatak			
Belgaum	71	27	30
Bijapur	64	41	42
Dharwar	71	23	26

SOURCE: Appendix A, Tables A-2 and A-3.

of the limitations of this index. First, the estimates of year-to-year change (i.e., the condition factors) are by their very nature not precise; small variations (say, three to five points) almost certainly have no meaning. Second, I have not called it an index of *output* (although it is only a linear transformation away from producing a series in tons of grains and pulses) because that might subject it to uses that the quality of the data will not bear. In particular, neither this index nor any linear transformation of it should be used to calculate food production per person. The results would be spuriously precise. With these limitations in mind, let us consider Table 2.3.

The first column in the table gives the mean weighted condition factors for the thirteen districts. Whatever the standard to which village-level revenue officials were comparing current crops, the differences in the WCF's suggest two possibilities. Either the standard differed from district to district or, if it was the same for all districts, some districts came close to it more often than others.

The highest values of the WCF are for the cluster of Surat, Khandesh, and Nasik (see Map 2.4). The remaining districts of the Deccan and Karnatak are divided into two groups. Those lying closest to the Ghats (Poona, Satara, Belgaum, and Dharwar) have higher condition factors than those lying farther to the east (Ahmednagar, Sholapur, and Bijapur). To the north, Ahmedabad, Kaira, and Broach have mean condition factors of about the same level as the Karnatak. This pattern suggests that village-level revenue officials in all districts had similar standards and that differences in WCF's are due to the occurrence of more bad years in the driest districts (Ahmednagar, Sholapur, and Bijapur) than in the less dry districts. It should be noted that these figures do not mean that yields per acre were highest in Surat and Khandesh (although that may have been the case) but rather that they suggest there were fewer bad or more good years (climatically speaking) in these districts, so that the average of all years taken together was better than for a district like Bijapur or Ahmednagar.

The second column gives the coefficients of variation for the weighted condition factors, and the third, the standard deviations of the IQAS.[18] These two measures of dispersion are quite highly correlated ($r = .82$), as would be expected given their construction. The greater variation in the IQAS is due to year-to-year changes in acreage planted. Drought, for instance, not only reduces the weighted condition factor; it also reduced the total acreage farmers could plant. As the coefficients of variation of the WCF and the standard deviations of the IQAS indicate, the variation of the condition of crops and of the overall quality of the foodgrain and pulse harvest (as measured by the IQAS) was as great as that of the rainfall patterns.

In Figure 2.2, the weighted condition factors for each year for three selected districts are graphically represented. The graphs show very dramatically how much the quality of the harvest could change between two years. They also indicate that for these districts, the years between 1896-1897 and 1910-1911 contained not only the lowest condition factors for the entire period, but also more below-average years than the ten preceding or succeeding years. The specific historical importance of these fluctuations and of those in the IQAS series will be discussed in later chapters. It is enough here to have demonstrated the enormous variability in rainfall and condition of crops to which the people of the region had to adapt.

[18] Since the mean IQAS has been set equal to 100, there is no need to "standardize" the standard deviations by dividing them by their respective means to produce the coefficients of variation.

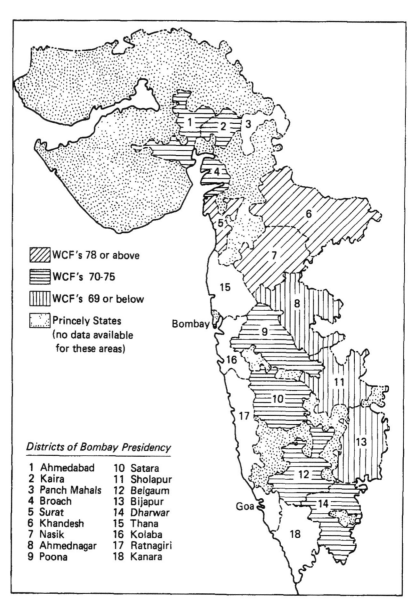

MAP 2.4 Districts of Bombay Presidency Showing Average of Weighted
Condition Factors for 1887-1920

SOURCE: Appendix A, Table A-2.

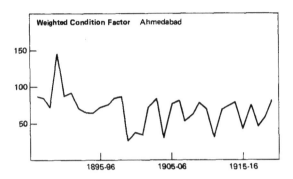

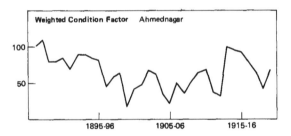

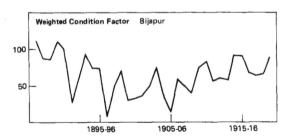

FIGURE 2.2 Annual Weighted Condition Factors in Selected Districts
of Bombay Presidency, 1886-1887 to 1919-1920

SOURCE: Appendix A, Table A-2.

III. Coping with Instability

The variability of agricultural seasons *per se* is not the cause of concern in South Asia. Rather, in this densely populated, low-income region, the concern with the variability of the rains and the seasons arises because years can occur when the quality of the season is so bad, the output of crops so low, that significant proportions of the population face the risk of hunger and starvation.[19] The overwhelming bulk of the qualitative and quantitative evidence suggests that agriculturists in western India have tried to avert that risk. The task is to decide on a reasonable theoretical formulation for strategies to avert risk and to examine the kinds of behavior actually generated.

Protection against risk—i.e., insurance—can rarely be achieved cheaply and may be particularly costly in poor agricultural societies. The costs of various kinds of actions to reduce the probability of disaster help to determine both the degree to which particular behaviors are used and the total amount of risk-reducing behavior that occurs. Even when agriculturists have a good sense of the risks that they face and when they have taken all of the precautions against disaster that seem reasonable and affordable to them, the probability that disaster will occur is unlikely to have been reduced to zero. Crises will, therefore, still happen. When they happen, another set of behaviors is called into play which is designed to enable the agriculturists to fall as little as possible below their disaster level.

Put more formally, agriculturists are attempting to maximize their utility subject to the constraint that the probability that consumption (net income) will fall below some disaster level $\underline{d}$ is less than $\underline{a}^*$. If/when there is no way that this constraint can be satisfied, then agriculturists maximize "the minimum return that can be attained with some fixed confidence level equal to α."[20]

The utility function need not be a simple function of net income. It can include separate arguments for food, money, time free from agricultural work, or any other arguments that appear to be especially important in understanding the behavior of a particular set of

---

[19] From the point of view of anyone concerned with the long-term development of the region, there are other reasons to be interested in variability and strategies used by agriculturists to cope. Some of these will be discussed later.

[20] This is Roumasset's Lexicographic Safety First$_2$. For a discussion of this decision rule and for a good discussion of the virtues of LSF models, see James Roumasset, *Rice and Risk* (Amsterdam: North-Holland, 1976), chap. 2.

agriculturists.[21] The choice of a disaster level for analytic or policy purposes is a complex problem. One possibility is to set the disaster level so that the family can remain in good nutritional condition and can retain those assets necessary to continue agricultural operations. Alternatively, a more austere disaster level could be set that enables the family to survive, but only by the sale of all assets and with some decline in the nutritional status of family members.[22] Obviously, more families will more often fall below the higher disaster level than will fall below the lower. However, the higher level is the one which seems relevant to the continued functioning of the agricultural system. The lower level focuses attention on the survival of individuals. Bad years coming in close proximity to each other could threaten an increasing number of cultivators as they reach the limits of assets that can be drawn down without affecting their ability to continue their current kind of cultivation (if we think of the higher disaster level) or as they reach the end of their assets (if we think of the lower disaster level).

The discussion of strategies to avert risk is limited in two ways. First, it is confined to cultivators—persons who as owners or tenants had some control over decisions about agricultural operations. Within this category, the discussion has most relevance to those whose wealth was sufficiently limited that they and their families could be directly and sharply threatened by one or several bad seasons. The limitation of the discussion to cultivators is not made either because there were no agricultural laborers in Bombay Presidency or because they were not affected by crop failures. Indeed, their usually limited assets probably meant that they suffered first and most severely.

[21] Food and money are specified as separate arguments because in most drought-prone areas the paucity of transport facilities and the high cost of transport practically prohibited the movement of grain among regions. As a result, money could not necessarily be used to acquire grain in these regions when the harvest was short.

[22] It is a conflict over the appropriate choice of a "disaster" or "distress" level that seems to be at the heart of N. S. Jodha's criticism of M. D. Morris's work. Morris argued that the sale of ornaments and the migration of agriculturists should not be viewed with alarm because they "are ordinary devices which agriculturists utilize in order to survive the statistically predictable fluctuations of water supply." Morris David Morris, "What is a Famine?" *Economic and Political Weekly* 9 (November 2, 1974):1857. Jodha argues that these actions *should* be viewed with alarm because they indicate that agriculturists have reached a level of distress where they are compelled to actions which reduce their chances to continue agricultural operations. Morris is concerned that relief come in time to save lives, Jodha is concerned that it protect "the farmer's own production base reflected through his own capital assets, including livestock." N. S. Jodha, "Famine and Famine Policies: Some Empirical Evidence," *Economic and Political Weekly* 10 (October 11, 1975):1614.

They are excluded from this discussion, however, because of another of the disadvantages under which they suffered: They exercised little if any role in making farming decisions. Second, since this discussion is intended to provide a baseline of the options available to a pre-modern agricultural sector, it is limited to those options that existed in the period before the large-scale development of railroads, government-administered relief works, and alternative sources of seasonal employment.

Obviously we must work inferentially for much of what we would like to know about peasant behavior in nineteenth-century western India. Our earliest significant records tend to come from the middle of the nineteenth century, at best, and some on which this section draws are from considerably later periods. This would not really be considered a problem in dealing with medieval or early modern Europe, but the fact that nineteenth-century India is so much closer to us in time leads to more uneasiness about mixing data sets that are 50 to 100 years apart. Actions taken by cultivators to reduce the probability that disaster will occur are discussed first. Actions taken to conserve assets and eventually life in years where net output looks as if it will fall below the disaster level are discussed afterward.

IV. Coping with Variability

There were four sets of actions that had as their chief purpose the assurance of a harvest large enough to keep the cultivators above the disaster level. First, varieties of crops were selected that were drought-resistant. The specific choices were responses to very specific ecosystems. For example, most of the districts of Bombay Presidency subject to drought have black soil of varying depth. Wherever this soil is deep, it will hold moisture even during a considerable break in the rains. But to reach that moisture, plants must have deep root systems, like that of the major variety of cotton grown in the 1840s. This plant's long taproot guaranteed its survival through a break in the rains that would wither a plant with more shallow roots.[23]

Second, mixtures of crops with different responses to rainfall patterns were planted.[24] The reasons why farmers in western India

---

[23] It was American cotton's lack of such a taproot that limited its spread in western India until it was successfully crossed with local cotton.

[24] For the proportions of some mixtures common in the late 1850s in Khandesh district, see Lieut. P. A. Elphinstone's report on agriculture in the Settlement Report for Khandesh, SRGB N.S. No. 93 (1865), p. 131. For mixtures current in Poona

mixed crops in a single field have been widely debated. Some have argued that the function of the mixtures was to help maintain soil quality (hence the inclusion of pulses), others that it was to assure some or most of the subsistence products needed for a farm family or to spread the work of harvesting over a longer period. While all of these reasons may have had some role, the importance of crop mixes for reducing the variance of output from a plot of ground cannot be ignored.

Third, if there was a variety of soil types available in the village, a farmer might attempt to diversify his holding to include some of each kind of land. Thomas Marshall, gathering information in the Karnatak in the 1820s, found farmers concerned with two main soil types, black and red, which they described as needing very different patterns of rainfall through the season to produce optimally.[25] And McCloskey has argued quite convincingly, for medieval England, that plot scattering even beyond that adequate to hold some of each major type of soil may be desirable because the variations in a microenvironment can have significant impact on the yield of different plots of land even as small as one acre.[26] Fourth, farmers adjusted the crops they planted according to the way the monsoon season began. Using their accumulated knowledge of seasons and crops, farmers might decide that "when the rains begin as they have this year, then it is better to plant this kind of pulse rather than that kind of pulse because this kind does better in this sort of year."

For farmers in relatively secure regions, these tactics might have been sufficient to reduce the probability of disaster to an acceptable level. For others for whom these techniques were not sufficient, one more was available. They regularly planted grain in excess of their current consumption requirements and planned to store that grain to consume in years when the extent of harvest failure would otherwise cause them to fall below their disaster level. The storage

district in the early twentieth century, and for their analysis of the reasons for planting mixtures of crops, see H. H. Mann and N. V. Kanitkar, *Land and Labour in a Deccan Village* (Bombay: Oxford University Press, 1921), p. 71. For instructions from the Director of Agriculture's office on how fields planted with mixed crops were to be counted for the preparation of agricultural statistics, see Bombay Presidency, *Annual Report of the Director of Agriculture*, 1884-1885 (Bombay, 1886), p. 13.

[25] Bombay Presidency, *Statistical Report on the Pergunnahs of Padshapoor, Belgam, Kalaniddee, and Chandgurh, Khanapoor, Bagalkot and Badamy, and Hoondgoond in the Southern Mahratta Country* by the late Thomas Marshall (Bombay Presidency, 1822), p. 123 (hereafter *Marshall's Report*).

[26] McCloskey, "English Open Fields," pp. 145-152. Research in village records could tell us if this were also the case in western India.

of grain beyond that needed for a current year's consumption was a very expensive activity, and it is therefore reasonable to ask why farmers did not sell grain and store some asset less likely to rot or be eaten by rodents. The answer seems to be that storage of grain was the cheapest or even the only feasible way of being sure of a supply of grain when the harvest failure was severe. Before rail transport became efficient (near the end of the nineteenth century or the beginning of the twentieth century), transport of enough grain into a region to relieve a famine was either prohibitively expensive or simply not possible. In addition, markets for the export of grain from these drought-prone regions were very limited, resulting in a low opportunity cost for storing grain.[27]

All of the forms of behavior described so far took place in "normal" years. They had as their objective a reduction of the probability that disaster would occur. Either because of the variation of the size of harvests or because of the generally low level of income in the region, disasters did and do continue to occur in dry South Asian agriculture.[28] Before the days of railroads, urban employment, and government relief, what options did agriculturists in western India have in a year when the rains failed?

First, they could undertake whatever "conservation" methods were available. As soon as it became clear that the *kharif* harvest could not be "normal," say in late July or August, discretionary expenditures of all sorts could be postponed. Fuel and food could be gathered from sources that might be neglected in better times.[29] In the period before the harvest was due, cultivators may have been more concerned about finding fodder for cattle than food for their families, since the remains of the last year's harvest could continue to feed humans. But as the time of harvest passed with only a fraction of

[27] For evidence on the prevalence of grain storage, see Michelle Burge McAlpin, "Railroads, Prices, and Peasant Rationality: India 1860-1900," *Journal of Economic History* 34 (September 1974): 677-679.

[28] Independent India has experienced droughts severe enough to provoke declarations of famine in 1966-1967 (Bihar), 1970-1973 (Maharashtra), and 1974-1975 (Gujarat and Rajasthan).

[29] "For example, while doing field cleaning or weeding as core activities for a crop, other activities like the collection of cleaned material (fodder or fuel about which nobody bothers during a year of plenty) are performed. Such activities . . . are justified because of the reduced opportunity cost of labour and increased value of products thus salvaged during a drought year." Jodha, "Famine and Famine Policies," p. 1620. Jodha's data are for Rajasthan, but can probably be safely extrapolated to other drought-prone regions.

the normal yields harvested, food for humans could become an increasing problem.

As a second tactic, stocks of stored grain could be drawn upon, when these existed, to supplement the scanty harvest. Considerable efforts could be directed towards finding enough fodder to keep cattle alive. In a mild to moderate scarcity, these actions might suffice to get the family through until the next harvest. In a more severe scarcity or in a second scarcity that followed close upon the heels of a first, a third option, the sale and mortgage of assets, could become necessary.[30] Goods like jewelry were usually thought of as among the first assets to be sold. Subsequently, land could be mortgaged or sold and cattle would also be sold. The efficacy of sale of assets depended on the size and nature of the market for both assets and grain. In Bombay Presidency during famines as late as 1876-1878, it appears that extra-local movements of grain were insufficient to bring supplies in badly hit districts up to levels that would provide food for everyone in the district. The rate at which assets could be exchanged for grain under these circumstances was very much less than in "normal" years, making sale of assets a poor form of insurance.

Although they have already been alluded to, it may be useful to summarize two of the options that were *not* available to farmers attempting to insure themselves against the consequences of crop failures in this pre-railroad era. First, the smallness of markets—both for the export of goods they could produce and for the import of grain when their own crops failed—limited the insurance that could be provided by storing non-grain assets. It was difficult to accumulate such assets, and the virtual absence of a transport network which could move substantial amounts of grain into a region where the crops had failed meant that assets could not be converted into food at any predictable rate.

Second, the possibility of borrowing grain, or money to buy grain, during a season of severe crop failure was also very limited. Persons who had larger than normal stocks of grain might have shared them (either from fear or other motives) with others who had less, but in general these "loans" of grain would have followed lines of existing and well-recognized social and economic ties. Various kinds of reciprocal behavior in years when crops did not fail probably were demanded in return. It is worth noting that such patterns of "loans"

[30] For the variety of inventories the Rajasthani farmers sold in the 1963-1964 drought, see Jodha, "Famine and Famine Policies," p. 1620.

would have been most viable in areas where the distribution of land was rather unequal, so that some could accumulate much larger stores of grain than others. Under these circumstances, persons tied to a "big man" might have had little need to migrate and little chance to store for themselves. But where distribution of control of land and labor was fairly even, the probability that one man would have the resources to maintain many others was small.[31]

When these circumstances limit the relief that can be achieved from the sale and mortgage of assets, a fourth option is migration out of the area, with or without livestock. The essential purpose of migration was to find areas where food and fodder were available, where any remaining liquid assets might be sold for more grain, and where work might be available. In any period before the 1890s, migration appears to have been a strategy of last resort and a dangerous one. Information on areas where conditions were better was limited; the movement of large numbers of people tended to spread cholera and other diseases; agriculturists found themselves far from home and exhausted when sowing operations for the next season had to be undertaken. In a famine severe enough to induce large numbers of people to migrate, mortality was high and the disruption to ongoing agricultural operations was significant.

[31] N. S. Jodha makes much the same point in his discussion of informal reciprocal aid networks in drought-prone areas. "The efficiency of all traditional systems of reciprocal aid is probably higher against life cycle risks than drought risks. Life cycle risks do not have a high covariance among residents of a small geographic area within which the traditional systems operate. On the other hand, drought affects the whole reciprocal group similarly, as all members experience the drought at the same time, although to various degrees," N. S. Jodha, "Effectiveness of Farmers' Adjustments to Risk," paper presented at a Workshop on the Effects of Risk and Uncertainty on Economic and Social Processes in South Asia, University of Pennsylvania, 1977, p. 22.

3. The Demographic Consequences of Famines

For 50 years after the initiation of decennial censuses in 1872, India's rate of population growth averaged only 0.37 percent per year. The rate of increase between 1872 and 1921 was even lower in Bombay Presidency—only 0.26 percent per year. These rates of growth are of the same magnitude as those that probably characterized a wide variety of pre-modern societies. But India is unique in the volume of good quality demographic data that are available to study this period, when major subsistence crises and epidemics were still a regular feature of the society. The first sections of this chapter present a population history of Bombay Presidency, laying out both the changes in aggregate population and those in age and sex composition. The second half of the chapter focuses on the demographic consequences of specific periods of harvest failures and epidemics.

I. Population Change in Bombay Presidency, 1872-1931

In his classic study of the population of the Indian subcontinent, Kingsley Davis wrote:

> The greater part of the census period conforms to the pattern of sporadic growth believed to have existed in earlier times. . . . In the decades of negligible growth, the trouble lay in [famine or disease]. During the 1871-81 period there occurred the great Indian famine of 1876-78; during the 1891-1901 decade, another famine; and during the 1911-21 decennium, the influenza epidemic of 1918.[1]

The effects of the events Davis mentions are clearly evident in Table 3.1 both for India as a whole and, in more extreme form, for Bombay Presidency. The decade 1911-1921 was the last in which the growth of population in the Indian subcontinent was negligible. To continue

---

[1] Kingsley Davis, *The Population of India and Pakistan* (Princeton: Princeton University Press, 1951), p. 28.

TABLE 3.1. Population and Rates of Growth of Population in India and Bombay Presidency, 1872-1931

Year	Population (thousands)		Rate of Population Growth (compound annual)		
	India	Bombay Presidency	Decade	India	Bombay Presidency
1872	255,166	14,074			
			1872-1881	0 10	−0.03
1881	257,380	14,040			
			1881-1891	0.92	1.29
1891	282,134	15,961			
			1891-1901	0.11	−0.42
1901	285,288	15,304			
			1901-1911	0 60	0.52
1911	302,985	16,114			
			1911-1921	0.09	−0.06
1921	305,679	16,015			
			1921-1931	1.02	1.17
1931	338,171	17,995			
			1872-1921	0.37	0.26
			1872-1931	0.48	0.42

SOURCES· India−Davis, *Population*, p. 27.
Bombay Presidency−Appendix B, Table B-1.

quoting from Davis, "Something appears to have happened after 1920, however, for the alternating process stopped."[2]

Because Bombay Presidency contained some of the districts where monsoon rainfall was and remains particularly capricious and because very little of its cultivated area was irrigated (always less than five percent), it was one of the provinces of British India in which fluctuations in harvests and changes in the rate of population growth were most marked. The importance of the port of Bombay and its increasingly good connections with its hinterland also facilitated the spread of the plague and influenza epidemics in the Presidency. As a result, we can see from Table 3.1 that when the rate of population growth for all of India was low (1872-1881, 1891-1901, 1911-1921), it was negative in Bombay Presidency. When growth in all of India was rapid (1881-1891, 1921-1931), it was even more rapid in Bombay.

The two major sources of demographic data for Bombay Presidency are the *Census of India* and the reports of the Sanitary Com-

[2] Davis, *Population*, p. 28.

missioner. Neither of these sources contains consistent and good series on all the variables on which information is desired. In general, the quality of the figures gathered by the census (i.e., how many people there were in a given region in a given year) is better than that of the figures in the Sanitary Commissioner's reports (how many people were born or died in a region and of what they died).

While migration might, in theory, be a major cause of changes in the rates of population growth, this seems unlikely in fact. For the period under consideration here, data available in the Census for sorting out migration flows are rather weak, but the general indication is that, relative to the size of the populations, migration flows between and among provinces were small.[3] In general, when discussing Presidency and divisional data, migration will be ignored as a source of population change. In discussions of district and *taluka* data, migration will be considered.

Once migration is set aside as a major source of changes in population, data that will permit inferences to be made about changes in vital rates become crucial. There are registered birth and death rates for Bombay Presidency from at least 1881 (data for earlier dates are fragmentary), but information from the census indicates severe under-reporting of vital rates. Inference from the census data backwards to what vital rates "must" have been is difficult because of the deplorable quality of the age data. Confronted with this set of problems, demographers like S. B. Mukherjee have ignored all or most of the vital-rate data and used the censuses and model life tables and other demographic models developed by Coale and Demeny and the United Nations to estimate what vital rates "must" have been.[4]

While one must admire the energy and skill with which Mukherjee has regrouped and analyzed data to provide consistent population series for the areas that comprise modern India's states, his work has a number of lacunae for the economic historian. Mukherjee essentially dismisses the short-run variations in birth and death rates that might be caused by famines and epidemics as both uninteresting and unimportant for the study of the age distribution of the population.[5] For some of his numerous tables, Mukherjee is unable to produce figures for various parts of India (often western India) because the number of males declined between two cen-

[3] Davis, *Population*, p. 107 and passim.

[4] S. B. Mukherjee, *The Age Distribution of the Indian Population* (Honolulu: East-West Center, 1976), Ch. 6.

[5] Mukherjee, *Age Distribution*, p. 158.

suses,[6] or because the level of mortality was very different from that allowed for by the model life tables.[7] The work of Mukherjee requires us to make some large and crucial, if unstated, assumptions about demographic patterns in India—namely, that they are and always have been like the models demographers use.[8] But if the ahistoricism that characterizes Mukherjee's book is to be redressed, vital registration data known to be defective must be used. How bad (or good) are these data? For what purposes can they reasonably be used?

The vital-rate data for Bombay Presidency were collected in the villages by an officer who also was part of the revenue-collection system. Above him was a "circle sanitary inspector" whose tasks included supervision of the collection of vital-rate data. As the department supervised by the Sanitary Commissioner became better organized over time and as the reliability of the village-level revenue personnel improved, the quality of vital-rate data improved. It is important to note that Bombay Presidency had the most extensive revenue operation in the field of any province of British India. This operation was an integral part of the Bombay Settlement and Survey system, of which the Presidency was very proud. The efforts to perfect this system and to increase the reliability of the numbers generated by it (mostly about crops planted, output, land cultivated, and changes in tenure) do appear to have produced agricultural statistics in Bombay Presidency that are generally of high quality— i.e., equivalent to those of many Western countries at the same time and much better than those of, say, Bengal where the form of land revenue settlement did not generate a record-keeping bureaucracy at the village level. Given the improvement in vital-rate statistics over time, using them to determine trends in rates is problematic. If, over time, we find an increase in either the registered birth rate or the registered death rate, it is impossible to separate this increase into a "real" component and a "statistical" component attributable to increasing coverage of the registration system. If rates are found to be decreasing, while we can be sure that some decrease did occur, the vital-rate data will tend to underestimate this decrease to the degree that registration improved over the same period. However, the vital-rate data, whatever their defects for determining trends, can reasonably be used to examine fluctuations in rates that might be anticipated from the impact of exogenous forces. So long as the

---

[6] Mukherjee, *Age Distribution*, p. 207, Table 7.11.

[7] Mukherjee, *Age Distribution*, pp. 211-214, Table 8.22.

[8] Mukherjee, *Age Distribution*, pp. 166-167.

rate of improvement in the overall coverage of the statistics was slow, the fluctuation between, say, 1896 and 1897, is going to reflect real changes rather than changes in the quality of the data. In this chapter, therefore, the vital-rate data will be used to chart annual fluctuations in birth and death rates.

For my purposes, the reliability of cause-of-death statistics also has to be considered. Most of the published statistics separate out only deaths due to cholera, smallpox, and, after 1896, plague. In the reports of the Sanitary Commissioner, detail on other deaths is sometimes available, but the breakdown itself (dysentery and diarrhea, fevers, respiratory diseases, etc.) leaves much to be desired. And even if the breakdown of reporting categories were all that could be desired, village officials can hardly be assumed to have had much skill in assigning deaths to these categories. Because, however, of their very distinctive symptoms, the Sanitary Commissioner's office generally viewed the statistics for cholera, smallpox, and plague as reasonably reliable. If we accept that view, we can use those data.

Very few deaths, even in the worst famines, were reported as due to starvation. Deaths that were so reported during a period of declared famine had to be explained on a one-by-one basis to superior authorities by the officials within whose territory such deaths occurred. More important, the proximate causes of famine-induced deaths are typically diseases to which acutely malnourished persons are particularly likely to be both exposed and susceptible. "Famine mortality" will be estimated, therefore, by observing the excess of deaths over "normal" (generally the average of the previous five or ten years), rather than by counting deaths from starvation. This is the technique that was used by the administrators of Bombay Presidency and, indeed, the rest of India. It makes certain assumptions about the effects of acute malnutrition on mortality that will be explored at greater length somewhat later.

Because published data for *districts* are not as consistently available as published data for *divisions* of Bombay Presidency, and since the latter can be constructed from the former but not the reverse, analysis in this chapter is generally done at the divisional level. Even where district-level data were available, they have been aggregated to produce divisional data.

Table 3.2 gives the population and rates of growth of the four major divisions and Bombay City, and for Bombay Presidency as a whole, for the census dates from 1872 to 1931. In 1872 the Presidency consisted of three divisions of nearly equal population (Gu-

TABLE 3.2. Population, Rates of Growth, and Indexes of Change for
Bombay Divisions and Bombay City, 1872-1931

	A. Population (thousands)						
Year	Gujarat	Deccan	Karnatak	Konkan	Total Brit. Dists.	Bombay City	Total Bombay Presidency
1872	2,814	5,249	2,752	2,615	13,430	644	14,074
1881	2,857	5,315	2,386	2,709	13,267	773	14,040
1891	3,098	6,213	2,861	2,967	15,139	822	15,961
1901	2,702	5,944	2,843	3,039	14,528	776	15,304
1911	2,804	6,387	2,833	3,111	15,135	979	16,114
1921	2,959	6,061	2,787	3,032	14,839	1,176	16,015
1931	3,225	7,194	3,049	3,366	16,834	1,161	17,995
	B. Rate of Growth (compound annual)						
1872-1881	.17	.14	−1.57	.39	− .13	2.05	− .03
1881-1891	.81	1.57	1.83	.91	1.33	.62	1.29
1891-1901	−1.36	− .44	− .06	.24	− .41	− .57	− .42
1901-1911	.37	.72	− .04	.23	.41	2.35	.52
1911-1921	.54	− .53	− .16	− .26	− .20	1.85	− .06
1921-1931	.86	1.73	.90	1.05	1.27	− .13	1.17
1872-1921	.10	.29	.03	.30	.20	1.24	.26
1872-1931	.23	.54	.17	.43	.38	1.00	.42
	C. Index of Population Change (1872 = 100)						
1872	100	100	100	100	100	100	100
1881	102	101	86	104	99	120	100
1891	110	118	104	114	113	128	113
1901	96	113	103	116	108	120	109
1911	100	122	103	119	113	152	114
1921	105	115	101	116	111	183	114
1931	115	137	111	129	125	180	128

SOURCES· Panel A–Appendix B, Table B-1. Panels B and C–computed from Panel A.

jarat, Karnatak, Konkan) and one (Deccan) that was much larger.
Over the next 50 years, until the 1921 census, the annual growth
rates of the four divisions were 0.03 (Karnatak), 0.10 (Gujarat), 0.29
(Deccan), and 0.30 (Konkan). For all divisions there was at least
one decade when population declined; for the Karnatak there were
four such periods. In the decade 1921-1931, all four regions had
positive rates of growth for the first time since 1881-1891. The four

regions together had a population increase between 1872 and 1921 of only 11 percent (an annual growth rate of 0.20), but growth between 1921 and 1931 was so rapid (1.17 percent per year) that by 1931 population was 25 percent greater than in 1872. For the individual regions, growth of total population between 1872 and 1921 ranged from 1 percent (Karnatak) to 16 percent (Konkan) and between 1872 and 1931 from 11 percent (Karnatak) to 37 percent (Deccan). The diversity of the patterns and magnitudes of population change in these four divisions encourages close examination of their vital rates in general and their experiences in famines and epidemics.

Population change during any time period equals the difference between births and deaths added to net migration. While both famines and epidemics can affect all three, only changes in the birth and death rates will be intensively examined here. Migration was not important for large units, and for smaller units it was a largely temporary phenomenon.[9] In any case, the data available to examine migration patterns are much scarcer than data on vital rates.

Demographers have generally attributed the relative constancy of pre-modern populations to the combined effects of high, stable birth rates and variable death rates. In the specific case of India, a typical argument runs as follows:

> During the two thousand years that intervened between the ancient and the modern period India's population could not have grown very rapidly. It must have remained virtually stable. The usual course was surely a gradual growth for a short period followed by an abrupt decline. The population would tend to grow slightly in "normal" times, because the customs governing fertility would provide a birth rate slightly higher than the usual death rate. This would build up a population surplus as a sort of demographic insurance against catastrophe. Inevitably, however, the catastrophe would come in the form of warfare, famine, or epidemic, and the increase of population would be suddenly wiped out.[10]

Demographers working on pre-modern periods tend to quickly dismiss changes in birth rates as possible causes of fluctuations in the rate of population change. This may be a sensible strategy if

[9] The exceptions to this statement would include the out-migration from Bombay City in 1896-1901, as workers fled the plague epidemic, and perhaps some of the migration into Ahmedabad City between 1911 and 1921 or 1931.

[10] Davis, *Population*, p. 24.

what one seeks to explain is long-run changes in the rate of growth. The argument is that most societies in pre-modern periods have not effectively practiced any kind of fertility limitation but rather have had their rates of increase kept low by high mortality, especially during the first five years of life.[11] The probability of a significant rise in the birth rate, under these conditions, is small. Therefore, any major increase in the rate of growth must come from reduced mortality.

The significance of the birth rate has not been explored, however, in short periods when population growth in pre-modern societies is declining or when populations themselves are declining. The tendency has been to dismiss changes in the birth rate in times of calamity and to concentrate instead on the elevation of mortality. This may be justifiable in terms of the relative importance of the two influences, but few data have ever been presented to indicate that it is indeed warranted. If the argument is that when the birth rate is high, little increase is possible, the corollary must be that significant decrease is possible in the face of stress.

Data on Bombay Presidency are sufficient to permit an examination of changes in divisional birth and death rates over the 40-year period from 1891 to 1930. Table 3.3 presents five-year averages of birth and death rates calculated from the vital registration data. As pointed out above, these data are underestimates of the true rates.[12] However, their fluctuations and relative levels are still useful to us.

Five-year average death rates ranged from a low of 23 per thousand in Konkan in 1921-1925 and 1926-1931 to a high of 55 per thousand in Gujarat in 1896-1900. For the entire period, the average death rate was lowest in Konkan (27.8 per thousand), while the average death rates for the other three regions are sufficiently close together (35.9, 36.9, and 37.0) to suggest that real differences among them were trivial. The coefficient of variation of death rates in Konkan was 20 percent, while for the other three regions the coefficient of variation was 24 to 27 percent. In other words, death rates in the Konkan, the one region of the four that was secure from famine,

---

[11] Thomas McKeown, *The Modern Rise of Population* (New York: Academic Press, 1976).

[12] Davis cites estimates of the birth rate in Bombay Presidency of 50.3 for 1881-1891, 43.9 for 1891-1901, and 50.8 for 1901-1911. He gives estimates of death rates for all of British India for the same three decades of 41.3, 44.4, and 42.6. Davis, *Population*, pp. 68, 36.

TABLE 3.3. Quinquennial Average Birth and Death Rates
by Divisions, 1891-1930[a]

| | Gujarat | | Deccan | | Karnatak | | Konkan | |
Quinquennium	BR	DR	BR	DR	BR	DR	BR	DR
1891-1895	34	34	42	34	41	29	31	25
1896-1900	33	55	38	45	36	39	30	32
1901-1905	34	45	37	40	32	52	30	28
1906-1910	38	33	41	32	36	28	33	27
1911-1915	41	31	43	33	40	35	35	25
1916-1920	38	42	38	54	37	48	31	39
1921-1925	37	26	39	28	37	27	33	23
1926-1930	38	30	41	29	39	29	33	23
Average	36.6	37.0	39.9	36.9	37.3	35.9	32.0	27.8
Standard deviation	2.7	9.6	2.2	8.9	2.8	9 7	1.8	5.4
Coefficient of variation	7	26	5	24	8	27	6	20

[a]Rates are numbers of births and deaths per 1,000 population. After averaging, the rates reported in Tables B-5 and B-6 have been adjusted for changes in population. This correction is necessary because the Sanitary Commissioner's *Report* used the population from, say, the 1901 Census, as the denominator of the birth and death rate ratios for the entire decade 1901-1910. In periods when population (and therefore the numbers of births and deaths) was increasing, this method generated an increasing upward bias in birth and death rate series over the decade. To correct the vital rate series it was necessary to adjust the reported birth and death rates for changes in the population base (see Appendix B, Table B-4). Such correction works well only when the rate of population change (whether growth or decline) was fairly steady. When, as was the case in Gujarat between 1891 and 1901, the difference between the endpoints is large and negative but all the decline in population occurred in the final year of the decade, this method of correction gives ridiculous results. Therefore, Gujarat data for 1891-1895 and 1896-1900 have been corrected using the growth rate of population for 1881-1891. The problem confronted in the data for Gujarat is not severe in any of the other divisions, where negative rates of change were closer to zero or where (as in the Deccan) the change was attributable to several famines, only one of which occurred at the very end of the decade.

SOURCE· Calculated from Appendix B, Tables B-4, B-5, and B-6.

were both lower on average and less variable than for the other three regions.

The lowest quinquennial average birth rate in the four divisions was 30 per thousand in the Konkan in 1896-1900 and 1901-1905, while the highest was 43 per thousand in the Deccan in 1911-1915. For the entire period, the birth rate for the Konkan was 32 per thousand. The Karnatak and the Gujarat had very similar average birth rates (37.3 and 36.6), but that for the Deccan was substantially greater at 39.9 per thousand. The coefficients of variation for the four regions varied only from 5 percent to 8 percent.

It is noteworthy that the two regions that grew most rapidly over this period—the Deccan and the Konkan—had, respectively, the highest and the lowest average birth rates. Coupled with the available information on death rates and their fluctuations, the birthrate data suggest that the pattern of population growth was different in the Konkan than in the Deccan. With lower birth and death rates, the Konkan's pattern implies less wastage of human life—fewer children born, but more surviving to adulthood. Correspondingly, if desired family size could have been reached with fewer births, then the stress on women of frequent childbearing would have been reduced. Further work using other local records from this region would be useful to test the hypothesis that in the Konkan, where the population was less subject to abrupt rises in the death rate due to famine, society had evolved norms for somewhat lower fertility resulting in lower birth rates.[13] For the remaining divisions, while it is clear that death rates vary about three times as much as birth rates over a cycle of good and bad years, changes in population over this cycle cannot be explained fully if variations in the birth rate are ignored.

II. Changes in the Age and Sex Composition of the Population, 1872-1931

To the extent that famines and epidemics produce reductions in birth rates and non-random changes in mortality, the population after these events will differ from the pre-famine, pre-epidemic population by more than just size. There may be changes in the ratios of adults to children and to old people; there may also be changes in the sex ratio. What are the biological and social factors that might lead to changes in the age and sex composition of a population subject to famines?

There is some evidence that females are "stronger" than males.

---

[13] The tentativeness of this hypothesis must be stressed. It may be that the registration of vital rates was more defective in the Konkan than elsewhere because of the difficulty of implementing the Bombay survey and settlement system in this division (see Chapter 4). It may be that malaria was the chief cause of lower birth rates, if those rates are real and not a function of the defective reporting agencies. However, if they are real, they are interesting. They may suggest how long birth and death rates in these rather secure but poor western districts of India have been low relative to the rest of India. In other words, the very low birth and death rates in the state of Kerala—so widely remarked upon today—in the same ecological niche as the Konkan, may be due to its history of climate as much as or more than to its history of widespread education.

Male infants have higher mortality than female infants.[14] In addition, females have hormonally determined higher immune resistance that can reduce their mortality from infections.[15] To the extent that the rise in mortality observed in years of food shortage is due to spread of infections, females might thus survive these more frequently than males. There is also some evidence from animal studies that females adapt more rapidly than males to protein deprivation by altering certain of their metabolic processes.[16] While inference from studies of rats to humans is risky, this evidence suggests that females, all other things being equal, may have a higher probability than males of surviving famine. With respect to age, very young children might be more vulnerable during a famine because of their low initial body weights. The very old might have lowered ability to tolerate nutritional stress simply because of their age. And both the aged and the young are less physically able to care for themselves.

Both the very young and the aged might also be victims of social discrimination in South Asia. Mortality among children, always high, may be further elevated during food shortages by a cultural pattern in which adult males eat first and women and children eat what is left.[17] Among children, females may be less valued by the family and relatively more neglected, so that social discrimination might offset whatever biological advantages they may have.[18] The aged may also be less valued members of the family. Women in childbearing ages may be vulnerable to famine, again in spite of being biologically somewhat stronger than males, because of frequent childbearing. Males may be expected to venture out of their villages to try to find food for their families, thereby exposing them to the

[14] Ingrid Waldron, "Why do Women Live Longer than Men?" *Social Science and Medicine* 10 (nos. 7-8, 1976):349.

[15] Waldron, "Why Do Women," p. 355.

[16] Catharine Stevens, M.D., personal communication.

[17] Paul R. Greenough, "The Ultimate Insurance Mechanism: Patterned Domestic Break-Up During the Bengal Famine, 1943-44," paper presented at a Workshop on the Effects of Risk and Uncertainty on Economic and Social Processes in South Asia, University of Pennsylvania, 1977, pp. 22-23.

[18] Gopalan and Naidu found that death rates for females under five were higher than for males in India (95.7 per 1,000 live female births vs. 86.7 per 1,000 live male births), although for developed countries the rates for males are higher than for females. Among children admitted to the hospital for treatment of kwashiorkor, there was no significant difference in mortality rates for male and female children. They conclude that the higher death rates for female children are due to relative neglect. C. Gopalan and A. Nadamuni Naidu, "Nutrition and Fertility," *Lancet* 2 (November 18, 1972):1077-1078.

dual risks of coming into contact with more diseases than if they remained in one place and of exhaustion from the act of wandering.

Both biological and social factors would tend to make famine mortality higher among young children than among other groups in the population. However, in the case of female children, inherent biological strength, tending to make their mortality lower than that for male children, might be offset by social discrimination tending to raise their mortality. For adults, while women appear to have the biological advantage, social patterns exist that might elevate the mortality of both sexes. Given the complexity of possible causal factors and their interactions, statistical data must be used to determine the effects of famines on the age and sex structure of the population.

The most severe famine in Bombay Presidency during the first twenty years after the British Crown assumed the governance of India came in 1876-1878. In an attempt to ascertain the seriousness of the famine, special famine censuses were conducted in parts of Bombay and Madras Presidencies in early 1878. These partial censuses are particularly useful for providing information on the population immediately after the end of a famine.[19]

The 1878 census was taken in a set of *talukas* which were thought—on the basis of mortality returns—to represent those of greatest and those of average distress in five of the most severely affected districts (Sholapur, Satara, Belgaum, Bijapur, and Dharwar). Within the districts, *talukas* were supposed to have been selected (1) for the highest death rate in the district, and (2) for the death most closely corresponding to the average for the district. The place of each *taluka* on a scale from least to most distressed—as the author of the report on the 1878 census ranked them, distress and mortality are clearly not perfectly correlated—is indicated in Table 3.4. This table also includes the population of each of the *talukas* in 1872 and 1878, an estimate of what the population would have been in 1878 if "normal" population growth had occurred at an annual rate of one percent, the difference between this estimate and the actual 1878 population (labeled "decrease due to famine"), the "decrease" converted into a ratio per 1,000, and the registered death rate for 1877. The compiler of the census formed the estimate of the population expected in 1878 in the absence of the famine in order to

---

[19] The censuses of 1881 and 1921 both occurred several years after a famine; that of 1901 occurred during a famine. On the other hand, since the census referred to above was taken in January 1878, some persons who had migrated in search of work or food may not have returned yet to their home villages.

attempt to ascertain the total impact of the famine (i.e., the effect on births as well as on deaths). However, because of the unreliability of the registered-death statistics, he did not actually attempt to partition the change in population into the portion due to higher death rates and that due to lowered birth rates.[20]

For the ten *talukas* taken together, the actual decrease in population was 11 percent. While all but Kod *taluka* in Dharwar district showed decreases, the specific decreases ranged from 4 to 21 percent. Similarly, in all *talukas* except Kod, the decrease per thousand due to famine (column 6) exceeded the registered death rate (column 7) by a wide margin. The difference between columns 6 and 7 represents (a) declines in the birth rate, (b) underregistration of deaths, and (c) net migration. In these terms, Kod *taluka* may have felt two effects of famine—elevation of death rates among children and in-migration of adults. Data in Table 3.5 confirm this hypothesis by showing that while the number of children under age 12 decreased in Kod, the number of adults increased.

For the remaining *talukas*, a clear pattern emerges in Table 3.5. There is a greater percentage decrease for children under 1 than for those 1 to 12. Both of these percentages are larger than those for persons ages 12 to 50, except in the Satara *talukas* of Man and Khatav. Finally, percentage decreases rise again for persons over 50. These data support the hypothesis that the very young and the aged are more vulnerable to both starvation and the diseases which accompany disruption of normal life and eating habits. In addition, both of these groups are forced to depend on others (in the age group 12 to 50) for assistance.[21]

The mortality patterns in the 1878 census suggest that the famine caused changes in the dependency ratio. Because of the way the

[20] The total effects on births could not have been evident as early as January 1878 in any case. Cornish found in Bellary district of Madras Presidency that birth rates had not regained their 1876 levels (or the average of the five years ending in 1875) as late as April 1879. Madras Presidency, *Review of the Madras Famine, 1876-78* (Madras: Government Press, 1881), Appendix B, unpaginated graphs of birth rates.

[21] There are some puzzling data on changes in population in each age group: in the Satara *taluka* of Khatav, the number of children under one year was 22 percent larger than in 1872, and in the Bijapur *taluka* of Bagalkot, the number of persons over 50 increased by 15 percent. For Khatav, a severe undercount of infants in 1872 may be the explanation. Another possibility is that malnourished children ages 1-4 were classified as infants in the 1872 census. For Bagalkot, the increase in persons over 50 years old could be due to immigration (conditions were reported better in Bagalkot than in some other Bijapur *talukas*), or it could be due to errors in reporting ages in one or both censuses.

TABLE 3.4. Change in Population in Selected *Talukas* Due to the Famine of 1876-1877

Division, District, and Taluka	Condition	(1) Pop. 1872	(2) Pop. 1878	(3) Percent Change	(4) Pop. 1878 with Normal Growth[a]	(5) Decrease Due to Famine (4-2)	(6) Decrease per 1,000 (5/4×1,000)	(7) Registered Death Rate, (1877)
Deccan Sholapur Madha	Most distressed	103,981	83,317	-20	110,378	27,061	245.2	41.8
Sangola	1 of 3 most distressed	62,960	60,640	-4	66,833	6,193	92.7	66.7
Satara Man	Most distressed	62,198	54,686	-12	66,024	11,338	171.7	65.3
Khatav	1 of 4 most distressed	81,950	73,668	-10	86,992	13,322	153.1	50.6
Karnatak Belgaum Athni	Most distressed	114,677	99,554	-13	121,732	22,178	182.2	75.7

Sampgaon	Average (conflicting reports)	131,504	125,804	-4	139,594	13,789	98.8	70.9
Bijapur								
Bagalkot	Average	110,185	97,177	-12	116,964	19,787	169.2	95.7
Badami	1 of 3 least distressed	114,288	90,489	-21	121,319	30,830	254.1	104.3
Dharwar								
Ron	Most distressed	73,503	68,065	-7	78,025	9,960	127.7	106.8
Kod	Least distressed	79,099	80,472	+2	83,965	3,493	41.6	70.5
Total		934,345	833,872	-11	991,824	157,951	164.3	—

[a]Growth of one percent per annum assumed for the six years, 1872-1878.

SOURCE: "Note on the Census Taken in January 1878 of Certain Talukas Within the Area Affected by Famine in 1876 and 1877," appendix.

TABLE 3.5. Population Change by Age Group, and Dependency Ratios, 1872-1878

Division, District, and Taluka	Percent Change in Population, 1872-1878[a]				Dependency Ratio[b]	
	Under 1 Year	1-12 Years	12-50 Years	Over 50 Years	1872	1878
Decca						
Sholapur						
Madha	−55	−20	−17	−18	.84	.77
Sangola	−34	− 5	(+)	−14	.80	.73
Satara						
Man	−48	− 3	− 9	−40	.91	.83
Khatav	+22	− 9	− 7	−33	.88	.83
Karnatak						
Belgaum						
Athni	−57	−11	−10	−16	.76	.68
Sampgaon	−34	− 7	(−)	− 3	.80	.65
Bijapur						
Bagalkot	−55	−24	− 7	+15	.82	.75
Badami	−74	−25	−14	−34	.85	.77
Dharwar						
Ron	−57	−11	+ 1	−23	.87	.71
Kod	−23	−12	+ 7	+37	.81	.73
Total	−45	−14	− 6	−14	.86	.74

[a] − = reduction in population, + = increase in population.

[b] Dependency ratio = $\dfrac{\text{population 0-12 years + population over 50 years}}{\text{population 12-50 years}}$.

SOURCE· Same as for Table 3.4.

data from this census were grouped for presentation, the dependency ratios have to be calculated as the number of persons under 12 and over 50 divided by the number of persons between 12 and 50. The last two columns of Table 3.5 show the dependency ratios in the ten *talukas* for the 1872 census date and for the period immediately after the partial census of 1878. While the dependency ratios in 1872 vary from a low of 0.76 to a high of 0.91, and those for 1878 vary from a low of 0.65 to a high of 0.83, the direction of change for all the *talukas* is the same: toward a lower ratio. Among the total population of these ten *talukas*, the dependency ratio declined from 0.86 to 0.74. These changes reflect the fact that dependents—children under 12 and adults over 50—accounted for 68 percent of the total decline in population.[22]

[22] This figure was calculated from the figures on population change in each age

A priori, we would expect changes in the sex ratio as well as in the dependency ratio to result from a famine. In Table 3.6, sex ratios (number of females per 1,000 males) are given for the ten *talukas* in which the special famine census of 1878 was taken, for the districts in which these *talukas* are located, and for the four divisions of Bombay Presidency. Except for Kod *taluka* (where in-migration is suspected on the basis of the age data and the reported good condition of the district), the sex ratio is uniformly higher in 1878

TABLE 3.6. Sex Ratios in 1872, 1878, and 1881

Division, District	Females per 1,000 Males in.		
and Taluka	*1872*	*1878*	*1881*
Deccan			
Sholapur	943		973
Madha	945	987	
Sangola	956	978	
Satara	968		996
Man	948	983	
Khatav	964	987	
Karnatak			
Belgaum	954		989
Athni	958	992	
Sampgaon	972	991	
Bijapur	954		1,013
Bagalkot	962	996	
Badami	958	1,003	
Dharwar	951		998
Ron	972	1,020	
Kod	953	943	
Deccan	947		973
Karnatak	954		997
Gujarat	911		974
Konkan	989		998
Presidency	932		975

SOURCE· Same as for Table 3.4, and *Census of India* (for citations, see Appendix B, Tables B-2 and B-3).

group. Of a total population decline of about 100,000 in all ten *talukas*, 68,000 was in age groups under 12 years and over 50 years. It might also also be noted that large-scale out-migration from a famine-stricken region would tend to raise the dependency ratio by reducing the number of people ages 12 to 50.

than in 1872. Since severe underreporting of women was suspected in the 1872 census, it is not obvious how much of any change between that census and later figures should be attributed to better coverage of women on successive enumerations, rather than to differential mortality during the famine. However, given the evidence W. R. Cornish, Sanitary Inspector in Madras Presidency, gathered from the Madras famine relief camps, it would be unwise to dismiss the entire change as the result of better counting of women in successive censuses. Cornish found that in the Madras famine relief camps the death rate among males was 796.4 per thousand while among females the death rate was 595.3 per thousand. In general, the districts of Madras Presidency that were affected by the famine showed the same kind of change in the sex ratio as indicated by the statistics from Bombay Presidency.[23] To the extent that the change in the sex ratio reflects real changes in the numbers of males and females, it supports the hypothesis that females have greater biological capacity to resist the rigors of periods of famine— a capacity that is not offset by social factors.

The special famine census of 1878 covered a relatively limited region and, of course, only one famine. For the effects of dearth over a wider region and for the effects of other famines, data from the decennial censuses must be used. Changes in both the age and sex distribution of the population that appear in the comparison of the special census of 1878 with the census of 1872 also appear in comparisons of data in the decennial censuses. Table 3.7 gives the number of male and female children under five per 10,000 population at the censuses from 1881 through 1931. The most striking feature of the table is the oscillation in the proportions of children of both sexes in the three famine-prone regions. In Gujarat and the Karnatak, the proportions of boys and girls under five dropped to less than ten percent each after famines with very high mortality, such as 1901 for Gujarat and 1881 for Karnatak. The fluctuations in the proportion of children were smaller in the Deccan but followed the same pattern as for the Karnatak and Gujarat. In contrast, the changes in the Konkan, a region not subject to famine, were smaller and differently distributed. The effects of high prices of foodgrains may be visible in the lowered proportion of children in 1901 in Konkan. However, the Konkan had the highest percentage of children even in that year, and overall had the smallest fluctuations in this percentage.

---

[23] *Review of the Madras Famine*, p. 122.

TABLE 3.7. Number of Male and Female Children Ages 0-5 per 10,000 Population, 1881-1931

Division	1881		1891		1901		1911		1921		1931	
	M	*F*	*M*	*F*	*M*	*F*	*M*	*F*	*M*	*F*	*M*	*F*
Gujarat	1,202	1,276	1,338	1,446	910	931	1,438	1,553	1,216	1,354	1,351	1,513
Deccan	1,295	1,421	1,493	1,648	1,154	1,244	1,434	1,550	1,233	1,358	1,534	1,641
Karnatak	972	989	1,556	1,606	1,233	1,295	1,333	1,405	1,252	1,345	1,428	1,519
Konkan	1,431	1,517	1,469	1,548	1,286	1,342	1,386	1,393	1,253	1,277	1,517	1,548

SOURCES: Gujarat, 1881-1931 – *Census of India*, 1931, vol. 8, pt. 1, p. 101.
Deccan, Karnatak, Konkan, 1881-1911 – *Census of India*, 1911, vol. 7, pt. 1, pp. 82-83.
Deccan, Karnatak, Konkan, 1921 – Calculated from *Census of India*, 1921, vol. 8, pt. 2, pp. 71-73.
Deccan, Karnatak, Konkan, 1931 – Calculated from *Census of India*, 1931, vol. 8, pt. 2, pp. 103-105.

A second measure of the effects of famine on the lower end of the age distribution is the ratio of children of ages 0-5 to women of ages 15-40. The numerator of this ratio reflects the two effects of famine on the number of children—fewer births and higher mortality. Ideally, this measure should be calculated for periods which are the same number of years after famines or were preceded by equal numbers of good years. Unfortunately, decennial census data do not permit this. The ratios have nonetheless been constructed for each of the census years and are shown in Table 3.8. As might be expected, the variation in the ratio is greatest in the Karnatak and the Gujarat, where famines were the most serious. Gujarat has the lowest value and the Deccan the highest. It is impossible from these data to sort out whether the differences are due to the number of children born or to the rate of survival of these children. However, the results are consistent—for the Deccan, the Karnatak, and Gujarat—with their relative birth rates (see Table 3.3). But the Konkan, which had a birth rate considerably lower than that of the other three regions, had a higher ratio of children 0-5 to women of ages 15-40 than did the Gujarat in 1881, 1891, and 1901, the Deccan in 1881 and 1901, and the Karnatak in 1881, suggesting that children had a better chance of surviving in the Konkan than in these other, more famine-prone regions.

Table 3.9 contains data on changes in the ratio of males to females for the entire period from 1872 to 1931. (The figures for 1872 must

TABLE 3.8. Children Ages 0-5 per 1,000 Women Ages 15-40, 1881-1931

Year	Gujarat	Deccan	Karnatak	Konkan	Bombay Presidency[a]
1881	619	684	466	731	639
1891	691	797	777	743	761
1901	420	597	679	658	589
1911	715	740	694	665	711
1921	732	684	694	614	673
1931	729	792	744	728	758
Mean	651	716	676	690	689
Standard deviation	121	76	109	52	68
Coefficient of variation	19	11	16	7	10

[a]Excluding Bombay City.

SOURCE Appendix B, Table B-8.

TABLE 3.9. Sex Ratios for Divisions, 1872-1931

Year	Females per 1,000 Males in:				
	Gujarat	Deccan	Karnatak	Konkan	Bombay Presidency[a]
1872	911	947	954	989	949
1881	942	974	997	998	976
1891	945	967	989	1,011	976
1901	955	990	986	1,012	987
1911	928	983	975	1,038	982
1921	915	970	960	1,037	970
1931	916	964	956	1,012	962

[a]Excluding Bombay City.
SOURCE: Appendix B, Tables B-2 and B-3.

be viewed with caution because of the possibility of undercounting of women in that first census.) The ratio is lowest in Gujarat and highest in Konkan throughout the 60-year period. In general, the ratio rises over the first four censuses and then declines over the last three. The contrast is again provided by Konkan where the ratio rises through 1911 and only then begins to decline. The sharp rises in the ratio in divisions with high mortality from famine—Karnatak and Deccan, 1872-1881, and Gujarat and Deccan, 1891-1901—offer further support for the hypothesis that females may be better able than males to withstand the trials of a period of famine. The rise in the ratio in Gujarat between 1872 and 1881 suggests, as does evidence to be presented in Chapter 4, that Gujarat may have experienced famine conditions in 1876-1878 even though no famine was reported.

Overall, periods of famine (i.e., periods when mortality is greatly increased due to food shortages) create a population which has a lower dependency ratio (fewer young and old relative to adult workers) than the pre-famine population and one with more females relative to males. Periods of food shortage that do not result in heavy mortality may still reduce the dependency ratio somewhat by reducing the ratio of children to adult women. This is probably due both to fewer births and to some increase in infant and early childhood mortality. Because such a high proportion of famine deaths is concentrated among dependents—both children and elders—the productive capacity of the labor force may not be very much reduced after a famine. At the same time, the reduction in the population of adults will tend to make labor somewhat more scarce relative to land. Overall, if there is little destruction of *capital* (bullocks, wells, good tilth of land), per capita income may be somewhat higher after a famine. Some such rise, when coupled with the relatively small reductions in numbers of women in childbearing years, may explain why population growth after famines has frequently been very rapid,— for instance, in the 1881-1891 period, 1.57 percent per year in the Deccan and 1.83 percent per year in the Karnatak. However, if a famine were to be accompanied by widespread destruction of capital, the situation afterward might well be less conducive to rapid recovery of population.

In the course of studying the demographic impacts of famines, the question naturally arises: Why did not the populations of affected regions simply control their population so that their limited food supplies in bad years would be adequate for their survival? Since decisions on population control are made at the level of the family, it is appropriate to translate this question to: Why did not families have only the number of children for whom they could store enough grain to feed them during a famine? There may be a number of factors that need to be considered in a comprehensive answer to this question. For instance, how many people would it have taken to grow· enough grain to store to assure survival of children during a famine? But here the only aspect to be considered is: How many children did a couple want to have and how likely was it that they could fulfill this desire?[24]

For most Indians, even today, children that survive to adulthood are basically the only form of old-age insurance that exists. Incomes are too low to permit savings in lieu of children. In addition, the marginal contribution of children to family income may exceed what it costs to raise them until they are old enough to do some work. In viewing children as social security, only sons count for most persons. Married daughters are usually regarded as members of their husbands' families, not of their natal families. They are lost to the family labor force and cannot provide for aged parents. In addition, for Hindu males a son is essential to the proper performance of the death rites. All of these factors argue that there exists and existed a very strong desire to have at least one son survive to adulthood.

Infant and child mortality, however, even in the best of years, were and are high in South Asia. During a period reported to have

[24] This form of analysis derives from the work of Richard A. Easterlin. See especially his "An Economic Framework for Fertility Analysis," *Studies in Family Planning* 6 (March 1975):54-63.

been free from bad harvests and to have had no more illnesses than usual, recorded deaths among males less than one year old averaged 205 per 1,000; the recorded death rate among those aged one to five was 52 per 1,000 and among those five to ten, 12 per 1,000. These registration figures have generally been regarded as too low, perhaps by as much as 25 percent. Using the registered rates, the probability that a male infant will survive to age ten is 0.61. If all of the rates are increased by 25 percent, the probability falls to 0.53.[25] These estimates probably come close to bounding the true value of the probability. For example, Davis calculated the age to which one-half of male children survived to have been 14 in 1881-1891, 12 in 1891-1901 and 10 in 1901-1911.[26]

The probabilities of the survival of a single son or two sons have been used to make estimates of the number of births necessary to produce one or two sons. These estimates are given in Table 3.10. The figures there indicate that to have 95 percent chance of having one son survive to age ten, a couple would need to produce three or four male births, i.e., six or eight total births. To have two sons survive to age ten with 0.9 probability, five or six sons would have to be born, implying a total of ten or twelve births.

Data on number of children ever born to Indian women are not very plentiful or very good, particularly if an approximation of late nineteenth- and early twentieth-century conditions is wanted. However, using data on registered births and on the age distribution of

TABLE 3.10. Estimation of Number of Births to Produce One or Two Surviving Sons

Number of Births	Expected Number of Sons	When 53% of children survive to age 10, probability that at least:		When 61% of children survive to age 10, probability that at least:	
		1 son survives	2 sons survive	1 son survives	2 sons survive
2	1	0.53	—	0.61	—
4	2	0.78	0.28	0.85	0.37
6	3	0.90	0.55	0.94	0.66
8	4	0.95	0.73	0.98	0.83
10	5	0.98	0.84	0.99	0.92
12	6	0.99	0.91	1.00	0.98
14	7	0.99	0.93		

SOURCE: See text.

[25] See Appendix Table B-4, for sources and methods.
[26] Davis, *Population*, p. 63.

the female population, the numbers of births per 1,000 women aged 15-40 have been calculated for the four divisions of Bombay Presidency for 1891-1895. Using these numbers as the probability that any given woman bears a child in a given year and assuming a reproductive life span of 24 years, estimates of the expected number of births per woman have been made. Since the data on registered births may be underestimated, a second set of estimates has been made by increasing the expected number of births by 25 percent. The results are summarized in Table 3.11. They suggest that the demand for at least one son surviving to adulthood may often have gone unmet. Even when adjusted for underreporting, the number of births per woman barely rises above six, the minimum necessary to provide a high likelihood that a single son would survive beyond the life span of his parents.

In circumstances like those depicted in Tables 3.10 and 3.11, the demand for surviving children exceeds the supply, or as Easterlin writes, "Since desire exceeds potential output, parents would, however, have as many children as possible. . . ."[27] The occurrence of periodic crop failures resulting in at least dearth and sometimes famine would serve only to widen the gap between the desired and the likely actual number of surviving sons both by raising mortality among children above its already high level and by reducing the fecundity of couples.[28]

TABLE 3.11. Estimates of Number of Births per Woman

	Births per 1,000 Women Ages 15-40, 1891-1895		Expected Children Ever Born per Woman	
Division	Registered	+ 25%	Based on Registered Births	Based on Registered Births + 25%
Gujarat	176	220	4.22	5 28
Deccan	213	266	5.11	6.38
Karnatak	202	252	4.85	6.07
Konkan	152	190	3.65	4.56
Total	191	239	4.58	5 73

SOURCES· Births – Census of India, 1911, vol. 7, pt. 1, p. 109.
Women ages 15-40 – Census of India, 1891, vol. 8, pt. 2.
See text for calculations.

[27] Easterlin, "Fertility Analysis," p. 59.

[28] While Kessinger's work on Vilyatpur focuses on general "insecurity" of life rather than the difficulty of raising sons to adulthood, his results generally support my argument. In 1884, 1898, and 1910, 24, 20, and 28 percent of households, respectively, contained a single male adult who had no heir. Of all the property groups at

III. The Role of Famines and Epidemics in the Slow Growth of Population, 1872-1931

In the previous section we examined the changes in the shape of the population of the divisions of Bombay Presidency between 1872 and 1931, laying particular stress on changes in the age and sex composition caused by famines. In this section we will see what role specific famines and epidemics had in producing slow rates of population growth between 1872 and 1921.

Very different amounts of data are available for the study of changes in birth and death rates induced by periods of dearth, famine, and epidemic. The concern of the government of India with the prevention of deaths from starvation during "declared famine" meant that attention was paid to the collection of mortality statistics and to the estimation of mortality in excess of normal during periods of famine. No such concern was extended to severe malnutrition that might have prevented couples from conceiving and bearing children. Famine reports therefore rarely contained any information on changes in birth rates.[29]

While it is clear that changes in the birth rate can be expected to alter the rate of change of the population, the precise impact of such changes is much more difficult to isolate than that of changes in the death rate during famines. The decision on what portion of deaths in a given year is attributable to famine conditions is relatively easy, although the computation may be laborious. The reduction in the rate of growth of population due to these deaths can be inferred directly.[30] At most, part of the additional deaths that occur during

---

these dates, 51, 45, and 55 percent had a single male adult. Tom G. Kessinger, *Vilyatpur, 1848-1968: Social and Economic Change in a North Indian Village* (Berkeley and Los Angeles: University of California Press, 1974), pp. 189-190.

[29] There were exceptions. W. R. Cornish, Sanitary Commissioner for Madras, wrote on the decline of births during and subsequent to the famine of 1876-1878. Some data on birth rates were included in the reports of the famine of 1899-1902. The report of the 1881 census for Bombay Presidency also discussed declines in the birth rate during 1876-1878.

[30] Of course, if there is a disproportionate number of deaths among members of the population in childbearing years, then population growth could be slowed due to (a) fewer women in childbearing ages and (b) fewer sexually active women if many were left widows by a famine. However, as we saw in the previous section, the evidence from a variety of sources indicates that the very young and the old were the chief victims of famine. Among groups of prime childbearing age, somewhat more men than women usually succumbed to famine. If anything, this suggests that population growth after recovery from a famine might be somewhat more rapid than before.

a famine (or during an influenza epidemic) may have occurred only a year or two before they would otherwise occur. If the only additional deaths that occurred during a famine (or even a major portion of the deaths in a famine) were of this sort, the long-term effect of famine deaths on the population would be negligible. Of course, for India the data certainly indicate that deaths during famine periods were great enough to have a substantial impact on the rate of change of population.

The impact of birth rates is more complicated for several reasons. First, it is not absolutely clear over what period lowered birth rates should be attributed to the effects of a famine. Decline in nutritional status may cause an increase in pregnancy wastage which could begin to appear within several months of a crop failure. This same decline in nutritional status may result in temporary sterility of both males and females. Fecundity might continue to be depressed for some months after a good harvest had eliminated the possibility of further famine-related deaths. In any case, birth rates themselves could not be expected to recover from famine-induced reductions until at least nine months after the return of adequate food supplies.[31] This suggests that birth rates need to be examined in the year of a famine and the subsequent year as well in looking for the impact of famine on birth rates.

But what we want to know is the impact of the fall in birth rates on the population at the time of the next census. Even if we know the diminution in birth rates attributable to a famine (the number of births prevented by a famine), we cannot infer directly from this number the diminution in *population*, say five years later, that is caused by the lowered birth rates. Rather, total number of births prevented by the famine has to be adjusted to allow for the high (but unknown) mortality among children aged zero to five years. In other words, even had these births occurred, many of the children born would still have died before the next census. Only after the number of births prevented has been adjusted by the age-specific mortality can the decrease in population attributable to reduced birth rates be determined.

To deal with this complex of problems, the following method was

---

[31] This discussion ignores the possibility suggested by Rose Frisch's stimulating work, that poor nutrition may shorten the reproductive span for both men and women, and concentrates instead on the effects on fecundity (that is, the ability to conceive and to produce a live birth) of relatively short-term but severe nutritional stress. See Rose Frisch, "Population, Food Intake, and Fertility," *Science* 199 (January 6, 1978):22-29.

used to estimate the impact on the population of lowered birth rates in quinquennia in which famines occurred. The quinquennium 1891-1895 was taken as the standard, the "normal" period against which the birth rates of successive periods were to be measured. That period was chosen because it is the first one for which birth rates by divisions are available and also because it was a period generally reported to be free from dearth and famine. Whenever a division's birth rate for a given year was lower than in the standard period, the difference was multiplied by the census population for the division, and this product was then multiplied by five to convert the data from annual to quinquennial figures. This process yielded estimates of the number of births less than "normal" for each quinquennium.

In order to take account of the mortality to be expected among these unborn persons, a simple life table was constructed for ages zero to nine (i.e., from birth to tenth birthday). This table is reproduced as Appendix Table B-7. The proportions of children surviving to different ages were calculated from this table and these proportions were applied to the number of prevented births to yield estimates of the number of persons who would have been expected to survive to the next census if they had been born during the preceding ten years. The resulting estimates are shown in Table 3.12.

It should be noted that this methodology does not permit discrimination between declines in birth rates due to famine and declines due to other causes (e.g., the plague in Bombay Presidency from 1896 to 1920). Furthermore, construction of the life table required the use of the age- and sex-specific death rates reported from the 1891 census for the entire Bombay Presidency. These data (a) are not exactly the ones that should ideally be used for the different divisions and (b) are uncertain as to accuracy, although they seem reasonable. Finally, it was assumed that birth rates were lower for the entire quinquennium, not just for the specific years of famine; consequently, the calculated distribution of the impact of lowered birth rates over time may differ from the actual distribution.

Table 3.12 indicates that the impact of lowered birth rates on the population at the next census was non-trivial. Population in the three famine-prone divisions of Bombay Presidency would have been larger by 155,000 persons in 1900, by 262,000 in 1911, and by 145,000 in 1921 if birth rates in all quinquennia had been no lower than those of 1891-1895. These estimates should, of course, be treated with caution. If child mortality was greater than that recorded, the impact would be smaller. And interpretation of the fig-

TABLE 3.12. Impact of Lowered Birth Rates on Population[a]

Division and Year	Births "Prevented"	Population Impact at Succeeding Census
Gujarat		
1896-1900	15,000	11,000
Deccan		
1896-1900	124,000	91,000
1901-1905	149,000	101,000
1906-1910	30,000	22,000
1911-1915	--	--
1916-1920	128,000	93,000
Karnatak		
1896-1900	72,000	53,000
1901-1905	128,000	87,000
1906-1910	71,000	52,000
1911-1915	14,000	10,000
1916-1920	57,000	42,000
Total		
1896-1900	--	155,000
1901-1910	--	262,000
1911-1920	--	145,000

[a]For methods of calculation, see text.

SOURCES: Tables 3.2 and 3.3.

ures depends on the assumption that while the level of registered births may be incorrect, the fluctuations underlying the series are real and reasonably accurate.

Not all of the fluctuations in observed birth rates automatically can be attributed to declines in food supplies and subsequent declines in fecundity. The crude birth rate would also decline if the proportion of women in the childbearing ages declined or if a significant number of women did not enter into sexual unions to produce children. Given the mores of Indian agricultural castes, most women did marry; declines in the birth rate due to changes in the percentage of women married will therefore be ignored.[32] In 1921,

---

[32] It should be noted that while hard times might force the postponement or scaling down of elaborate marriage celebrations, the joint family structure meant that marriages did not have to wait upon a young man's securing an independent means of livelihood. In any case, between 1901 and 1931 the percentage of unmarried women aged 15 to 40 varied only from 3.2 to 3.7 percent. Government of India, Commissioner of the Census, *Census of India*, 1901, vol. IX-A, pp. 72-74; 1911, vol. 7, pt. 2, pp. 78-80; 1921, vol. 8, pt. 2, pp. 71-73; 1931, vol. 8, pt. 2, pp. 103-105.

however, women aged 15 to 40 were only 39 percent of all women (compared to 41 percent at all other census dates), due to the influenza epidemic of 1918, which killed disproportionate numbers of adults and particularly women of childbearing age.[33] The decline is large enough to have affected birth rates during the quinquennia 1916-1920 and 1921-1925. This suggests that the influenza epidemic had two effects on the size of the population of Bombay Presidency: It increased the death rate, and it decreased the birth rate, not by reducing fecundity but by altering the proportion of women of childbearing years in the population.

Having estimated the effects of lowered birth rates on slowing the rate of population growth, we turn to the effects of increased deaths. The impact of famine, plague, and influenza on the population were of sufficient concern to administrators that there is available more than one set of figures to estimate mortality from these causes. The first set of estimates comes from the famine reports and from reports of the Sanitary Commissioner and the census on plague and influenza. "Excess" mortality from famine and from influenza has been obtained by subtracting the average mortality in the previous five years during the same months as the famine or epidemic from the registered deaths during the demographic calamity. However, if some of the previous five years had been "exceptional," they were usually eliminated from the calculations. In the case of plague, deaths were registered separately after the outbreak in 1896. The total deaths attributed to plague in the Presidency were accumulated by the Sanitary Commissioner and published in his reports and in the census reports. All other death rates and figures on deaths were usually given two ways—one including and one excluding deaths from plague.

The estimated mortality from famine calculated from the famine reports is presented in Table 3.13. These figures are very much what would be expected given the census figures on population change. For the period between the censuses of 1872 and 1881, the estimated mortality of 66,000 in the Deccan and 150,000 in the Karnatak is consistent with the very slow growth of population in the former (0.14 percent annually) and the decline of population in the latter (negative 1.57 percent annually). Gujarat also experienced very slow growth (0.17 percent annually), which may indicate that mortality was elevated in this period even though no deaths were reported as due to food shortages since a famine was not officially declared. For the decade 1891-1901, the figures are in accord with

[33] Calculated from Appendix Table B-8.

TABLE 3.13. Estimates of Mortality from Famines[a]

Division	1876-1878	1896-1897	1899-1900	1900-1901	1901-1902	1905-1906	1911-1912	1912-1913	1918-1919
				Number of Deaths					
Gujarat	—	—	289,000	92,000	15,000	—	6,000	—	4,000
Deccan	66,000	88,000	166,000	5,000	—	22,000	53,000	3,000	25,000
Karnatak	150,000	33,000	7,000	7,000	—	6,000	13,000	—	—
Total	216,000	121,000	462,000	104,000	15,000	28,000	72,000	3,000	29,000
				Rate per 1,000 Population[b]					
Gujarat	—	—	93.3	34.0	5.6	—	2.1	—	1.4
Deccan	12.6	14.1	26.7	0.8	—	3.7	8.3	0.5	3.9
Karnatak	54.5	9.9	2.4	2.5	—	2.1	4.6	—	—
Total	20.0	11.5	37.9	9.0	1.3	2.4	6.0	0.2	2.4

[a]Estimated as the difference, net of plague deaths after 1896, between registered mortality in famine period and average of mortality for the same months in previous 5 years (generally). No estimates are given for the famine of 1913-1914 because there was no table of deaths in the report on that famine. No report appears to have been published on the 1915-1916 famine in North Gujarat. No retrievable death figures have been found for the famine of 1891-1892 in Karnatak, but the elevation of the death rate for 1892 over the average of 1891, 1893, 1894, and 1895 suggests about 19,000 "excess" deaths in Karnatak during that famine.

[b]These rates are not directly comparable with those in Table 3.3 and Appendix B, Table B-6, because they cover a "famine" year from September to August rather than a calendar year or an agricultural year (April to March) and because they include only famine-related (as opposed to all) deaths in the year.

SOURCES: 1876-1877 – "Mortality from the Famine of 1877 in the Bombay Presidency," Minute by the Governor of Bombay, dated 20 August 1878, *Proceedings of the Public Works Department,* L/PWD/3/580.

1896-1897 – Famine Commission, *Report of the Indian Famine Commission, 1898,* Appendix vol. III, p. 209. The report does not state that the figures are net of plague deaths. However, comparison with excess mortality estimated from the average annual death rates from all causes, 1891-1895, and death rates from all causes, 1896 and 1897, indicates that plague deaths are not included, since excess mortality from all causes was 24,000 in 1896 and 136,000 in 1897 for all famine districts except Dharwar. (*Report of Indian Famine Commission,* Appendix vol. III, p. 239.)

1899-1900, 1900-1901, 1901-1902 – *Report on the Famine in Bombay Presidency, 1899-1902,* Appendix 60, pp. 179-192.

1905-1906 – *Report on the Famine in Bombay Presidency, 1905-1906,* Appendix, pp. 22-23.

1911-1921 – *Report on the Famine in Bombay Presidency, 1911-1912,* Appendix, pp. 22-23.

1912-1913 – *Report on the Famine in Bombay Presidency, 1912-1913,* Appendix, p. 6.

1918-1919 – Calculated from *Review of the Famine Administration in Bombay Presidency, 1918-1919,* Appendix 10, pp. 32-33. Excess mortality for November 1918 has been excluded because it appears to have been due to the influenza epidemic rather than the famine.

the rates of change of population derived from the census for all three divisions. Gujarat's deaths from famine were 381,000; Deccan's, 259,000; and Karnatak's, 47,000. Gujarat's rate of growth during that decade was negative 1.36 percent, the Deccan's, negative 0.44 percent, and the Karnatak's, negative 0.06 percent. However, the next two decades were also periods of slow growth of population (relative to the decades 1881-1891 and 1921-1931). The estimated total of 147,000 excess deaths from famines in these three divisions between 1901 and 1919 is much too small to account for the slowness of growth.

The explanation of these two decades of slow growth must lie with three other phenomena—plague, influenza, and reduced birth rates.[34] Plague appeared in Bombay City in 1896 and, in spite of efforts to contain it, it spread inland where it caused heavy deaths for a decade and then became endemic. As late as the quinquennium 1931-1935, Bombay Presidency reported an annual average of 12,000 deaths from plague.[35] Registered deaths from plague for the entire Presidency, including Sind and Bombay City were 265,000 in 1896-1900; 1,113,000 in 1901-1910; and 565,000 in 1911-1920.[36] Not all of these deaths occurred in the three divisions that were subject to famine. These divisions constituted between 61 and 62 percent of the population of Bombay Presidency including Sind, to which the statistics purport to correspond. Lacking a divisional breakdown of plague mortality, 61 percent of plague deaths have been assigned to the divisions of Gujarat, Karnatak, and Deccan.[37] By this method, 162,000 deaths from plague are attributed to the three divisions for 1896-1900; 679,000 for 1901-1910; and 345,000 for 1911-1920.

The influenza epidemic, part of the pandemic that swept the world in 1918-1919, appears in Bombay Presidency to have been confined to the second six months of 1918. It began in Bombay City in May

---

[34] The argument is that periods of crop failure sufficient to provoke declarations of famine might, with relief efforts, result in little elevation of mortality, yet the decline in nutritional status could have been sufficiently severe to reduce fecundity. The role of government relief efforts in reducing mortality during famines is discussed in Chapter 6.

[35] Calculated from data in Bombay Presidency, *Annual Reports of the Director of Public Health for the Government of Bombay*, Nos. 70 (1933) and 77 (1940).

[36] *Census of India*, 1921, vol. 8, pt. 1, p. 20.

[37] This rough method is not particularly satisfactory, since plague initially tended to spread in waves out from Bombay City, causing heavy deaths and then moving on. It apparently did not become endemic everywhere. Given time and effort, materials probably do exist in the reports of the Sanitary Commissioner to reconstruct district-level series on plague mortality.

but reached truly epidemic proportions only in September, when 60,000 deaths in excess of normal were reported in the Presidency. The epidemic peaked in October, with over 600,000 deaths in excess of normal reported, and then receded fairly quickly—less than 200,000 deaths in the Presidency in November, and almost none after that except in Bombay City. Of the total estimated excess deaths of 1,030,000 for the Presidency, 102,000 occurred in Gujarat, 452,000 in the Deccan, and 159,000 in Karnatak.[38]

Table 3.14 summarizes the various causes of slow growth of population in the famine-prone divisions of Bombay Presidency from 1891 to 1921. Mortality from famines, plague, and influenza are included as well as the impact of lowered birth rates calculated in Table 3.12. From both Table 3.14 and Table 3.13, it appears that famine played a declining role in producing excess mortality, only 18 percent of famine mortality occurring after 1901. (Although deaths from famine were greater in 1911-1921 than in 1901-1911, they dropped off virtually to zero in the succeeding decades.) Over the entire period, plague accounted for 1,186,000 deaths, while famine accounted for 834,000, and influenza, 713,000. Over the three decades there was also a reduction of population (below what it would have been without famine and epidemics) of 562,000 due to lowered birth rates. Some of this reduction is probably attributable to plague and influenza as well as to famine, but more precise statements for this period await future research.

It is possible to form a second set of estimates for total excess mortality during this period using the quinquennial death-rate data from Table 3.3. Taking the death rate from 1891 to 1895 as the standard, excess mortality can be calculated as the difference between that rate and any rate higher than that. When these differences are multiplied by the population at the previous census and converted from annual to quinquennial figures, the results are estimates of excess mortality. These estimates for Gujarat, the Deccan, and the Karnatak are given in Table 3.15.

The last column in Table 3.15 indicates how closely these estimates correspond to the estimates of total mortality arrived at previously. (E.g., for 1896-1900, the estimate of 810,000 in Table 3.15 is 95 percent of the estimate of 849,000 shown for 1819-1901 in Table 3.14.) The high degree of agreement is reassuring, since the two estimates come from the same underlying data on the registration of deaths in countless villages. Some of the discrepancy is

[38] *Census of India*, 1921, vol. 8, pt. 2, p. 24.

TABLE 3.14. Determinants of Slow Growth of Population in Gujarat, Deccan, and Karnatak, 1891-1921

1891-1901		
"Excess" mortality		
Famines:		
1896-1897	121,000	
1899-1900	462,000	
1900-1901	104,000	
Total famine mortality		687,000
Plague		162,000
Total Excess Mortality		849,000
Impact of Lowered Birth Rates		155,000
		1,004,000
1901-1911		
"Excess" mortality		
Famines		
1901-1902	15,000	
1905-1906	28,000	
Total famine mortality		43,000
Plague		679,000
Total Excess Mortality		722,000
Impact of Lowered Birth Rates		262,000
		984,000
1911-1921		
"Excess" mortality		
Famines		
1911-1912	72,000	
1912-1913	3,000	
1918-1919	29,000	
Total famine mortality		104,000
Plague		345,000
Influenza		713,000
Total Excess Mortality		1,162,000
Impact of Lowered Birth Rates		145,000
		1,307,000

SOURCE· See text.

probably due to the tendency of both famines and epidemics to have had disproportionate effects on members of the population whose general health was sufficiently poor that they could be expected to die within a year or two anyway. In the data used to prepare Table

TABLE 3.15. Estimates of Excess Mortality from Registered Death Rates

	Excess Deaths from All Causes				Percent of Total Excess Mortality[a]
Decade	Gujarat	Deccan	Karnatak	Total	
1891-1900	325,000	340,000	145,000	810,000	95
1901-1910[b]	150,000	180,000	325,000	655,000	91
1911-1920[b]	110,000	640,000	355,000	1,105,000	95

[a]Total excess mortality from Table 3.14.

[b]For all three divisions in 1906-1910, and for Gujarat and Deccan in 1911-1915, death rates were below the 1891-1895 standard.

SOURCE· Calculated from Tables 3.2 and 3.3.

3.14, the deaths of these persons would be reported as due to famine, plague, or influenza. In the data used for Table 3.15 (that is, in quinquennial averages), the effect would be to move their deaths from, say, 1920 in the absence of an influenza epidemic, to 1918 because of the epidemic. In other words, the method used to estimate deaths due to famine, plague, and influenza in Table 3.14 would, if the registration data were correct, overstate somewhat the total impact of such deaths on the size of the population.

The null hypothesis of this inquiry, drawn from the work of Kingsley Davis, is that in the absence of famine and epidemic, population in India would have grown at the same rates in all decades as it did in decades that were free of these scourges. To test this hypothesis, the estimates of the impact of these events on population can be used to reconstruct what the population would have been if they had not occurred. Table 3.16 contains such a reconstruction. It should be stressed that this table does not show *estimates* projected from vital rates; rather, it shows an actual *reconstruction* from estimated mortality and birth-rate reductions. The average annual population growth rate for the two least affected decades, 1881-1891 and 1921-1931, was 1.23 percent (compounded annually). The decade for which the reconstruction yields the most similar rate of growth is that of 1901-1911, when the rate was 1.25 percent.

There are a number of statistical problems that might account for the differences between these reconstructed rates of growth and the rate during the "standard" decades. First, the registration data for the Presidency (on which all estimates ultimately rest) may have chronically failed to capture all changes in population. Second, registration may have been unusually deficient during the famine of 1899-1902. The indications are that this was the worst famine in

TABLE 3.16. Reconstructions of Population of Gujarat, Deccan, and Karnatak
As If Famine, Plague, and Influenza Had Not Occurred

Decade	1891-1901	1901-1911	1911-1921
Initial population	12,171,000	11,490,000	12,023,000
Final population	11,490,000	12,023,000	11,805,000
Growth rate (compound annual)	-0.57	0.45	-0.18
Final population	11,490,000	12,023,000	11,805,000
+ Excess mortality	+ 849,000	722,000	1,162,000
+ Effect of lowered birth rates	+ 155,000	262,000	145,000
Reconstructed population	12,494,000	13,007,000	13,112,000
Growth rate	0.26	1.25	0.87

SOURCES: Calculated from Tables 3.2, 3.3, and 3.14.

Bombay Presidency's history (although not in western India's history), and the burdens on the administrative structure may have rendered it less efficient in registration than usual. Third, migration has been ignored throughout. It is certainly possible that in 1901 some persons had left the three most affected divisions of the Presidency to escape the famine. However, there does not appear to be any reason why an unusual number should have been out of the Presidency in 1921. Another possibility is that the 1901 census had a fairly severe undercount because it was taken in the midst of a famine and a plague epidemic. The census of India made use of regular government personnel as enumerators and the government of Bombay used them as famine workers. This triple demand on their time and energies in 1901 may have led to greater than normal errors. If this were the case, then some of the growth attributed to the decade 1901-1911 really occurred in 1891-1901. Again, however, there is no reason why the census of 1921 should have had such difficulties. Of these four possible sources, the most important one is probably the chronic underregistration of both births and deaths.

Non-statistical factors may also play a role. For instance, in the quinquennium of 1891-1895, the registered birth rate for Gujarat is the same as the division's death rate. Even with due regard for the frailties of the registration data, this nonetheless suggests that there was no growth of population in Gujarat during the first part of the decade 1891-1895, when neither famine nor epidemic was noted in that division. However, slow or no growth in Gujarat is unlikely to completely account for the large differences between the reconstructed rates of growth and that of the decades 1881-1891 and 1921-1931. After all, the Deccan and Karnatak both have large surpluses of registered births over registered deaths in the quinquennium of 1891-1895. Research at a more disaggregated level is needed to determine what was causing the slow growth of population in Gujarat.

The data presented in this chapter have shown a surprising pattern. While mortality from periods declared to be famines was high up to 1901, subsequent declared famines produced *much* smaller increases in mortality. The high mortality of the decades 1901-1911 and 1911-1921 was due not to famines but to plague and influenza. (Although droughts and crop failures continued into the 1920s and 1930s, they rarely resulted in either declarations of famine or elevations of mortality.) We are therefore compelled to ask what changes had occurred after the beginning of the twentieth century that could be responsible for the sharp diminution in mortality from famines. In order to explore that question, we must begin by studying the patterns of the agrarian system that permitted mortality from those earlier famines to be so great. Chapters 4 and 5 undertake that study. Chapter 4 examines changes in the agrarian system under British rule from 1818 to about 1895. Chapter 5 explores aggregate changes in the agricultural and industrial sectors. Then Chapter 6 confronts directly the question of what changed—or why a society that had once suffered enormous elevations in mortality as a result of crop failures later developed the capacity to deal with such crop failures in ways that reduced excess mortality.

4. *The Agrarian System and the Impact of British Rule*

Between 1803 and 1818 the East India Company conquered significant parts of western India from its Maratha rulers. The Company's officials knew then, and we know now, relatively little about the organization and functioning of the agrarian economy before this conquest. This limited knowledge made it difficult if not impossible for those men to determine in advance the results of the policies they adopted (or, as a corollary, to know what policy to choose to obtain a specific result). For modern researchers, the lack of a baseline that describes how things were before modern influences—new systems of revenue assessment and collection, railroads, increased integration into world markets, new sources of employment, and new famine relief policies—affected the structure and functioning of the agrarian system frustrates attempts to determine the impact of colonial rule.

The first section of this chapter develops, from rather fragmentary information, such a baseline for the Deccan and the Karnatak. It will be a somewhat speculative picture, a somewhat hypothetical construct. But I shall try to sort out fact from myth, to be explicit about what we do and do not know, and to generate a consistent picture that further research in new sources can challenge or confirm. The second section of the chapter traces the revenue and cultivation history of twelve *talukas* in the Deccan and Karnatak from their takeover by the British through the expiry of the first 30-year settlement, done under the Bombay Survey and Settlement System (or from about 1818 to the 1870s and 1880s). The final sections of the chapter use the baseline and the history of these twelve *talukas* to make some statements about the impact of British rule during this period.

I. The Baseline

Of the four natural regions that comprised Bombay Presidency (Gujarat, Konkan, Deccan, and Karnatak), the Deccan and the Karnatak have been, over a long period of time, subject to more years of food crisis than the other two regions. The Konkan region, located along the coast, tends to have high, stable levels of rainfall and to report few if any food crises. The Gujarat region, while it has known famine, was free of food crises of famine magnitude for much of the nineteenth century.[1] It is not clear whether a more highly developed commerce, a richer agriculture, and a greater degree of patrimonial relationships made food crises both easier to survive and less visible than in the Deccan and the Karnatak, or whether absolutely fewer years of severe food shortage occurred in the Gujarat.[2] Whatever the reason for the lower incidence of reported famine in Gujarat, that lower incidence has been used to exclude Gujarat from the portion of this study that focuses on the conditions of the period before colonial rule and the impact of the first 60 years of that rule.

Generally speaking, the literature on the Deccan and the Karnatak has been concerned with the *structure* of villages and not with the functioning of the agricultural system or with the functioning of the state with respect to villages. We have, therefore, descriptions of the village members and their duties and privileges, but little information on how these were determined or sustained and under what conditions they changed. The image has, overall, been one of a largely unchanging system that had evolved into an "equilibrium" at some past time. As an example, virtually every writer on these regions has discussed permanent members of the village land-owning strata—variously called *mirasdars* and *chali ryots*—and contrasted them with others—called *upris* or *uparis*—who farmed some land in the village on a temporary basis but who were not full members of the village community. Nowhere, however, do we find any sustained discussion of the origin of the *uparis*. The impression

---

[1] No famine was *declared* in Gujarat until 1899-1900. The last severe famine before that date was either in 1812, as reported by Bhatia, *Famines in India*, frontispiece map; or in 1833-1834, as reported by R. D. Choksey, *Economic Life in the Bombay Gujarat 1880-1939* (Bombay: Asia Publishing House, 1968), p. 170. However, evidence from the demographic materials in Chapter 3 (see especially Table 3.2) indicates almost no growth of population between 1872 and 1881, and other evidence from Choksey (*Bombay Gujarat*, p. 152) suggests that the famine of 1876-1878 was felt to some extent in Gujarat even if no famine was declared by the administration.

[2] It would obviously be worthwhile to study in some detail all of these possibilities. I have not chosen to do so for two reasons. When I commenced this study, two colleagues were engaged in close study of the social and economic history of the Gujarat, and I had no wish to duplicate their work. Even had this not been the case, the Deccan and the Karnatak are sufficiently large and diverse to more than occupy my research time. Where comparisons among the four regions of Bombay Presidency have been possible from published data collected for other projects, I have made them.

is commonly left that they were both deprived (because they were not full members of the village community) and courted (because of a general shortage of labor and a desire on the part of the *patel* or of the community to have more land in the village tilled). To further complicate the picture, several authors sometimes argue that *uparis* could, under certain conditions, become *mirasdars*. And it is generally agreed that *mirasdars* or *chali ryots* paid higher rates for their lands than *uparis* paid for lands they cultivated.[3]

It is possible to generate, from the extensive data available on western India before the British conquest, a more integrated analysis than yet exists. To do so, I will make use of two sets of sources and some economics. The first of the sources is the able descriptive work derived from documents, commonly referred to as the Peshwa Daftar, of the Maratha administration. The second are the reports, written between 1818 and 1850, of early East India Company administrators in the Deccan and the Karnatak. Since these men sometimes used records from the Peshwa Daftar in writing their reports, the two sets of information are not completely independent. However, the Englishmen also relied heavily on informants, village documents, and their own observations, sources of information that are separate from the Peshwa Daftar. The economics will be drawn upon to move from description of villages and village-state relations to analysis of the functioning of the institutions. My use both of sources and of economics will be informed by some of what anthropologists and sociologists have told us about the crucial elements that hold a rural society together. Landholders and revenue assessments will be discussed for the two regions separately; other members of the village community will be discussed for the regions together.

It is difficult to separate the Karnatak and the Deccan in works

---

[3] For examples of the kind of work summarized in this paragraph, see I. J. Catanach, *Rural Credit in Western India, 1875-1930* (Berkeley and Los Angeles: University of California Press, 1970); H. Fukazawa, "Land and Peasants in the Eighteenth Century Maratha Kingdom," *Hitotsubashi Journal of Economics* 6 (June 1965):32-61; H. Fukazawa, "Rural Servants in the Eighteenth Century Maharashtrian Village—Demiurgic or Jajmani System?" *Hitotsubashi Journal of Economics* 12 (February 1972):14-40; A. R. Kulkarni, "Village Life in the Deccan in the 17th Century," *Indian Economic and Social History Review* 4 (March 1967):38-52; Ravinder Kumar, "The Rise of Rich Peasants in Western India," in *Soundings in Modern South Asian History*, ed. D. A. Low (Berkeley and Los Angeles: University of California Press, 1968), pp. 25-58; Ravinder Kumar, *Western India in the Nineteenth Century: A Study in the Social History of Maharashtra* (London: Routledge & Kegan Paul, 1968).

that draw on the Peshwa Daftar. However, a report by Captain (later Sir) George Wingate, published in 1853, does deal specifically with the Maratha revenue system in the Karnatak. Wingate gives a somewhat idealized version of the system "during its best period . . ."[4] Even so, the system he describes is a confusing one, as a long quote from his report will show.

A district yielding two or three lakhs of rupees was placed under a SurSoobhedar, with dependent Mamlutdars, who fixed annually, according to the extent of cultivation and circumstances of the ryots, the amount to be paid by each village. The distribution of this amount was left to be settled by the village officers and cultivators amongst themselves, though appeals were open to higher authorities, when any individual thought himself unfairly burdened.

The assessment was made up of the "Rukhum" [Rakam] or "Einatee," that is, the original standard rate; the "Mamool Puttee" [mamul patti], or accustomed cesses; and the "Jasthee Puttee" [jasti patti], or extra cesses, necessary to bring up the village rental to the amount settled by the Mamlutdar for the year's Jummabundee [jama-bandi].

There was also a classification of the lands under cultivation into "Chalee" [chali], "Khutgoota" [katguta], "Khundmukta" [khandmakta], and "Cowl" [kaul], or other denominations of the same import.

The "Chalee" alone was subject to the payment of all the cesses above described; the "Khutgoota" generally paid the "Einatee" or standard rate, and the "Mamool Puttee"; while the amount payable for "Khundmukta" was a low fixed rate, according to previous agreement with the holder. "Cowls" were granted when the land had long been waste, and secured its enjoyment for a certain number of years rent free.

A ryot was not allowed to relinquish any part of his chalee land; but, to enable him to pay the heavy assessment on it, he was always allowed to hold a certain portion of khutgoota and khundmukta, or cowl land. He was also permitted to cultivate the lands of Enamdars [inamdar], which were always obtainable on much more favorable terms than Government lands. When a chalee ryot, from poverty, could not contribute his quota, it was made

[4] SRGB No. 12 (1853), p. 5.

up by others, and recovered by them from him, as circumstances would permit. All the chalee ryots were permanent residents in the village, and had a voice in the management of its affairs. A ryot refusing to cultivate his chalee land was liable to be deprived of the privilege of grazing his cattle on the common waste lands, and of cultivating the land of Enamdars. He was also frequently subject to a house tax, and generally looked upon by his neighbors as a person who had meanly endeavored to shift his share of the general burthen upon the shoulders of his fellow villagers.

Temporary residents, or cultivators residing in neighboring villages, were not required to hold chalee lands; but neither were they entitled to interfere in the management of the village affairs, nor to the privilege of cultivating cowl or enam lands. They usually cultivated on the khutgoota or khundmukta tenures.[5]

Part of the difficulty in understanding the system Wingate describes arises from the lack of clarity, both in this statement and in the ways that scholars have usually approached similar documents, about which authority "required," "permitted," and "did not allow." Three authorities are clearly present in this system—the state or overlord represented by the *SurSoobhedar* and the *mamlatdars*, the village officials, and the cultivators—but their relative spheres of influence are not well defined. I am going to argue that the system described by Wingate, as well as its analog in the Deccan, emerged from a process of continuous negotiation between the state or overlord and the village officials and cultivators, ignoring for the time being the relationships between the latter two groups.

It is important to state at the outset that I reject the notion that all revenue was collected by force and that threat of reprisal was the primary reason that payments of revenue were made. The process of petition and contract between village and overlord that is documented for this region from the seventeenth century onwards is inconsistent with a state operated entirely by force.[6] For whatever

---

[5] SRGB No. 12 (1853), pp. 5-6. I have attempted to locate all of the revenue terms Wingate used by searching H. H. Wilson, *A Glossary of Judicial and Revenue Terms*, 2nd ed. (Delhi: Munshiram Manoharlal Oriental Publishers and Booksellers, 1968). *SurSoobhedar*, however, has eluded me; perhaps a lack of imagination on my part in transforming Wingate's spelling is at fault. All the other revenue terms in the quote from Wingate are followed by Wilson's spellings, in brackets, the first time they occur, unless the two spellings are the same.

[6] Kulkarni, "Village Life"; Fukazawa, "Land and Peasants" and "Rural Servants"; Stewart N. Gordon, "Recovery from Adversity in Eighteenth Century India: Rethinking 'Villages,' 'Peasants,' and Politics in Pre-Modern Kingdoms," *Peasant Studies* 8 (Fall 1979):61-82.

reasons, the belief structures of the people who lived in villages and those who were their overlords included some norms about what rights each had in land and its produce and what duties each owed the other.[7] These beliefs were not immutable; they could and did change. They formed a framework within which state and peasants related to each other. But in this unstable region of western India—unstable in terms of climate and of political control—periods of order alternated with periods of disorder. In the periods of disorder, the rights of both state and peasants may have been abridged—their contract may have become void because of the failure of one side (most often the state) to be able to fulfill its role. For example, peasants who were not protected from raiders did not have crops to hand over to their overlord.[8] States could not collect revenues from peasants whose crops were short because of droughts—but this may have diminished the capacity of the state to protect those peasants if drought struck a large part of its domains at once. In periods of disorder, villages probably paid only because of threats of violence; after all, the state had failed them. But in periods of order it was otherwise.

In times of order, the two major decisions that had to emerge from whatever system obtained were: How much revenue would the village pay? and who would pay what share of that revenue? The following paragraphs argue that the first question was settled by negotiation between the *mamlatdar* and the village and that the answer to the second was generated by the interaction of the internal structure of the village and the negotiations with the state.

The basis of the negotiation between the state and the villages it embraced was the *right* of the state to a part of the produce of the land so long as it succored the peasantry. But this did not determine the share of produce; it just formed the background against which a bargain could be made. While the aims of the state or its ruler were not expressed entirely in a demand for revenue from the villages, revenue was, of necessity, a major goal. The very existence of the state required that some revenue be raised to pay for defense and administration. It might have been desirable for the state to have moved inside the village to determine the rates of taxation on each field or each cultivator in order to have better information about

[7] Textual studies of kingship certainly support the notion that kings and subjects had reciprocal rights and duties. Ronald Inden, "Ritual, Authority, and Cyclic Time in Hindu Kingship," mimeo., 1977.

[8] Records for Khandesh show that the Maratha overlords permitted villages to deduct tribute they had paid to a passing army from the *jamabandi* they normally paid to the overlord. Gordon, "Recovery from Adversity," p. 64.

the ability of the village to pay, but the administrative costs of doing so were high in terms of personnel needed. In addition, even if the state did make such a determination once (and there is evidence from diverse parts of the subcontinent that such determinations were made), a strong and undistracted government was required to maintain the system.[9] In times of peace, rulers with adequate resources might work to restore regions damaged by drought or war, to increase the cultivated area within their lands, and to gain more information about and control of the surplus produce, but these activities could not be sustained when war was sought by or thrust upon the state or when other forms of crisis reduced the resources available to it.[10] Faced with frequent warfare and limited numbers of good administrators, their own administrative constraints left the eighteenth-century states of western India little choice but to bargain with the village for the highest sustainable revenue or tribute and leave the allocation of that demand within the village to the villagers.

If we accept for the moment that the allocation of revenue demand within villages was determined inside the villages, how might we interpret the pattern of tenures and assessments that Wingate describes? The picture or pictures that we generate cannot encompass all possible variations, because the material with which we work (even when we expand our sources beyond Wingate) encompasses only a very limited number of patterns, though we hope they are the major ones. Bearing this caveat in mind, let us attempt to explain the data at hand.

Villages in the Karnatak, like those in many other parts of India, appear to have had their individual origins as settlements of independent, fairly coequal agriculturists on empty land. Such groups may have settled because population pressures impelled them to

[9] For evidence on an attempt by Madhav Rao Peshwa to impose direct taxes on *kunbis* in the 1760s, see R. Kumar, "Rise of Rich Peasants," p. 28. For a discussion of the Maratha government in Malwa, see Stewart N. Gordon, "The Slow Conquest: Administrative Integration of Malwa into the Maratha Empire, 1720-1760," *Modern Asian Studies* 11 (February 1977):1-40.

[10] The amounts of resources and personnel needed to restore a district ravaged by famine and war are illustrated by the efforts of the Peshwa in Khandesh in the mid-eighteenth century. The fate of regions so devastated when such resources were not forthcoming can be seen in the condition of Khandesh in 1818. Gordon, "Recovery from Adversity," pp. 69-73, 76. Wingate's description of the regions that became Dharwar district suggests that a similar deterioration in that region's economy occurred before 1818 and was not ameliorated by early British rule. SRGB No. 12 (1853), pp. 47-48.

move from their place of origin, because crisis of some form (drought, war, pestilence, predatory ruler, epidemic) drove them away from their former homes, or because they were lured by promises of new lands at lower rates or by hope of new lands beyond the reach of a taxing authority. We will probably never have a general answer to why they came.

When they settled, they generally practiced exclusively rainfed agriculture. The rivers of the region do not lend themselves to the easy construction of irrigation works. The British did find evidence that tanks had been widely built, but they appear more often designed to provide the village with water through the dry season than to irrigate any considerable amount of land.[11] Population seems generally not to have been very dense, nor cultivation very intense (in the Boserupian sense).[12] Waste lands were plentiful and supplemented village grazing lands and woods. While the region obviously yielded some of its surplus to an overlord or state, it does not appear to have also supported a class of landlords who did not cultivate. (This statement is, unfortunately, based largely on the lack of reported landlords rather than direct statements that most agriculturists followed the plow on their own lands.) Power inside the village presumably, therefore, rested with the set of agriculturists who were permanent residents in the village—those Wingate refers to as *chali ryots*—and perhaps with the village headman or *patel* if one had emerged who was more than *primus inter pares*.

If power rested with the agriculturists to distribute the revenue demanded by the overlord or state among themselves, what goals and objectives governed the distribution of obligations? At the risk of being taken for an economist-bull in a historian's china shop, I am going to suggest that maintenance of the corporate identity of the founding group of agriculturists was one primary goal and that a second goal was the maintenance or increase of this group's social and economic status.[13] If Wingate's statements about tenures and

[11] SRGB Irrigation Series No. 5 (1866), p. 7.

[12] For a full discussion of intensity of cultivation, see Ester Boserup, *The Conditions of Agricultural Growth* (Chicago: Aldine, 1965). Population clearly had waxed and waned with periods of order and disorder. Deserted villages were reported in several parts of the lands that became Bombay Presidency. At the time of East India Company's takeover in the Deccan and the Karnatak, deserted villages appear to have been most common in the "march lands" of the Peshwa—Khandesh and the southern and eastern parts of the Karnatak. SRGB No. 1 (1852), p. 406; SRGB No. 12 (1853), p. 48.

[13] Such groups probably already had a corporate identity when they settled a village—the corporate identity of their shared caste membership.

assessments are reinterpreted with this in mind, the following picture seems reasonable.

When a village was first settled, its lands were divided among the families of the settling group. In areas where the village included several types of soils, or lands with different degrees of access to water, each family received some of each kind of soil and land. Thomas Marshall, travelling in the Karnatak in the early 1820s, reported that each cultivator tended to have some *regur* (deep black soil) and some *musub* (light red soil). The two types of land were suitable for somewhat different crops, responded differently to rainfall, and required major inputs of labor at different points in the agricultural cycle. The *musub* lands most often cultivated were those near the village where the availability of manure was greatest. *Regur* lands could be chosen for other desirable characteristics, since they did not require manure under usual conditions.[14] It is not clear if all of the land in a village was allocated among the families, or only enough to allow each family to meet its current needs and perhaps have some land for expansion if several sons grew to maturity. In either case, some common land or waste was preserved for grazing village animals, and some land was set aside for the village site. Even without the exactions of the state or an overlord, the village had some collective expenses (defense, celebrations, religious observances), assessments for which were levied on individual families.[15] To maintain status as a member of the founding collective, a family had to contribute to these expenses unless poverty prevented it (see the fifth paragraph of the quote from Wingate).

When an overlord entered the picture to collect his share of the produce from the village, the total amount of payment was settled by negotiation between the village's representative and the over-

[14] *Marshall's Report*, pp. 114, 117. Scattering of holdings among several qualities of land has been reported for a village in Satara district. Further, the scattering of holdings is observable in the earliest records of holdings in the village, dating from the early seventeenth century, not long after the settlement of the village. Lee I. Schlesinger, "Agriculture and Community in Maharashtra, India," in *Research in Economic Anthropology*, vol. 4, ed. George Dalton (Greenwich, Conn.: JAI Press, 1981), p. 238. Village maps prepared at the time of the settlement and survey operations (after 1840) sometimes show field patterns that appear to be designed to give as many owners as possible access to a stream. The fields are long and narrow, with one shorter side along a stream. *Official Correspondence on the System of Revenue Survey and Assessment* ... (Bombay: Education Society's Press, 1850) (hereafter *Joint Report*), appendix, p. 15; *The Survey and Settlement Manual*, vol. 2 (Bombay: Government Central Press, 1902), maps nos. 1-5.

[15] Fukazawa, "Lands and Peasants," pp. 45-47.

lord's, and this total was apportioned among the *chali ryots* in the same way as assessments for ordinary village expenses. Being a *chali ryot*, a member of the privileged group that founded the village or a descendant from that group, meant being required to help meet this demand. Once the village had negotiated its revenue payment for the season, it would be profitable for the *chali ryots*, as a group, to rent out land they were not currently cultivating to people from outside the village. The collections from this land would reduce the amount they had to raise among themselves for the revenue payment. The outsiders to whom the land was rented would be the ubiquitous *uparis*, about whose possible origins more will be said later.

The renting of land to outsiders raises two problems. First, if, as was generally the case, these lands were rented at rates below those that were paid by *chali ryots*, why should the latter not give up the lands they already cultivated and take up some of these other lands—if not in their own village, then in a neighboring village? Yet this does not seem to have happened. I think that the records suggest one reason why this might be the case, and common sense suggests another. Wingate is quite clear that anyone who did not cultivate *chali* land was not a full member of the village and not entitled to the privileges of such membership (a rent-free housing site, grazing rights on common lands, a voice in village affairs). He also suggests that failure on the part of a *ryot* to cultivate "his" *chali* land was regarded as shirking by other members of the village. The combination of denial of certain privileges and the institution of social sanctions (who would marry the daughters of a shirking ryot, smoke with him, help him out when his bullock died half way through plowing time?) was sufficient to keep members of the corporate group from trying to avoid making their full contribution to the village's revenue payments.[16] The second, but probably less important, reason why *chali ryots* continued to cultivate their *chali* lands was that they were in all probability the best lands in terms of fertility, location with respect to water and to the village, and all the other variables farmers value in their lands.

But the second problem was one between the village and the overlord rather than one within the village. Why should the overlord be content to permit the village to have all of the profits from renting

[16] The importance of adhering to caste norms to preserve a network of social relations is documented by many anthropological studies of India. See, for instance, A. C. Mayer, *Caste and Kinship in Central India* (Berkeley and Los Angeles: University of California Press, 1970).

out its land to outsiders? A loyal or ambitious *mamlatdar* should logically have considered the expansion of cultivation in a village as ground for reopening negotiations about the revenue to be paid. Let us hypothesize that *katguta* and *khandmakta* tenures both had their origin in such negotiations.[17] In return for giving up to their overlord some of the revenue they derived from renting out lands to outsiders, the *chali ryots* were guaranteed the right to cultivate some land, in addition to their *chali* land, at lowered rates of revenue. In effect, they negotiated with their overlord for a larger share of the produce from these additional lands to remain with them, the cultivators. It is by a process of interaction between overlord and village that a range of tenurial types was created in each village.

In the same way, villagers negotiated with the overlord to bring new lands into cultivation under a *kaul,* an agreement that the land should pay no revenue for some years. The fact that the right to cultivate both *kaul* land and the land of *inamdars* was reserved to *chali ryots* (Wingate, above, paragraph five) reflects both the power of the corporate group of agriculturists and one of the resources they had to maintain their privileged status and their corporate identity. While the precise allocation of such profitable lands among the members of the brotherhood was a function of the relative strengths of the individual families and the factions into which they were divided, and perhaps of the power of the *patel* or headman as well, the availability of these resources to the group as a whole and the ability to deny them to members who violated the norms of the group increased the potential for preservation of the group as a group.

We have here a process by which the tenures that Wingate observed in the Karnatak could have developed. It is both speculative and hypothetical. However, it is also the only such attempt that has been made for the Karnatak. This description does not yet explain how these various tenures were sufficiently formalized to have survived in village and state records, and to have been the basis on which the East India Company's officers began to try to collect taxes. Consider another hypothesis. In several of the periods of peace in this region, its overlords had attempted to gain a more secure hold on villages and their revenue payments by writing down what each village paid (so much for *chali* land, so much for *katguta*, so much

---

[17] See the quote from Wingate (pp. 87-88 above) for one definition of these terms. H. H. Wilson has *katguta,* tenure of land held at a fixed rate of revenue, usually lower than the ordinary rate, and *khandmakta,* land leased at a fixed and usually favorable rate.

land held *kaul* until *fasli . . .*). But these records merely reflected the existing variety of tenure and rights of access to privileged tenures that had grown up from the village's internal structure and from negotiations between *mamlatdars* and villages. They were *not* imposed by the state, nor were they all part of one overall plan. They were recorded by the state in what one might call an attempt to move from a personal to a bureaucratic administration. Such attempts appear to have been short-lived.

This story is a fairly complex one; the historical remains it seeks to explain are equally complex. But before dismissing these conjectures, it would be well to remember that European peasants evolved very complex systems of cultivation and tenure—in particular, open field systems with two- and three-field rotations—over major portions of western Europe with no guidance from above. They also related to their overlords in a variety of ways including the payment of some portion of their labor and the crops as tribute.[18] The hypotheses that have been developed here about the process of creation of tenures in the Karnatak may be wrong—but they should not be rejected either because they are hypotheses or because the overall system is judged to be too complex to have evolved without a grand design from above. Villages were not supine collections of individuals upon whom an all-powerful overlord or state could impose. The relations between village and state emerged as a result of negotiations and conflicts in which each side made some gains.

The structure of villages and revenue assessments in the Deccan did not, in the large, differ very much from that of the Karnatak, although there were shifts in both detail and vocabulary. The balance of the source materials available on the Deccan includes many more records from the Peshwa Daftar than are available for the Karnatak. These records give us fuller information on the interactions between the state and the village than Wingate's work does for the Karnatak, but somewhat less information on the range of tenures inside the village.

The permanent cultivators of Deccan villages held *miras* lands and were themselves called *mirasdars*.[19] The most reasonable as-

[18] Richard C. Hoffman, "Medieval Origins of the Common Fields," in *European Peasants and Their Markets: Essays in Agrarian Economic History*, ed. William N. Parker and Eric L. Jones (Princeton: Princeton University Press, 1975), pp. 23-71.

[19] In the Deccan, the term *thalkari* seems both to have meant the same things as *mirasdar* and to have been used with it, as in the phrase *kunbi thalkari mirasdar*. Fukazawa, "Land and Peasants," pp. 35, 39.

sumption is that the origin of this tenure paralleled that which I have suggested for the origin of *chali* lands and *chali ryots*. While the government had the right to collect some revenue from *miras* lands, they were the inheritable, saleable property of the *miras- dars*.[20] It is not clear what rights in his *miras* land remained to a *mirasdar* who could not pay the revenue due. In most areas it appears that population, not land, was the scarce factor. This is indicated by the concern that the Maratha states displayed with encouraging peasants to settle and to return to areas that had been ravaged by drought or war and with keeping taxes below the level that would have led peasants to leave. In such areas of population scarcity, the state would not have gained by denying a peasant the right to cultivate some land and thus becoming able to pay some revenue. Consequently, the *mirasdars* may have retained the right to cultivate their lands even during periods when they could not pay the revenue.[21]

The classification of lands that existed in the Deccan in the eighteenth century and the rights of disposal of these classes support the argument that *mirasdars* were or had been corporate groups. Four major classes were discernible—*miras* lands, *inam* lands, state lands, and the lands of extinct *mirasdar* families and waste lands.[22] The lands of extinct *mirasdar* families (*gatkul jamin*) could be disposed of in a variety of ways and by a variety of interests. First, they might be absorbed by other *mirasdars* into their own holdings, but in that case they paid full *miras* revenue, which appears to have been a heavy demand.[23] Unless there were major differences in the quality of the lands, *mirasdars* in need of more land to cultivate might prefer to take up lands from *inamdars*, from the state (perhaps on terms comparable to the *katguta* and *khandmakta* reported in the Karnatak), or in neighboring villages.[24] But the significant point is that the *mirasdars* and their headman appear to have had first claim on lands that had belonged to departed *mirasdar* families. These villagers could also create an *inam* out of waste lands if they

[20] Fukazawa, "Lands and Peasants," p. 40.

[21] Kulkarni, "Village Life," pp. 42-44; Gordon, "Recovery from Adversity," pp. 64-65, 71, 75.

[22] Fukazawa, "Lands and Peasants," pp. 38-39. This is consistent with Gooddine's classification in SRGB No. 4 (1852), pp. 3-5.

[23] Fukazawa, "Lands and Peasants," pp. 45-48.

[24] Gooddine reported a class of people called *owandkuree* (H. H. Wilson has *owandekari*), who cultivated land in a village but resided in and belonged to another village. SRGB No. 4 (1852), p. 3.

needed to pay a debt or to attract some special class to the village.[25] If the villagers did not dispose of such lands, the state could. The records that have survived represent only long-term disposal of such lands; their year-to-year use may have been granted by local state officials without generating the sort of records preserved by the state. In disposing of them, the state might have created *inams*, or might have rented the lands on favorable terms to promote cultivation and increase of population.[26] Again we see that both the village and the state had some recognized rights over uncultivated, unclaimed land in the village.

Overall, the similarities between the Karnatak and the Deccan in the patterns of access to land and responsibility for land revenue appear to have very substantial. Some of the differences that are perceived may have been a function of the longer, tighter control in which the Maratha chieftans had held the Deccan. The Karnatak, like Khandesh, was a march land, where conflict with neighboring states often occurred.[27] For the Deccan and the Karnatak we find the following four similarities. (1) The village was built around a corporate group whose members were, generally, the only full citizens of the village. They had significant privileges denied to all others who resided in the village; they controlled some resources collectively, especially access to lands other than those already controlled by their members or already firmly granted to some other person or institution. The corporate group had at its disposal certain sanctions against members who violated its norms by, for instance, shirking their fair share of village expenses. (2) A second classification of cultivators (called *uparis*) was widespread in each region. (3) Records from each region document a variety of tenures, which can be summarized into three basic categories: (a) full tax lands (those in the *chali* and *miras* classes); (b) part tax lands (those held on *kaul, katguta,* and *khandmakta*); and (c) lands whose taxes had been assigned in full or in part (*inam* lands). (4) There is circumstantial evidence for each region that the revenue or taxes paid and the variety of tenures observed evolved through a process of negotiation between the state and the villages.

Since the similarity of the patterns of land control, of corporate structure of the dominant group of land owners, and of relationships

[25] Fukazawa, "Lands and Peasants," pp. 47-48.

[26] Fukazawa, "Lands and Peasants," pp. 48-49.

[27] For a summary history of such conflicts in the Karnatak, see *Gazetteer of the Bombay Presidency: Belgaum* (1884), chap. vii.

between the village and the state in the Deccan and the Karnatak have been pointed out, the remaining categories of people commonly associated with the village will be discussed only once. There are four such groups: the *patels*, or village headmen; the *inamdars*, or holders of grants of land paying specially reduced rates of revenue; the *uparis*, or nonresident cultivators; and the *balutedars*, or artisans attached to the village.

The patel

In the process of negotiation between a village and its overlord, the corporate group seems frequently to have been represented by one individual—the *patel*. The power and status of this individual relative to that of his fellow villagers varied widely from village to village. In extreme cases he might have so little power as to be only *primus inter pares*, or so much power as to be virtual ruler of the village.[28] These variations may have arisen from a number of disparate causes. In periods when the state (either the Maratha state or the Mughal state, which alternated with it in parts of the Deccan) was anxious to repopulate lands deserted because of famine or disorder, ambitious individuals had scope to promote settlements where they and their immediate followers had advantages.[29] While we would expect that settlers would generally have sought the best possible terms from such entrepreneurs, the final outcomes could differ widely due to the high costs of information-gathering. That is, uprooted peasants may sometimes have accepted terms relatively unfavorable to themselves simply because they lacked the resources to support themselves while they sought out other terms. In other cases, where the settlement of a village had been done by a corporate group, the varying fortunes (many sons, few sons, many daughters, untimely deaths, unequal distribution of talent and ambition) of the members might have tended either to preserve a high degree of equality or to foster the emergence of a single dominant family. Given the variety of terms on which the individuals designated *patel* and the villages they lived in dealt with each other, it is most reasonable to argue that these reflect the different histories of the villages in very particularistic terms. To try to place the relationship of village and *patel* on a strict historical continuum (first, like this; then, evolving like this; etc.) and perhaps to argue that these dif-

[28] SRGB No. 4 (1852), p. 15.
[29] Gordon, "Recovery from Adversity," pp. 70-71, 76-77.

ferences arise from contacts with markets or tax collectors seems to me to impose more order than in fact existed.[30]

Inamdars

Lands that were either revenue-free or that paid revenue to the state at a rate less than that paid on *miras* or *chali* lands were called *inam* lands; holders of such lands were *inamdars*. Most commonly, *inams* were granted as compensation for some services (e.g., to village officers or former soldiers) or to support worthy people or institutions. The state could create several forms of *inams*. For support of large institutions or of individuals who had provided significant services, whole villages might be designated as *inam*. In such cases it was not the *lands* of the village that were granted, but rather the right to collect all or a share of the revenue due the state from those villages. The state might also grant as *inam* either the waste lands of villages or the lands of *mirasdar* families that had died out. Most grants of *inam* by the state in these regions seem to have been of the more limited form—grants of specific lands in specific villages to people who might or might not have already been resident in the village. In these cases (as opposed to the grants of whole villages), *inamdars* received the right to cultivate the land (or to have it cultivated) and pay less than normal revenue.[31] *Inams* could also be granted by villages "for a debt, or some other purpose, the village continuing by paying the total revenue of such village, to make up the difference, and to ensure Government from loss."[32] Grants of small amounts of land as *inam* were sometimes forgiven by the government of the Peshwa.[33] The ability of villages to make grants of *inam* lands underscores the corporate nature and responsibility of the village. Villages could and did incur debts and agree to pay them off by capitalizing them and giving the creditor rent-free or rent-reduced title to a parcel of land.[34]

---

[30] For a careful discussion of the differences that may be found among villages in this region today, see Schlesinger, "Agriculture and Community," pp. 235-236.

[31] Fukazawa, "Lands and Peasants," pp. 41-43, 47.

[32] SRGB No. 4 (1852), p. 5.

[33] Fukazawa, "Lands and Peasants," pp. 47-48.

[34] Village officers (the *patel* and the *kulkarni*) and some of the *balutedars* (most often the Mahars?) held land at low or zero rates of revenue as part of the payment for their services to the village. This land was, in the Deccan, part of their *watan* (although Mann and Kanitkar refer to the land held by the Mahars as *inam*: Mann and Kanitkar, *Land and Labour*, p. 32). It is not clear whether the rest of the village paid the revenue that would have been due on lands held as *watan* or whether the state forgave such amounts. The purpose and structure of Gooddine's inquiry into

Uparis

Persons temporarily residing and cultivating in a village were called *uparis*. The tendency among students of western India has been to assume that *uparis* would have preferred to be full members of the village but "either from poverty or other causes, could not obtain the right of settlement."[35] Two matters seem unsatisfactory about the existing discussions of *uparis*: first, it is generally implicitly assumed that they would have preferred permanent to temporary cultivation; and second, no mention is usually made of their origin or their destination.

The *uparis* may have been the "surplus" sons of members of villages other than those where they tilled. But this explanation is not particularly appealing in light of the fact that most villages were not fully cultivated. Why would sons of its members go elsewhere, then, where they would be compelled to be second-class citizens? A more persuasive notion is the possibility that most *uparis* were drawn from a group which had other occupations as well as agriculture. *Uparis* appear generally to have come with their own cattle to the village where they became temporary cultivators. Perhaps they were engaged in breeding or raising cattle or in trade using cattle as carriers and may have taken up cultivation of light soils to supplement their income.

It is important in this context to remember that over most of the area being considered, two types of soil predominated. The first was *regur* (commonly called "black soil") and the second was *musub* (a light red soil). To get the former land into tilth when it had been out of cultivation (or never cultivated) was a process involving two years and access for several months together to large teams of bullocks and some hired labor.[36] Such lands seem unlikely candidates for cultivation on a temporary basis. On the other hand, *musub* soils were quite easy to plow and sow the same year with minimal aid from cattle and only the labor of the cultivator. But if they were to continue to yield well, they had to be heavily manured. These *musub* lands appear therefore to be ideal ones for temporary cultivators of the sort described above. They could be quickly brought into cultivation—essentially with no investment—but would also quickly decline in fertility unless some investment (in the form of manure)

---

the customary payments to village officers and *balutedars* seem to suggest that the British thought such amounts for at least the *patel* and the *kulkarni* were legitimate deductions from the revenue due the state. SRGB No. 4 (1852).

[35] SRGB No. 4 (1852), p. 3. For a slightly different view, see R. Kumar, "Rise of Rich Peasants," pp. 28-29.

[36] *Marshall's Report*, pp. 113-117.

was made in them in subsequent years. As long as such lands were plentiful, however, the sensible course might well be to shift from cultivating one plot of such land to another. In other words, the combination of the geology of the region and the ratio of people to land made it feasible to exploit some lands on a very extensive basis—cultivated only occasionally and then in a very casual way. But presumably they yielded well in terms of man-hours and cattle-hours expended so long as cultivation was shifted frequently.

The unsettled times through which much of the Karnatak and Deccan had passed and the arbitrariness and capriciousness of revenue systems may also have produced *uparis*. Since reports of desertion of lands and villages by farmers who felt either threatened or oppressed are common, it is reasonable to try to figure out where they went. One possibility is that some *uparis* were cultivators temporarily displaced from their own villages. They would come with their own cattle, and they generally would not have any interest in becoming permanent settlers or investing heavily in preparing lands to cultivate which they hoped to occupy for only a season or two. But in this case, as in that where the *uparis* may have been a separate group with other functions as well as cultivating, the point to be made is that it need not be assumed that *uparis* were a deprived group which was desperately seeking a plot of land. *Uparis* operated differently from permanent cultivators in villages—either because of a totally different life style or because of a temporary dislocation in their more regular operations.[37]

Balutedars

As in much of the rest of South Asia, so in western India each village contained a set of artisans and ritual specialists. In the Marathi-speaking villages they were called *balutedars*, and in Kannada-speaking villages, *ayakarru*.[38] The lists of those included among

[37] D. W. Attwood has suggested that in his work in Poona District he frequently encountered the term *pahune*, meaning "in-laws," for cultivators who were not full members of the village. Some *pahunes* had been resident in the village for several generations (Attwood, personal communication). Given the nature of the relationship that men have with their affines in Marathi- and Kannada-speaking areas, it does make sense that uprooted farmers might have sought out their wives' villages either for temporary shelter or for more permanent resettlement. David G. Mandelbaum, *Society in India*, 2 vols. (Berkeley and Los Angeles: University of California Press, 1970), 2:158.

[38] Wilson, *Glossary*, p. 53. It is worth noting that while the *balutedari* system was in one sense a variant of the *jajmani* system, in another sense it was fundamentally different from the classic *jajmani* system described in William H. Wiser, *The Hindu*

the *balutedars* vary from place to place but include a common core. In his study of 33 villages, Gooddine found that the most commonly included were: the carpenter, the blacksmith, the leatherworker, the potter, the barber, the washerman, the astrologer, the temple priest, the goldsmith, the *mahar* (scavenger, messenger, watchman), the *patel*, and the *kulkarni* (accountant).[39]

These village servants were remunerated for their several duties on a retainer basis rather than on a fee-for-service basis. That is, each of them was entitled to a certain fixed share of the harvest, perhaps some revenue-free land, and various other small perquisites. And each enjoyed a monopoly on the provision of his particular service in the village. In return, these servants provided all of the regular or ordinary needs of the agriculturists for their services. Extraordinary services—such as the construction of carts or houses by the carpenter—were paid for separately.

The three principal artisans of the village were the carpenter, the blacksmith, and the leatherworker. These three were most crucial to the continuance of agricultural operations. Perhaps for this reason, they had "the privilege of sowing in every farmer's field a strip of land each with ralla [a type of grain], each strip consisting of four furrows. The farmer tills the land, and these artisans merely bring each his basket of grain, which is sown by the farmer, and reaped by the recipient when ready."[40]

The association of these artisans and ritual specialists with villages rendered the latter almost self-sufficient in the provision of services. The method of payment (a share of the harvest) also provided insurance for the community as a whole to permit it to continue agricultural operations and to maintain the minimum necessary culturally determined level of consumption.[41] If these artisans had

Jajmani System: A Socio-Economic System of Interrelating Members of a Hindu Village Community in Services (Lucknow: Lucknow Publishing House, 1936). The *balutedars* in Maharashtrian villages were servants (employees) of the village and not the servants-clients-employees of specific families. For the fullest treatment of this difference, see Fukazawa, "Rural Servants." This is not the place to enter into a full discussion of how this crucial difference may have influenced the nature of relationships between castes in these villages or the potential for the widespread development of factions inside the village. But given the long-continuing difference in performance of the rural sector in Maharashtra from that in many other states, this difference in village organization is certainly one that merits more attention than it has generally received.

[39] SRGB No. 4 (1852), pp. 11-18.

[40] SRGB No. 4 (1852), p. 11.

[41] In the context of Hinduism this minimum level of consumption sometimes included a certain amount of services by scavengers, washermen, barbers, and priests.

been paid on a fee-for-service basis as, for instance, weavers were, their incomes would have declined drastically when crops were short. Farmers would have made do, done for themselves, or done without. But in succeeding years, the artisans would no longer have been available to the village. The *balutedar* system and the variations of it found throughout South Asia helped to ensure that any village which harvested enough of its crop for the agriculturists to survive would also have all of the categories of people it needed to continue its normal life.[42]

II. The Early Years of British Rule

The previous section has described how the relationships between state and villages may have functioned in fairly peaceful periods. But by the last decade of the eighteenth century and the first decades of the nineteenth century, as Maratha chiefs warred among themselves and Maratha power ebbed, parts of the Deccan and the Karnatak were subject to military incursions and the concomitant extractions and dislocation. In addition, there were years of cholera and years of famine. In these trials, the always rather brittle system of relationships between the state and the villages tended to degenerate towards anarchy. The state and its representatives became one of many powers ready to take by force whatever grain and other goods a village could yield. As disorder spread, villages were abandoned, minor irrigation works fell into disrepair, and population probably declined. The farmers from now deserted villages sometimes became part of the bands of disaffected soldiery that contributed to the disorder of the countryside. Much of the area with which this study is concerned was, therefore, rather chaotic in 1818, when the East India Company replaced the Peshwa as ruler.

The new administration was faced with a host of problems. Groups of soldiers still roamed parts of the Company's new territories; they had to be disarmed and persuaded to return to their agricultural pursuits. The rights of numerous petty rajas who had helped or

---

[42] Weavers were nowhere included among the village servants. There appear to have been two reasons for this. First, weavers were not necessary to the continuance of the agricultural process. Potters, blacksmiths, leatherworkers, and carpenters were. Second, weavers did not provide any services that could not be obtained through the market. Cloth was available from itinerant merchants or at periodic fairs. Services provided by scavengers (rubbish and night-soil removal), washermen, brahmins (rituals for life-crisis rites), barbers (not only haircutting and shaving, but frequently also marriage brokering) could not generally be obtained in periodic markets in premodern India.

hindered the English cause had to be determined.[43] But the greatest task of all those that faced the new government was "to devise an effective and economical administration" for these newly conquered lands.[44]

At the center of any such administration there was a need for people responsible for determining how much land revenue was due from the subregions and who was to pay it. The very tendency of the East India Company's servants to use the word *revenue* instead of the word *tax* helps to exemplify how important a part of the support of government was drawn from these collections from the land. By 1818 there were already several revenue systems in force in the conquered parts of India, and debates were raging about the proper form and function of a revenue system. In Bengal, a set of persons (*zamindars*) who the English had hoped would become "improving landlords" had been given proprietary rights in great tracts of land, and their land revenue had been permanently fixed (the Permanent Settlement). In Madras, an attempt was being made to grant proprietary rights to persons actually involved in cultivation (the *ryotwari* settlement). In other parts of northern India, a settlement for the revenue was being made with whole villages (the *mahelwari* settlement). In the first of these settlements (in Bengal), the fixity of government demand for land revenue was intended to make government depend on the taxation of activities other than agriculture for its increased tax needs. But that principle had been quickly abandoned, and the settlements going on in other parts of the East India Company's territory retained the option of the government to raise its demand at some point in the future.[45] These three patterns of settlement shared a concern for the preservation of the old landed classes, even though individual administrators disagreed about who these classes were and how much effort should be made to preserve them.

It was against this background that Mountstuart Elphinstone, placed in charge of all the Deccan and Karnatak territories conquered from the Peshwa (with first Thomas Munro and later William

[43] For the best account of these problems, see Kenneth Ballhatchet, *Social Policy and Social Change in Western India, 1817-1830* (London: Oxford University Press, 1957).

[44] Eric Stokes, *The English Utilitarians and India* (Oxford: Clarendon Press, 1959), p. xv. Stokes is the best source for the administrative and intellectual history of the East India Company's servants' efforts to find the ideal revenue system. See especially pp. 81-86.

[45] Stokes, *English Utilitarians*, p. 83.

Chaplin of the Madras Civil Service to assist him in the Karnatak), began to lay plans for the collection of the land revenue. During his long tenure as Political Resident in Poona while the Peshwa was a British dependent, Elphinstone had acquired both some knowledge of the administration of the regions under Maratha rule and a strong desire to preserve this system if it could be rid of certain abuses. With this end in mind, officers engaged in "settling" the country were advised to treat the hereditary village officers (the *patel* and the *kulkarni*) with respect and to strive to gain their cooperation. Since these men were the persons most likely to have access to whatever records of assessment for individual villages existed (especially any that dealt with the internal partition of the land revenue among villagers), their cooperation was clearly a necessity if the attempt to retain the existing revenue system was to be successful.[46]

Elphinstone had probably overestimated the degree to which the ideal revenue system described later by Wingate (see above) was still a reality in the rather ravaged countryside. In any case, expediency and the availability of personnel led to an attempt to put into effect the same *ryotwari* settlement already being used in Madras. A number of officers, both Indian and European, were brought from Madras to help in the settlement operation.[47] The instructions issued to them on the conduct of the settlement were of the most general kind. To quote from those written by Chaplin, when he had replaced Elphinstone as commissioner of the Deccan:

> There are two modes which are commonly observed in making the Ryotwar, or as it is sometimes called, the Koolwar Settlement of Villages. . . . The first is to fix the amount of the settlement of the whole village in the first instance and afterwards, to distribute in detail the constituent parts of it amongst the body of the Ryots. . . . The second is to settle the rent of each individual Ryot, and the whole being completed, to form from the aggregate, the Jumma or Beriz of the village. Either of these modes may be adopted, as may be most convenient and best suited to secure the interests of Government and the cultivators. . . . In following the mode first pointed out, it will be requisite to inquire what has been the settlement of the village, in each year, for a long succession of preceding years. . . . The village settlement, being thus formed . . . individual repartition of it should as far as time will admit of it, be made by the Collectors Cutcherry [office, establishment];

[46] Ballhatchet, *Western India*, pp. 9-10, 28-31, 105.
[47] Ballhatchet, *Western India*, pp. 91-93.

but as this operation can be only partially accomplished, the remainder must be completed by the Mamlutdar and his establishment, under strict injunctions to that Officer, not to leave the duty to be performed at the discretion of the district or village functionaries.[48]

Chaplin's instructions go on to state the importance of getting from the *kulkarni* accurate records of cultivation in the village in current and preceding years and to suggest methods for overcoming the difficulties most likely to be encountered in securing such information.[49]

Elphinstone, Chaplin, and their subordinates were trying to establish (or, they thought, trying to preserve) a revenue system which would not interfere with the usages of the country, which would prevent undue extortion of the *ryots* by members (native and European) of the revenue staff, and which would maintain revenue collections. In general, they failed to achieve any of these aims. In spite of their years in India (and Elphinstone's in Poona itself), the Company's officials do not appear to have understood the processes of determining revenue demand, whatever information they had about the forms which emerged. But even this information was often denied them, either because of their failure to gain the confidence and cooperation of locally powerful men or because the information they thought should exist had either never been created or had been lost in the troubled times that proceeded British conquest.[50] Given these combined lacks of understanding and information, the revenue establishment of the Company could have succeeded in pre-

---

[48] *A Report Exhibiting a View of the Fiscal Judicial System of Administration introduced into the conquered territory above the Ghauts under the Authority of the Commissioner of the Dekhan* (Bombay: Government Press, 1824; reprinted 1838), p. 3 (hereafter *Chaplin's Report*).

[49] *Chaplin's Report*, pp. 3-8.

[50] Chaplin's instructions are filled with sentences that illustrate the difficulty he and his subordinates faced in obtaining information. "In order to check abuses, it may be proper to state the most common modes in which these accounts of cultivation are falsified by the Koolkarnees. . . . Government lands are newly entered as Enams, which are often held or granted by the connivance and collusion of the village officers. . . . Any concealed resources may, however in general, be discovered throughout the agency of some of the partners in the Patel or Koolkarneeship, amongst whom, some jealousy, enmity, or rivalship, always subsists. . . . When the accounts of a village are incomplete and all the details of its resources are but imperfectly known, it is best perhaps to form the settlement of the village in the gross. . . . But as the Koolkarnee's accounts are never to be depended upon, and as every cultivator is accustomed to object to the amount of his rent. . . ." *Chaplin's Report*, pp. 4-5, 7.

serving the good features of the Maratha revenue system only by chance. Inevitably then, the settlements that were made did interfere with the usages of the country in greater or lesser degree.[51] The lack of information in the hands of the men in charge of the revenue system left power for considerable extortion from the *ryots* and their headmen with the lower levels of the imperial establishment. The system Chaplin described to his subordinates left enormous power in the hands of the Collector's Cutcherry and in those of the *mamlatdars*.[52] Not surprisingly, this power sometimes became a source of income as these men collected one amount of revenue from the *ryots* and reported a different amount to their superiors. Finally, lack of information about the previous level of revenue collected and the conditions under which it had been collected even impinged upon the government's ability to maintain the level of revenue collected. Revenue demands that were fixed too high or that were divided inequitably among *ryots* were increasingly difficult to collect, especially when the government took little if any of the ruler's traditional responsibility for the recovery of the country from the turbulent and destructive times through which it had passed.[53]

Various signs of these difficulties were soon visible in diverse parts of the Karnatak and the Deccan. By 1821, when St. John Thackeray had replaced Chaplin in charge of the Southern Maratha Country, disaffection with the imperial establishment was held to be widespread among the *ryots*. Thomas Marshall reported that the *ryots* complained of overassessments and harsh collection practices. In his reply to Marshall's report, Thackeray argued that the government was not injuring the *ryots*, but that the village officers might well be since the government had been unable to establish complete control over their exactions. To remedy the problem, Thackeray suggested that a survey be made to determine the actual extent of cultivation and the capacity of the area. Only with such a survey could the European establishment be freed from dependence upon the native revenue officers and their books.[54]

[51] In addition, the great freedom Elphinstone gave his collectors meant that they were free to introduce all sorts of innovations to get through their business. Ballhatchet, *Western India*, pp. 106 and passim.

[52] Ballhatchet, *Western India*, pp. 96-99.

[53] These responsibilities included assistance in reconstructing damaged irrigation works and encouragement of cultivators by granting periods of reduced revenue. For a discussion of the exercise of these responsibilities by the Peshwa in the eighteenth century, see Gordon, "Recovery from Adversity," pp. 69-71, 76.

[54] *Marshall's Report.*

In the Deccan district of Ahmednagar the revenue had been farmed since 1803-1804. Under the tax farmers, the land measures and rates that existed had become only nominal. In this area, villages had "usually" paid an assessment called *tunkha* (about one-fourth of the produce, but collected in cash). However, under some Maratha administrations they had also paid an additional assessment called *kumal*. When the East India Company took over the district, its representatives assumed that the total of the two assessments was the amount that could and should be collected. Attempts were made to ascertain from the village officers the rates assessed on the *bighas* of each holding, but when few such rates could be found, others were assigned. The officer who settled the Newasa *taluka* of Ahmednagar district in the early 1850s speculated that "from the absence of all trustworthy information, the whole plan of distribution of the rates must have been pure guesswork."[55] During the 1830s the government found it necessary to reduce the rates on groups of villages when *ryots* could not pay the assessed rates or when they protested vehemently. In Khandesh district as well, the initial attempts to settle the revenue pitched rates somewhat too high. Negotiations between the revenue establishment and the villages effected some reduction of rates after the first two years of British rule, but rates had to be reduced again in 1845 and 1848-1849.[56]

The difficulties that the revenue establishment faced in the Deccan and the Karnatak might have been dealt with entirely by episodic reductions of demand and alterations of rates. But there was a growing spirit of reform among the officials of the East India Company who dealt with revenue policy. Chief among these officials was James Mill, who wrote the revenue letters that the Board of Control in London sent to the Government of India. Mill and his fellow practitioners of the new science of political economy, Thomas Malthus and David Ricardo, fixed upon *rent* from agricultural land in their studies, and Mill conceived it to be the best source of taxation. Rent, they argued, was unearned income from land, and its taxation would not alter the efficient allocation of labor and capital. By the 1820s officials in all of the parts of India not covered by the permanent settlements were being pressed by the directives from London to calculate the rent of land and use it as the basis for levying government demand.[57]

In Bombay a decision was made to begin to reform the revenue

[55] SRGB N.S. No. 123 (1871), pp. 17-18.
[56] SRGB N.S. No. 93 (1865), p. 312.
[57] Stokes, *English Utilitarians*, pp. 93-98.

system. A new settlement would determine what share rent bore in the total produce of land, and government demand would be based on this share. The task of setting up this system was entrusted to R. K. Pringle, a young civil servant who had been one of Malthus' best pupils while at the East India Company's college at Haileybury. With a small staff, largely Indian, Pringle began to build his new system in the districts of Poona and Sholapur. His establishment was to measure land and to classify it according to quality. In the virtual absence of a rental market for land, he proposed to calculate the "net produce"—that which remained after all of the costs of cultivation including a fair return on capital and family labor had been deducted. What Pringle called "net produce" a contemporary economist would call Ricardian rent. Pringle proposed to claim 55 percent of the net produce as the government "rent" on land. He viewed this demand as a moderate one which ran no risk of exceeding the real rent and trenching on the returns to labor and capital. Pringle wrote up his efforts and presented them to the government in 1828, and his system went into operation.[58]

Almost immediately it failed. By the early 1830s cultivators were fleeing from the districts where the system operated to those of the Nizam of Hyderabad—where rates of taxation were thought to be extortionate. The ultimate cause of the failure of Pringle's settlement was lack of information. Because of this lack he severely overestimated the net produce and produced a general level of revenue demand that was too high. But with so small a staff, Pringle was also unable to ensure the honesty of his native subordinates, so that the resulting sets of assessments tended to favor their friends and oppress those who had not paid for friendship.[59]

The system that became known as the Bombay Survey and Settlement had its origins in the attempts, beginning in 1835, of H. E. Goldsmid and George Wingate to revive the Indapur *taluka* of Poona district from the disaster of Pringle's settlement. Goldsmid and Wingate shared with Pringle a belief in the Ricardian law of rent and with Mill a belief in the suitability of rent as a base for taxation in India.[60] Goldsmid and Wingate also shared with Mill the view that "unless the state defined the assessment for each peasant cultivator there was no security that a rapacious middleman would not exact

[58] Stokes, *English Utilitarians*, pp. 99-102.
[59] R. Kumar, *Western India*, pp. 96-114.
[60] Stokes, *English Utilitarians*, pp. 107-108, 122-123.

more than the true rent and do untold harm to the country. A detailed *ryotwar* settlement was therefore essential."[61]

But these men, imbued with the spirit of reform, wanted to do more than create a new revenue system that would regularize and rationalize government demand. They wanted to put into place a system which by its very operation would encourage—if not force— the growth and development of the agrarian sector. By this they meant quite specifically that they wanted to foster the accumulation of capital and the improvement of techniques of cultivation.[62] In effect, they were dedicated to the development of a process, devised and maintained by the state, that could yield not only revenues for the state but also sets of rates that would generate incentives for agriculturists to invest and to expand output.

Following Mill's lead, Goldsmid and Wingate viewed all land as the property of the state, which rented it out to cultivators.[63] But beneath this legal statement, cultivators *owned* land in the same way that an Iowa farmer does. So long as a cultivator paid the government rental, the land was his. He could sell it—in which case the new owner became responsible for payment of the rental. He could bequeath it—in which case his heirs became responsible for payment of the rental.[64] Cultivators were thus provided with a secure tenure for their land, one of the elements necessary to foster improved agricultural practices.

To further encourage good agricultural practice, the rental de-

---

[61] Stokes, *English Utilitarians*, p. 91.

[62] These concerns permeate the language of the *Joint Report*. "In determining, then, upon the extent of country to be assessed at uniform rates, we are of the opinion that the more permanent distinctions of climate, markets, and husbandry [as opposed to the condition of the cultivators], should receive . . . chief attention. We should not think of imposing different rates of assessment on a tract of country similarly situated in respect to these three points, in consequence of the actual condition of the cultivators varying in different parts of it. Were we to do so, we should depart from the principle, laid down by the Hon'ble Court of Directors, of assessing land according to its capabilities, and adopt the objectionable one of doing so with reference to the means of the person holding it. The effect of such a system, by creating different rates of profit upon capital employed in agriculture, would interfere with its natural and most advantageous distribution by diverting it from lands, actually in cultivation, to the lowly assessed waste of those villages of which the cultivators happen to be poor. By enabling the latter to meet the Government demands without application of the same degree of capital and skill required in the case of better cultivated villages, it would foster in the former a slovenly and unremunerative mode of husbandry." *Joint Report*, p. 15.

[63] Stokes, *English Utilitarians*, pp. 122-123.

[64] For rules of transfer, see *Joint Report*, revised edition (Bombay, 1859), pp. 157-160.

manded varied with the quality of the land. A man with good land would pay a high rental whether or not he cultivated the land well enough to get its full potential output. Wingate and Goldsmid strongly emphasized the importance of taxing on the quality of land, and hence on the potential output, rather than on the actual output. With their plan of rentals, land would pass out of the hands of poor and slovenly cultivators into the hands of those who would make the best use of it.[65] So in addition to providing security of tenure, the Bombay Survey and Settlement system was also designed to induce cultivators to make their land yield its full potential output.

Other systems of land revenue before this one had begun with equally high ideals, but most had faltered. That the Bombay Survey and Settlement system designed by Goldsmid and Wingate did not meet a similar fate is largely due to the attention that was paid to the details. For the first time, willing or unwilling, a branch of the government of India really devised a system that would yield the information needed to make a revenue system function as it was intended to function. As a result of this meticulous concern for detail, the settlement which began in the 1830s in the southern parts of the Deccan and in the Karnatak could not be extended to all parts of the Gujarat until the 1860s.

The operations of the Bombay Survey and Settlement, usually covering one *taluka* at a time, consisted of three phases, the first two of which were under the immediate personal supervision of European officers and the third of which was done completely by a European officer.[66] First, a complete field-by-field survey of each village in the *taluka* was done by one part of the survey department. The survey generally respected existing divisions of land and also divided the uncultivated land of each village into fields of 15 to 30 acres. When the outlines of each field had been determined, the

---

[65] In addition to the language quoted above in footnote 62, consider the following quote from a letter Wingate wrote in 1848, defending the *Joint Report*: "And if it be said that it would, however, occasion loss in the case of very poor cultivators, whose necessities might compel them to part with their whole produce before the last installment [of revenue] became due, and who had nothing besides from which it could be realized, I would reply that nothing more desirable could occur, and that the sacrifice of revenue here contemplated would be far more than counterbalanced by the advantage that would accrue from ejecting such paupers from their occupancies so as to allow of the land falling into the hands of substantial cultivators. I believe, however, that instances of this kind would very rarely occur." *The Bombay Survey and Settlement Manual* by R. G. Gordon, 2 vols. and supplement (Bombay: Government Central Press, 1917, 1922), 1:76-77.

[66] The details presented here are all drawn from the *Joint Report*.

villagers were required to put in place boundary markers at the corners of the fields. Then a second part of the survey department classified the soil in each field of the village. The survey used nine classes of soil, running from deep black soil (the highest class) to thin, stony red soil (the lowest class). Several examinations of the soil were made in each field, and the results were averaged to produce the classification for the entire field. The classification branch, which was completely separate from the measuring branch, also checked the work of that branch and reported and corrected any errors in measurement. When both the measurement of the fields and the classification of their soils had been completed, a settlement officer for the district—usually one of the men who had supervised the measurement operation—examined the condition of the *taluka* and wrote a report to the collector of the district, proposing rental rates for groups of villages within the *taluka* varying according to their access to markets and the dependability of the rainfall.[67]

In a system so firmly committed to the law of rent, it would seem only reasonable that the rates established by the settlement officer should be based on a determination of the amount of rent accruing to different classes of land. But Goldsmid and Wingate were men who could temper their theory with common sense to produce a workable system. Instead of trying to adhere to taking some portion of the "net produce" as Pringle had done, they built a system which rested on history. To determine what rates villages should pay, the settlement officer examined the past 20 or 30 years' collections from the villages and added his own observations of the condition of the *ryots* whom he saw in the process of measurement.[68] Once the rate that the best land should pay in each group of villages had been decided upon, the rate that should be paid for each lower class of land was calculated as a proportion of that maximum rate. In the assignment of taxes on specific fields, their general circumstances with respect to access to roads, to the village, and to water were also taken into consideration. However, capital improvements, such as the construction of wells, were not taxed.[69] The rates produced by the Bombay Survey and Settlement, after due correspondence between the settlement officer, the district collector, the divisional commissioner, and the Presidency government in Bombay, were

[67] For such a set of correspondences, see the opening pages of virtually any settlement report done before 1900.

[68] Stokes, *English Utilitarians*, p. 104. See any settlement report done before 1900 for relevant tables and diagrams.

[69] *Bombay Survey and Settlement Manual*, suppl. (1922), pp. 27-30.

guaranteed to the *ryots* for 30 years. As the end of that period approached, a new settlement would be prepared.

III. The Consequences of the Bombay Survey and Settlement System

The survey and settlement operations were not only intended to provide clear title to land and to end the reliance of the revenue officers on defective and deceptive Maratha records; they were also intended to reduce the level of revenue demand in most districts. In particular, there was a desire to make the demand on good soils somewhat low relative to their quality in order "to turn labour and capital preferentially on to the better soils" with the expectation that "the increase of wealth derivable from the cultivation of [the better soils] would ultimately bring the poor soils into occupation remuneratively."[70] It was, of course, also expected that systematization of revenue demands would tend to provide a stable and perhaps increasing collection of revenue.

In view of these high expectations, it is logical to ask how well the Bombay system fared compared to the rather *ad hoc* methods it replaced. To permit such a comparison, Figures 4.1-4.4 provide a set of revenue-related series for twelve *talukas* in the Karnatak and Deccan divisions of the Presidency. (The data from which these graphs have been prepared, as well as a discussion of the quality of the data, are contained in Appendix C.) Map 4.1 gives the locations of these *talukas*.[71] *Taluka*-level data have been used for several reasons. First, only at the *taluka* level are long, reasonably consistent series for government lands taken up by farmers for cultivation ("government lands occupied") generally available. Second, we may learn more about the effects of both revenue systems

---

[70] *Bombay Survey and Settlement Manual* (1917), vol. 2, p. 19.

[71] Because this is a study of famines, I initially wanted to use all of the *talukas* where the special famine census of 1878 had been done. Unfortunately, I was able to locate three successive settlement reports (an initial settlement and two resettlements) only for the *talukas* of Khatav and Man in Satara district, Sampgaon and Athni in Belgaum district, Bagalkot and Badami in Bijapur district, and Ron and Kod in Dharwar district. I could locate no *talukas* in Sholapur where three successive settlement reports were available. I then decided to broaden my search to include the districts of Khandesh, Nasik, Ahmednagar, and Poona. Each of the first three of these districts did yield some *talukas* for which three settlement reports were available. From these I selected Amalner and Erandol *talukas* in Khandesh and Ahmednagar and Shevgaon in Ahmednagar district. This is a convenience sample and *not* a random sample; powerful statistical tests are therefore unwarranted.

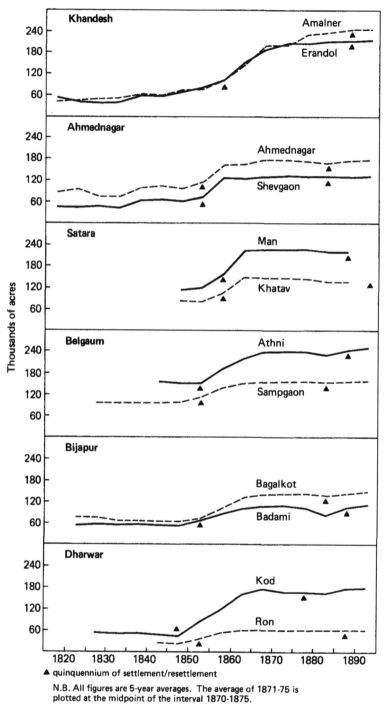

FIGURE 4.1 Government Lands Occupied in 12 *Talukas*, 1815-1895

▲ quinquennium of settlement/resettlement

N.B. All figures are 5-year averages. The average of 1871-75 is
plotted at the midpoint of the interval 1870-1875.

SOURCE: Appendix C.

FIGURE 4.2 Revenue Collected in 12 *Talukas*, 1815-1895

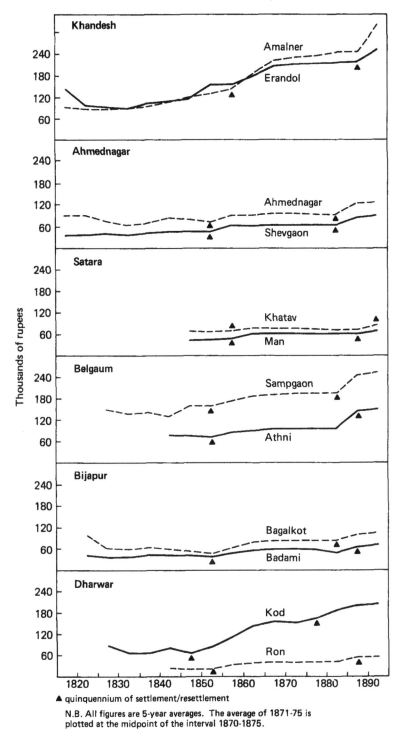

▲ quinquennium of settlement/resettlement

N.B. All figures are 5-year averages. The average of 1871-75 is
plotted at the midpoint of the interval 1870-1875.

SOURCE: Appendix C.

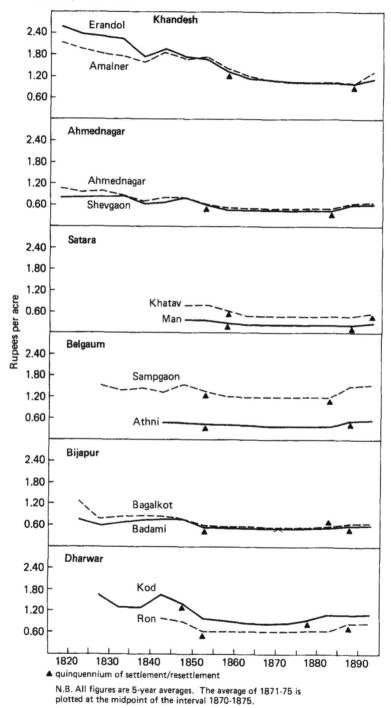

FIGURE 4.3 Revenue Collections per Acre in
12 *Talukas*, 1815-1895

▲ quinquennium of settlement/resettlement

N.B. All figures are 5-year averages. The average of 1871-75 is
plotted at the midpoint of the interval 1870-1875.

SOURCE: Appendix C.

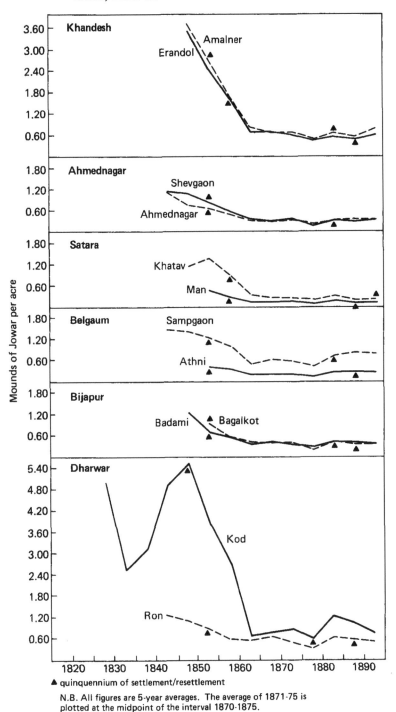

FIGURE 4.4 Real Value of Revenue Collections per Acre in 12 *Ta-lukas*, 1826-1895

▲ quinquennium of settlement/resettlement

N.B. All figures are 5-year averages. The average of 1871-75 is plotted at the midpoint of the interval 1870-1875.

SOURCE: Calculated from data in Appendix C.

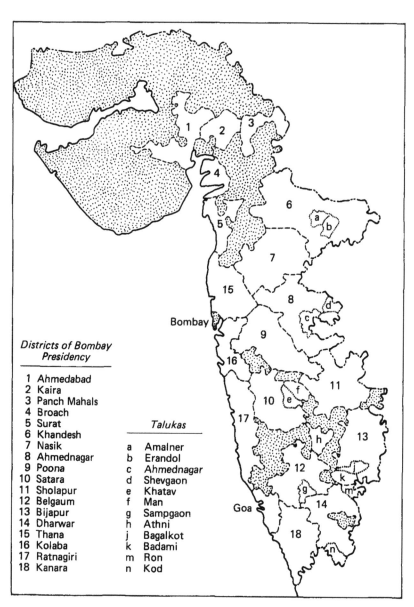

Districts of Bombay
Presidency

1 Ahmedabad
2 Kaira
3 Panch Mahals
4 Broach
5 Surat
6 Khandesh
7 Nasik
8 Ahmednagar
9 Poona
10 Satara
11 Sholapur
12 Belgaum
13 Bijapur
14 Dharwar
15 Thana
16 Kolaba
17 Ratnagiri
18 Kanara

Talukas

a Amalner
b Erandol
c Ahmednagar
d Shevgaon
e Khatav
f Man
g Sampgaon
h Athni
j Bagalkot
k Badami
m Ron
n Kod

MAP 4.1 *Talukas* from which Revenue History was Prepared

by looking at a number of fairly small areas instead of attempting (if it were possible) to construct aggregate data for a much larger region. Generally speaking, data for these *talukas* (or sections of *talukas*) are available in the first settlement report and two resettlement reports done about 30 and 60 years after the initial settlement. The first settlement report generally contains a revenue history of the *taluka* from the year it came under direct British administration up to the year of settlement. For some *talukas*, data are therefore available from 1818 forward. Several *talukas* were not under direct British control until some later date because they were originally granted to various chiefs and princes (and the Raja of Satara) and only later resumed for one of several reasons. The number of years of data before the introduction of the Bombay system varied from a low of about 10 years to a high of almost 40 years.

Figures 4.1-4.4 contain four series. The first (4.1) is that for the area of government lands occupied—that is, a series for all the lands that farmers had rented from the state, the ultimate owner of all lands. These lands might or might not be cultivated, but cultivators were obliged to pay revenue for them. The reliability of this series obviously improves after the first settlement date. To varying degrees, the estimates of lands occupied before the cadastral survey was complete were just that—rough estimates. The second series (4.2) is for land revenue collections. This series is self-explanatory and is probably about equally accurate in all periods. There are some minor anomalies in the late 1870s, when one level of collections was reported but large amounts of "arrears" were also reported. Apparently these arrears were not subtracted from revenue collections because the government anticipated that they would be paid eventually. Since whether or not they were in fact paid is not generally deducible from the settlement reports, some ambiguity remains.

The third series (4.3) is the quotient of the second divided by the first—i.e., revenue collections per acre. Changes in this series indicate both changes in the level of government revenue demands (particularly immediately after a settlement or resettlement) and various patterns of taking up and abandoning of fields by farmers. For instance, when collections per acre rise as a result of a larger decline in government land occupied than in revenue collections, we can infer that some lands paying below-average revenue and presumably having below-average productivity have been abandoned. The fourth series (4.4) converts nominal collections per acre into real collections per acre by dividing nominal collections by the price of a *maund* (82 pounds) of jowar. The resulting series is the number of *maunds* of jowar a farmer would have to sell to pay the revenue on an average acre of land. Obviously cultivators generally grew crops besides jowar and the majority of them may not have generally sold jowar to get the cash to pay their land revenue. But because jowar was grown in all of the *talukas* under consideration, because it was a staple of food crop, and because price series for it are among the most available price series, I have chosen to use it as the measure of real value.

The years before the first settlement under the Bombay Survey and Settlement system went into effect in these *talukas* were ones in which the experience of different *talukas* varied widely. In the Khandesh *talukas* of Amalner and Erandol, there was a period of decline in revenue collections and (in Erandol) in government lands occupied. These declines were followed by periods of increase in both these variables—increases that may have been partly or wholly caused by the reductions in the general level of revenue demands that were made in the 1840s. In Ahmednagar district, Ahmednagar *taluka* experienced some declines in both revenue collections and government lands occupied through the mid-1830s, after which these variables began to increase. However, Shevgaon *taluka* in the same district had constant or rising revenue collections and government lands occupied throughout the pre-settlement period. For Khatav and Man *talukas* in Satara district, we have information only from the mid-1840s, but over that period government lands occupied and revenue collections were both increasing, the former more rapidly than the latter so that the average collection per acre was falling.

When we shift our attention to the Karnatak division, we find that in Belgaum district, Sampgaon *taluka* had nearly constant occupation of government lands up to the quinquennium in which the settlement took place, but revenue collections fluctuated. In Athni *taluka* of Belgaum district, the fifteen years of direct British rule before the settlement were characterized by almost constant values for government lands occupied but by falling revenue collections. In Bijapur district, Bagalkot *taluka* experienced generally falling values for both government lands occupied and revenue collections from the early 1820s until the quinquennium of 1851-1855, when the new settlement was promulgated. In contrast, Badami *taluka*, in the same district, showed little if any trend in either of these variables over the period before the introduction of the new settlement. Finally, in Dharwar district, Kod *taluka* experienced fluctuations in both government lands occupied and in revenue collections, but these were fluctuations around a downward trend. In Ron, the other Dharwar *taluka* examined here, the short period for which data are available before the new settlement suggest slightly falling values for both government lands occupied and revenue collections.

In the quinquennia after the introduction of the settlements prepared under the Bombay Survey and Settlement system, we can see several noteworthy changes. First, for all of the *talukas*, government lands occupied and revenue collections increased. Second, revenue collections per acre, for all *talukas*, declined from their former levels. While the declines varied in size, they were present in all cases—and it is well to remember that they are somewhat masked by the process of averaging five years together. Yearly data have not been used because of the cumbersome length of the resultant series, but they would show more dramatic declines in many instances than the five-year average figures do. Third, the experiences of all *talukas* were much more similar *after* the introduction of the new settlements than they had been before. Fourth, the real value of collections generally declined more rapidly after the introduction of the settlement than nominal collections per acre did.

Before awarding the Bombay Survey and Settlement Department too many good-conduct medals, we again need to ask how confident we can be in the data used and what other forces besides the new settlement might have been affecting the environment in which cultivators were making decisions. The series in which I have the least confidence is that for government lands occupied before the introduction of the new settlements. If this series is biased downwards (due to concealment of cultivation, poor measurements, or measurement of cultivation rather than occupation of land), then Figure 4.1 tends to overstate the increases in lands rented from government after the introduction of the new settlements. There is little evidence now available or likely to become available that will shed light on the existence and extent of the underestimation of government lands occupied before introduction of the Bombay Survey and Settlement. For those *talukas* where the changes in this variable were large, a small degree of underestimation would not change our general conclusions. Where the observed changes were relatively small, they could be due entirely to improvements in measurements. The Karnatak districts had been at least partially surveyed in the 1820s, so we might expect that in those *talukas* the early figures are more likely to be reliable. When Sampgaon *taluka* of Belgaum district was surveyed, the settlement officer wrote:

In 1825/26 a survey of the talooka was made with considerable accuracy, judging from a comparison with the areas, as ascertained by our survey wherever the boundaries of the former were ascertainable. No general revision of the rates appears to have been made. The old rates were applied on the area ascertained by the former survey, with the exception of single cases here and there, where at different times some modification of the old assessment has been made by the officers in charge of the talooka.[72]

While this statement suggests that the figures on government lands occupied before the first settlement under the new Bombay system may have been quite accurate, information from other settlement reports suggests otherwise. Wingate included a quote from one of his subordinates on the old survey:

But the rates so obtained were found to vary materially from the rent actually levied, and the Cutcherry servants, actuated by dread of displeasing the Collector on the one hand, and by the difficulty of conciliating the ryots on the other, endeavored to modify the results by certain expedients of their own. Whenever the new rates effected an increase in the old rent, reductions were made on the score of imperfect cultivation, poverty. But if the survey fell short of former payments, a proportion of waste land was tacked to the reduced field, by which the total rent was kept up to its original amount. This patchwork assessment now exists in the talookas of Dharwar, Nuwulgoond, Dummul, and Purusghir.[73]

From his own examination of the revenue accounts, Wingate wrote:

In fact, it would be difficult to believe that a complete measurement of this Collectorate had been so recently executed, but for the circumstances of its results appearing in our revenue accounts, while the effect of these data being entered there is to render our accounts system more hopelessly perplexing than before.[74]

Taken together, these remarks suggest that any general conclusion about the quality of the data before the completion of the cadastral survey is impossible. It was good in some places, and less good to actually bad in others. Attempts to find the old village books might

---

[72] SRGB N.S. No. 94 (1865), p. 42.
[73] SRGB No. 12 (1853), p. 10.
[74] SRGB No. 12 (1853), p. 10.

yield enough information to resolve this issue for specific villages, but a great many such villages would have to be examined to make a firm conclusion possible. But even if we cannot arrive at an evaluation of the quality of the data on government lands occupied before the cadastral survey, we can examine them to see if they are consistent with what else we know about the economy of the region—and we shall do so below.

Whenever taxes on the agricultural sector are fixed and collected in cash, the real burden of taxation can be changed in two ways. First, the amount of taxes can be lowered. Farmers will then have to sell less of their crop to pay their taxes. Second, rising prices can also reduce the amount of their produce that farmers must market to get the cash to pay their taxes. The intention of the Bombay Survey and Settlement system was, initially, to lower rates of taxation and thereby to encourage cultivation. If farmers could keep more of the produce of each acre, the argument ran, then they would be able to accumulate resources to enable them to cultivate more land and they would have the incentive, in the form of higher earnings from cultivation, to take more land under cultivation. As additional fields were rented from the state, its income from the land revenue taxes would also rise. The data presented in Figures 4.1 and 4.2 show quite clearly that the events of the 30 years after the introduction of the new settlement system generally met these expectations. However, when we look at the value of revenue collections per acre in Figures 4.3 and 4.4, we see that while the changes in the revenue system resulted in some decrease in the tax burden (nominal collections per acre), rising prices further reduced the tax burden (real collections per acre) in all of the *talukas* studied. Reductions in the real burden of revenue collections are particularly striking in the quinquennium of 1861-1865, when speculation on cotton (because of the American Civil War) led to rising prices throughout the agricultural sector. Since we do not know how much extra incentive in the form of reduced real taxes cultivators needed to take up new fields, we cannot be sure of the relative roles of reductions in collections per acre and rising prices in stimulating the agricultural sector. In general, the expansions of cultivation both after the reductions in rates and during the rise of prices in 1861-1865 suggest that each played some role. The Bombay Survey and Settlement may have also contributed to growth in the agricultural sector by generating clear and constant expectations about revenue collections and thereby reducing the perceived risks of cultivation.

It should be noted that not all rises in prices can be expected to stimulate cultivation. Rises in prices that originate outside the agricultural sector—because of increasing demand from urban areas or from abroad, because of reductions in transport costs, or because of increases in the money supply—are all likely to stimulate expansion of cultivation. However, rising prices or, more accurately, periods of high prices that are due to harvest shortfalls that sometimes culminate in famine are likely to have the opposite effect. After such periods cultivation may decline because of decreases in available supplies of capital and labor due to the deaths of bullocks and people during a period of famine. The quinquennium 1876-1880 was a period of high prices caused by harvest failures in many parts of the Presidency in 1876-1877 and, to a lesser extent, in 1877-1878. Badami *taluka* in Bijapur district exhibits the sharpest declines in government lands occupied and revenue collections as a result of this famine, but smaller declines occurred in about half the *talukas* studied.

While Figure 4.4 clearly shows that the absolute amount of jowar a farm household would have to sell to pay the revenue on an average acre of land was quite low, we would also like to have some assessment of the relative importance of the taxes. That is, how large was the amount of jowar that had to be sold relative to the yield? In an ideal world, instead of using only jowar prices to convert the nominal revenue collections per acre into real values, we would like to use a price index that included all of the crops grown by the farm household, each price weighted by the share of the crop in total output. The data to form such an index for the entire period, however, either are not available, or are available in local sources so scattered that preparation of the index would be a major work in itself. Not desiring to undertake that task, I have elected to use jowar prices because (1) jowar was grown in all these *talukas*, (2) jowar prices are among the most commonly available prices in settlement reports, and (3) jowar was a major food crop. The use of jowar has another advantage when we want to estimate the share of produce that had to be sold to pay the land revenue: Crop-cutting yields for jowar for 1946-1954 are available for all of the districts in which these twelve *talukas* are located. As Chapter 2 made clear, there are no trustworthy figures on yields for any crop grown in Bombay Presidency for the colonial period. With the help of certain acts of faith, we can produce series that indicate the fluctuations in total output of foodgrains and pulses from year to year for part of the colonial period, but these figures tell us little about the absolute levels of yields per acre. For the latter figures we must rely on the crop-cutting experiments done in the 1940s and 1950s.[75]

These crop-cutting yields have been combined with the figures on real value of revenue collections from Figure 4.4 and Appendix C to produce Table 4.1, which gives the real value of collections per acre as a percentage of the crop-cutting yield. Use of the crop-cutting yields means that we implicitly assume that there were no changes in yields per acre over the period from 1826 through 1954—an assumption that we accept only because of the general paucity of evidence on changes in yields.[76] Further, we assume that the crop-cutting yields are a suitable average to use for a smaller section of the district like a *taluka*. Given these caveats, what trends do the figures in Table 4.1 show?

In general, not only were absolute levels of demand low after the introduction of the Bombay system, but revenue payments also formed a small share of the output of an average field. For all *talukas* the share of produce paid as land revenue declined, and frequently very dramatically and consistently, from the earliest dates for which data are available. Given the frequency with which *increasing* revenue demands have been cited as a major cause of poverty in the agricultural sector, these findings suggest that reconsideration of existing views of the nineteenth-century experience is urgently needed. However, there was a large amount of variation among the *talukas*, only some of it explicable in terms of the differing degrees of fertility and market access. If we accept the crop-cutting yield figures as correct, then by 1891-1895 the Satara *talukas* of Man and Khatav and the Belgaum *taluka* of Athni paid unusually low shares (four percent or less) of their produce in land taxes. The Ahmednagar *talukas* of Ahmednagar and Shevgaon and (to the extent that they depended on the *rabi* season rather than the *kharif* season) the Bijapur *talukas* of Bagalkot and Badami and the Khandesh *talukas* of Amalner and Erandol paid unusually high (14 percent or more) shares of produce in land taxes. The three *talukas* with unusually low shares of revenue demand have in common that they were taken over by the British in the 1840s from Indian rulers—Man and Khatav from the Raja of Satara and Athni from the Nepaneekur. The differences in rates tend to suggest that these Indian rulers were

---

[75] For the problems with even these data, see Heston, "Official Yields."

[76] For a discussion of the opinions advanced about the course of yields, see Michelle Burge McAlpin, "Railroads, Cultivation Patterns, and Foodgrain Availability: India 1860-1900," *Indian Economic and Social History Review* 12 (January-March 1975): 48-50.

TABLE 4.1. Real Value of Revenue Collections per Acre, 1826-1895, as a Percentage of Average Yield of Jowar in Crop-Cutting Experiments of 1946-1954

Real Value of Revenue Collections as a Percentage of the Crop-Cutting Yield[a]

	Deccan Division								Karnatak Division							
	Khandesh District				Ahmednagar District		Satara District		Belgaum District		Bijapur District				Dharwar District	
	Amalner		Erandol		Ahmednagar	Shevgaon	Khatav	Man	Sampgaon	Athni	Bagalkot		Badami		Ron	Kod
Quinquennium	K	R	K	R	R	R	K	K	K	K	K	R	K	R	K	K
1826-1830															80	20
1831-1835															40	
1836-1840															50	
1841-1845					41	43			20						79	20
1846-1850	52	94	48	89	29	41	17		20				34	48	88	18
1851-1855	38	69	33	61	25	31	20	7	17	6	25	36	19	27	61	14
1856-1860	24	44	23	43	19	22	14	4	14	5	16	22	15	21	43	10
1861-1865	11	21	10	18	12	14	6	2	7	3	11	16	10	14	11	9
1866-1870	9	17	10	17	11	12	4	2	9	3	11	15	11	16	13	10
1871-1875	9	17	8	15	13	14	4	3	8	3	11	15	10	14	14	7
1876-1880	7	13	6	12	9	7	3	2	6	2	6	8	8	11	10	5
1881-1885	9	17	8	14	13	13	5	3	10	4	12	17	12	17	20	10
1886-1890	8	14	7	13	14	12	3	2	11	4	10	14	11	15	17	9
1891-1895	11	21	9	16	14	14	4	2	11	4	10	15	10	14	12	8

[a]Crop-cutting yields, 1946-1954, were as follows (in maunds):
Khandeshi – kharif (K), 7.23; rabi (R), 3.95.   Belgaum – K, 7.17.
Ahmednagar – R, 2.65.   Bijapur – K, 3.66; R, 2.59.
Satara – K, 6.65.   Dharwar – K, 6.23.

SOURCES: Crop-cutting yields – Heston, "Official Yields." All other figures calculated from data in Appendix C.

collecting (at least into their general coffers) a smaller share of the produce than the East India Company was trying to collect from the *talukas* it administered directly from 1818 onwards. It is also noteworthy that the British further reduced the level of revenue demands—already low in the 1840s—when they introduced the Bombay system into these *talukas*.

The data in Figure 4.2 show that the Bombay Survey and Settlement system did achieve one of its objectives—a stable and increasing revenue. Table 4.1 suggests that this had been done while simultaneously lowering the share of produce collected as land revenue. While the figures in Table 4.1 certainly suggest that incomes were probably rising in the countryside, other information would be useful to provide confirmation of this, to indicate how increased incomes were being used, and, if possible, to show how widely distributed these income increases were. To this end, Table 4.2 contains the percentage change in a number of variables that are associated with the general level of prosperity in an agricultural system. These data have been drawn from the resettlement reports made at the end of the first 30 years of guaranteed rates. Figures are not available for all the *talukas* under study, but they are presented for all the *talukas* for which they are available. The numbers are not of such high quality that small changes in them should be accorded undue weight. Little information exists on how most of them were collected. What is clear is that even for the series into which the administration put the most effort—those on cultivation and on government lands occupied—data from different time points are often not comparable due to changes in methods of data collection or definition (see Appendices C and D). What follows is, therefore, an attempt to tell a story that is consistent with the data that exist, with economic theory (sensibly applied), and with common sense.

Table 4.2 shows that population, agricultural cattle, carts, wells, and superior houses (usually meaning those with flat or tiled roofs) increased for all seven of the *talukas* for which we have data. In all but one of the districts for which figures on area under cultivation are available, it, too, was increasing. In five *talukas* the number of sheep and goats had increased, and in two the number of milk cattle had also increased. How are we to interpret these various increases?

It would, of course, be desirable to have figures on areas of cultivation in each of these *talukas* instead of using figures for the districts in which they are located. However, as for many other pieces of *taluka*-level data, retrieval is not easy or even possible. If

TABLE 4.2. Changes in Population, Agricultural Capital, and Houses During the First 30-Year Settlement

Division, District, Taluka, and Dates of First 30-Yr. Settlement	Population[a]	Govt. Lands Occup.[b]	Land Cult. (Dist.)[c]	Percentage Increase (+) or Decrease (−) in:						Houses[a]	
				Agri. Cattle[a]	Other Cattle[a]	Sheep and Goats[a]	Carts[a]	Wells and Budkis[a]	Tanks[a]	Superior	Inferior
Deccan											
Khandesh											
Amalner, 1858-1888	+47	+142	+87	+23	− 8	−39	+ 52	+27	n.a.	+45	+22
Erandol, 1859-1889	+57	+110		+19	−25	−23	+ 51	+31	n.a.	+66	− 8
Ahmednagar											
Ahmednagar 1851-1881	+15	+ 48	− 1[d]	+30	+ 4	+58	+ 61	n.a.	n.a.	+25	+ 3
Satara											
Khatav, 1858-1888	+30	+ 33	+11	+12	0	+26	+232	+72	n.a.	+34	−31
Man, 1858-1888	+31	+ 41		+13	+14	+48	+515	+76	n.a.	+56	+ 7
Karnatak											
Belgaum											
Sampgaon, 1852-1882	+14	+ 39	n.a.[e]	+14	−36	+74	+216	+87	− 6	+23	
Dharwar											
Kod, 1846-1876	+29	+270	+44[f]	+24	−31	+21	+177	n.a.	+2	+58	− 5

n.a. = not available.
[a] Calculated from data in resettlement reports. See Appendix C for citations of reports.
[b] Percentage change calculated between quinquennia of settlement and resettlement – e.g. for Amalner, 1855-1860 and 1886-1890.
[c] Gross sown area plus current fallows for the appropriate district. Taluka-level figures for cultivation are not available.
[d] 1855 to 1881-1885.
[e] The transfer of three talukas from Belgaum district to Bijapur district in 1865 makes calculation of increases in cultivation in Belgaum district, 1855-1882, impossible.
[f] 1855 to 1876-1880.

we accept increases in cultivated areas in the appropriate districts as reasonable proxies for increases in the *talukas,* we can observe that these increases are uniformly *lower* than the increases in government lands occupied. This pattern is interesting for it suggests that cultivators were renting from the government land that they were not cultivating or having cultivated. While they may have done this for several reasons, one prominent possibility is that they were holding land in anticipation of either rising values of produce or rising land values. In an early defense of the Bombay Survey and Settlement system, Wingate wrote:

> The new settlements have nowhere been in operation for a sufficient period to admit of any certain or general conclusions being drawn regarding their effect on the value of land; but the eagerness of Mirasdars to become re-possessed of such portions of their estates as have fallen into the hands of others, and the competition of different cultivators for portions of waste, would seem to indicate that all descriptions of land are rapidly acquiring a value; and we have little doubt but that in the course of a few years they will become saleable with the same facility as other descriptions of property. [77]

The increases in agricultural cattle, wells, carts, and, to the extent that they were used to shelter animals and to process and store crops, superior houses all represent increases in the stock of agricultural capital. Given their sizes relative to changes in area of cultivation, the changes in the numbers of agricultural cattle and other cattle are somewhat difficult to interpret. Even if we assume that the settlement officers had successfully performed the task of counting and classifying all of the cattle, we have no information on how intensively agricultural cattle (essentially draft animals) were used or on how productive other cattle (essentially milk animals) were. For instance, in the Khandesh *talukas* of Amalner and Erandol it is impossible to know if the smaller increases in agricultural cattle than in areas of cultivation imply (1) that land was being cultivated less intensively, or (2) that animals were being used more nearly to capacity at the end of the 30-year settlement, or (3) that improved, more productive cattle were being used, or (4) that each of these possibilities was true in some degree. To the extent that cultivation expanded and waste lands for free grazing were reduced, cultivators certainly had incentives to get rid of use-

[77] *Survey and Settlement Manual* (1882), vol. 1, p. viii.

less animals (whether draft or milk animals) and to upgrade those that had to be fed. In these Khandesh *talukas*, where population growth was the most rapid and increases in areas of cultivation were even more rapid, farmers may also have had incentive to maximize the return to labor and capital (rather than to land) by farming somewhat less intensively.

The Satara *talukas* of Man and Khatav present a somewhat simpler picture: Growth of population and agricultural cattle (and of wells and carts) exceeded increases in cultivation in a pattern that is clearly suggestive of increased intensity of cultivation. It is important to realize that these differences in patterns between the Khandesh *talukas* and the Satara *talukas* (and the variations on these patterns that other *talukas* display) have to be interpreted in the context of their different conditions and different potentials at the time of the first settlement. Growth of agriculture in response to the stimulus of falling nominal and real revenue demands and increasing prices naturally followed different paths in different circumstances.

Taken together, all of these figures demonstrate rising surpluses in the agricultural sector. Agriculturists became sufficiently prosperous that they could simultaneously add to their stock of agricultural capital, increase their consumption as well as their capital by improving their houses, and afford to hold land from the government on which they paid taxes but which they did not cultivate.

All of these changes are compatible with a variety of patterns of distribution of benefits, although they do suggest some limits on these patterns. For instance, an increase of 66 percent in superior houses in Erandol *taluka* (an absolute increase of 7,599 houses) is not consistent with a narrow distribution of the gains from expansion of agriculture.[78] However, data from the settlement reports do place severe restrictions on how much we can learn about changes in the distribution of income and power. Part of the problem in tracing change over time comes from shifts in vocabulary between a time, shortly after the introduction of British rule in the Deccan and the Karnatak, when the announced objective of the administration was the preservation of the old order, stripped of certain abuses, and a time, after the introduction of the Bombay Survey and Settlement system, when the announced objective had become the encouragement of development and capital accumulation. The vocabulary of the former period drew upon the Maratha revenue

[78] SRGB N.S. No. 239 (1890), p. 5.

system, while that of the latter, although preserving a variety of terms, added new ones from the writings of Malthus, Mill, and Ricardo. In an attempt to answer the two basic questions of who gained from increased agricultural prosperity and how social and economic power was redistributed among groups, we will make use of the categories of persons described at the beginning of the chapter. The process of tracing the welfare of these categories of persons in the later British records is fraught with difficulties and risks, but some effort at it is necessary.[79]

The Upper Part of the Village: Chali Ryots, Mirasdars, and Patels

In the ideal world of the Maratha revenue system, *mirasdars* or *chali ryots* may have been heavily taxed, but they occupied a superior social position within their villages. Where they remained an effective corporate group they had the disposal of uncultivated village lands (and at least part of the earnings from leasing them out) in their hands. So long as revenue was demanded from the village as a whole, the corporate body of *ryots* with settlement rights in the village formed an arena for the exercise of social and economic power in the distribution of the burden of taxes among themselves. They also had an interest in acting collectively to reduce their joint revenue burdens by encouraging *uparis* to cultivate some of their otherwise vacant lands. Gooddine's work on the role of *patels* suggests that in some villages the corporate body of *ryots* had lost their power of acting collectively to a greater or lesser degree and that this power had been gathered up by the *patels*.[80] In favorable circumstances, the exercise of this power could bring the *patel* considerable economic gains.

The activities of revenue farmers in the Deccan and Karnatak after 1800 had probably begun to undermine the corporate groups in many villages as had some earlier attempts of the Peshwa's government to assign specific tax burdens inside the villages.[81] The first three decades of British rule probably further undermined the functional cohesion of the corporate groups by making individual

[79] The problem is akin to that so ably addressed by Dharma Kumar in *Land and Caste in South India: Agricultural Labour in Madras Presidency during the Nineteenth Century* (Cambridge: Cambridge University Press, 1965), where she works to connect castes in 1800 with landless laborers in 1900.

[80] SRGB No. 4 (1852), p. 15.

[81] R. Kumar, "Rise of Rich Peasants," pp. 27-29; Fukazawa, "Rural Servants," pp. 27-30.

ryots rather than the village responsible for the payment of taxes and limiting that liability to fields that *ryots* were cultivating.

Because of the degree to which it penetrated the villages, the Bombay Survey and Settlement may have completed the transformation of the old structure within villages. While it is difficult to determine the degree to which it was a direct objective of the Bombay system to alter the village structure, the careful carrying out of a field-by-field survey, the regularization of procedures for taking up waste fields for cultivation and for relinquishing title to fields already held, the institution of close supervision of all matters concerning title to land within villages, and the transference of many functions from the village officers to the offices of the *malkuri* or the *mamlatdar* had the effect of leveling the distinctions in economic power that came from differential access to land. In addition, the power of disposal over vacant lands was transferred from the village corporate body or the officers of the village to the state. Henceforth, all land was held directly from the government with no intermediaries and with no distinction in the title to one piece of land or another.[82] While these changes may not have stripped the *mirasdars* and *chali ryots* of their power, they did alter the ways in which they could exercise it.

The village social structures had shown considerable resilience in preserving their own interests in the century preceding the introduction of the Bombay Survey and Settlement. Attempts by the Peshwa, by Pringle, and by Thackeray's subordinates in the Karnatak had all come to grief because of the ability of the village corporate group to resist redistribution of burdens within the village and to maintain its dominance. The revision introduced by the Bombay Survey and Settlement did not end that dominance, in spite of ostensibly removing power over the disposal of unused lands from the village members to the state. As noted above, for the *talukas* discussed in depth in this chapter, increases in the occupation of government lands generally exceeded increases in cultivation of government lands during the first 30-year settlements. It seems likely that the lowering of the land tax, and the further reduction in the real burden of this tax as prices began to rise, encouraged the old *chali ryots* or *mirasdars* to lay claim to nearly all of the lands

---

[82] This does not imply that land could not be rented out. What it does imply is that no one in a village was given title to any land on which he was not paying revenue to the government. Title to all waste land (and ultimately to *all* land) rested with the government. A *ryot* wanting more land took it up from the government, not from the corporate group of the village.

of the village by paying the (rather low) revenue demanded by the government. This was indubitably motivated partly by speculation on rising land values (as I have argued above), but it may also have been the way that members of the village corporate group now were forced to continue their dominance. Formerly their dominance had come from the corporate group's social prestige and from its ability to deny non-members equal access to land. In effect, its dominance came from total power inside the village. The Bombay Survey and Settlement may have succeeded in stripping the corporate group of that total power. Now the corporate group had to sustain its power by exercising its economic advantage—an advantage it would not have had if revenue demand had continued high enough (in real terms) to absorb most of the surplus production from land. But that was patently not the case, and some of the surplus seems to have been invested in holding land well in advance of the need for cultivation—an effective way to maintain control of who settled in the village. Given the ability to exercise differential economic power, the distinction from the old system would be that now the unused land and the disposal of it resided with individual families rather than with the village's corporate group. Only with investigation into village-level records will it be possible to be certain how much more equally or unequally land was distributed after the survey and settlement process than before.

While longitudinal data on the size of holdings and the way in which they were cultivated are rare, the resettlement reports for ten of the twelve *talukas* under consideration here do provide information on the way holdings were cultivated at the end of the first 30-year settlement. Because holdings are not all of the same size, knowing the percentage of holdings that were cultivated by tenants will not tell us the percentage of *land* that was so cultivated.[83] If the holders who rented out their land all had holdings above the average, then the percentage of land rented out would exceed the percentage of holdings rented out. If the holders who rented out their land had smaller-than-average holdings, then the percentage of land rented out would be smaller than the percentage of holdings rented out. The shares of holdings (for lands paying full revenue and for *inam* lands) cultivated by their holders alone or in partnership with someone and those rented out for money or produce rents are given in Table 4.3. Since the legal fiction in Bombay Presidency

[83] In Vilyatpur, Kessinger found both large and small plots rented out—some plots of one acre or less and one as large as 33 acres. Kessinger, *Vilyatpur*, p. 65.

TABLE 4.3. Percentages of Holdings Cultivated by Their Owners and Rented Out at End of First 30-Year Settlement

Division, District, Taluka, and Date	(1) Cultivated: By Holder	(2) In Partnership	(3) Total of 1 + 2	(4) Rented for Money	(5) Rented for Produce	(6) Total of 4 + 5	(7) Total of 3 + 6	(8) Inam Holdings as % of All Holdings
DECCAN								
Khandesh								
Amalner, 1888								
Government land	91	3	94	5	2	7	101	
Inam land	70	4	74	22	4	26	100	
Total	89	3	92	6	2	8	100	8
Erandol, 1889ᵃ								
Total	—	—	89	8	3	11	100	n.a.
Satara								
Khatav, 1888-1889								
Government land	64	13	77	12	10	22	99	
Inam land	32	18	50	36	14	50	100	
Total	56	14	70	18	11	29	99	25
Man, 1888-1889								
Government land	67	16	83	8	9	17	100	
Inam land	35	18	53	37	10	47	100	
Total	62	16	78	13	9	22	100	16

KARNATAK

Belgaum								
Sampgaon, 1882								
Government land	63	4	67	15	18	33	100	
Inam land	47	6	53	20	26	46	99	
Total	59	5	64	16	20	36	100	26
Athni, 1882								
Government land	72	3	75	16	9	25	100	
Inam land	46	5	51	38	12	50	101	
Total	64	4	68	23	10	33	101	31
Bijapur								
Bagalkot, 1881								
Government land	77	4	81	14	6	20	101	
Inam land	42	5	47	45	8	53	100	
Total	63	4	67	26	7	33	100	39
Badami, 1886								
Government land	80	2	82	14	4	18	100	
Inam land	62	5	67	29	4	33	100	
Total	72	3	75	20	4	24	99	43
Dharwar								
Kod, 1876								
Government land	77	3	80	14	7	21	101	
Inam land	47	5	52	41	8	49	101	
Total	65	3	68	25	7	32	100	40

TABLE 4.3 (Continued)

Division, District, Taluka, and Date	(1) Cultivated: By Holder	(2) Cultivated: In Partner- ship	(3) Total of 1 + 2	(4) Rented for Money	(5) Rented for Produce	(6) Total of 4 + 5	(7) Total of 3 + 6	(8) Inam Holdings as % of All Holdings
Ron, 1886								
Government land	70	9	79	15	7	22	101	
Inam land	52	10	62	28	10	38	100	
Total	64	9	73	18	8	26	99	29
Unweighted Average of Nine Talukas[b]								
Government land	73	6	80	13	8	21	—	
Inam land	48	8	57	33	11	44	—	
Total	66	7	74*	17*	8*	25*	—	29

[a]Separation between government and inam lands not available in resettlement reports.
[b]Erandol missing except for figures marked *.
SOURCE: Resettlement reports, see Appendix C for citations.

was that the state owned all the land, everyone was first of all a tenant of the state and was referred to as a "holder." But if we were talking about Iowa farmers we would call these same people "owners," and I shall do so in the discussion that follows.

The first column in Table 4.3 gives the percentage of holdings cultivated by their owners. The second column gives the percentage of holdings cultivated "in partnership." We have no direct evidence on what "in partnership" means. I think that the most reasonable speculation is that it refers to the set of practices Schlesinger describes in modern Satara district, where a family lacking some necessary farm implements enters into a partnership with another family possessing those implements, and in return for the loan of implements (and labor to accompany them), the partner family receives a share of the harvest.[84] If we accept this definition of "in partnership" (which category, interestingly, was most common in the Satara *talukas* of Man and Khatav), then these holdings also belong in the category of "cultivated by owners" (as opposed to that of rented out). Columns 4 and 5 of Table 4.3 give the percentages of holdings rented out for either money or produce rents. Since all these statistics are provided separately for land paying the full revenue (government land) and for *inam* land, the percentage of all holdings in the *taluka* that were *inam* holdings has been provided in the final column.

While there is considerable variation among the *talukas* under consideration, the average share of government holdings cultivated by their owners (either singly or in partnership) is 80 percent. The percentage of *inam* holdings so cultivated is lower—57 percent— but for both types of holdings taken together, 74 percent were cultivated by their owners. Because of the nature of the Bombay Survey and Settlement, it seems reasonable to take these numbers at face value; when a percentage of holdings are reported as cultivated by their owners (or holders) we need not seek for a set of sub-holders to confuse the picture. All the evidence from both before and after the Bombay Survey and Settlement was introduced is that the Deccan and the Karnatak did not support a many-layered social and economic structure that could give rise to the complexities of tenure that are so often discussed in some other parts of India. But even if we agree to accept the data at face value, we are still faced with the problem of deciding whether these percentages of land rented out should be regarded as high or low, a problem made more acute

---

[84] Schlesinger, "Agriculture and Community," pp. 248-254.

by our inability to trace change over time in any given *taluka*. All that is possible is to examine the nonquantitative evidence from earlier periods and attempt to draw some inferences.

Consider *inam* lands first. Fewer *inam* lands were cultivated by their owners than were holdings paying full revenues to the government. People who held *inam* land in return for services (like the keepers of tombs) commonly did not cultivate that land themselves, nor could institutions (like mosques) have cultivated their *inams*.[85] *Balutedars* who held *inam* land as part of their remuneration from the village may or may not have cultivated their own lands as their time and caste allowed. The *kulkarni* and the astrologer, both commonly brahmins, would very probably have rented out their *inam* land. Further, since *inam* lands were held either rent-free or at low rents, the probability was greater for them than for lands held directly from the government and paying full revenue that the surplus they produced could maintain a landlord as well as a cultivator. All of this suggests that a considerable portion of *inam* lands had been rented out before the beginning of British rule in these areas— rented out as a normal part of the functioning of the agrarian system. Therefore, 44 percent of all *inam* lands rented out in the 1880s should probably not be regarded as a high level of renting out. It may not even have been much of an increase over time—something on which only village studies can provide definite information. But even if it were an increase over time, we need to consider how such an increase may have come about and whether it would indicate increasing or decreasing inequality, particularly since, before the British period, only *chali ryots* could cultivate *inam* lands in the Karnatak, while afterwards anyone could legally do so.

As with *inam* lands, the qualitative evidence suggests that some other (non-*inam*) lands in each village were rented out in pre-British times—commonly to *uparis*. No village-level data are currently available on the percentages of land that were rented out. Since this is so, it is important to examine briefly the reasons for tenancy in agricultural communities. One kind of tenancy was that of the *upari* who rented some land from a village that had more than it needed. This was a contract freely entered into, where both sides stood to benefit—the village by getting help in meeting the revenue demand and the *upari* by getting a piece of land to cultivate. A second kind of tenancy was that where one or several individuals or families had been able through whatever means to gain superior title to large

---

[85] Fukazawa, "Lands and Peasants," p. 48.

amounts of land which they then rented out to people without such rights. Depending on the competition for land among renters, the terms may have been either fair, probably when renters were scarce relative to land, or in some sense exploitative, when renters were plentiful relative to land. There was a third kind of tenancy which was part of the normal functioning of the agricultural community: tenancy among the coequal property groups of the village. Such tenancy came about because the males in some property groups were too young, too old, or too few to be able to work the group's land, or because the males in another property group were sufficiently numerous to work more land than their group owned. Over time the relative positions of such groups could change, as one had many surviving sons and another few. It is this kind of tenancy that may well have been most heavily represented in the Deccan and the Karnatak after the introduction of the Bombay Survey and Settlement. Throughout this area the majority of holdings were between 10 and 50 acres, with less than 3 percent larger than 100 acres.[86] Our problem, then, is to decide what percentage of tenancy was "normal" and how to interpret departures from this norm.

In his study of Vilyatpur, Kessinger found that almost all land that was leased out was leased from one Sahota property group to another. In 1848, 21 percent of land was so leased; in 1884, 30 percent; and after 1898, about 40 percent.[87] Given that some percentage of *inam* lands had always been cultivated by tenants, and given that some amount of tenancy in agricultural communities was normal, the range of tenancy found in the ten *talukas* examined in Table 4.3—from a low of 8 percent to a high of 36 percent—can reasonably be interpreted as the normal working of the agricultural system rather than as a symptom of pathological decay. All these rates are at or below the levels Kessinger found in his Punjab village. The usual hypothesis about Indian agriculture has been that tenancy increased in the nineteenth century because former landowners had been driven into debt, lost their land to their creditors, and become tenants on what had been their own lands.[88] But an average of 80 percent of land paying full revenue to the government being cultivated by its owners, either singly or in partnership, in the 1880s,

[86] Michelle Burge McAlpin, "The Effects of Markets on Rural Income Distribution in Nineteenth Century India," *Explorations in Economic History* 12 (July 1975):295.

[87] Kessinger, *Vilyatpur*, p. 140.

[88] Morris David Morris, "Economic Change and Agriculture in Nineteenth Century India," *Indian Economic and Social History Review* 3 (June 1966):185-195, gives a good summary of the classical view.

is clearly inconsistent with that process having occurred in the Deccan and the Karnatak during the first settlement period (about 1850 to 1880). The percentages of tenancy observed are low enough to suggest that nothing is represented but the normal operations of the agricultural system. However the Bombay Survey and Settlement altered the power of the old corporate groups and the ways in which they might exercise it, there is no evidence that the system, alone or in combination with market forces, produced any general impoverishment of these old landholders. The degree to which differentials among them increased awaits further study.

The Uparis

All of the available evidence seems to indicate that *uparis* were a normal part of the village in the Deccan and Karnatak in the early decades of the nineteenth century. The first section of this chapter suggested several hypotheses about the origin of the *uparis* and their role in the agrarian system. By the end of the first settlement period, the designation of *uparis* had disappeared from the administrative literature. What had become of them?

To the extent that *uparis* had been tenants of the village, the effect of the settlement operation was to change the status of land (removing it from control of the village to control of the state) and to change the legal status of the *uparis*. Fields cultivated by *uparis* may have been entered in the name of the field's owner (but who was this to be if it had been village land?), and *uparis* may have continued to cultivate land as the tenants of some individual instead of as the tenants of the village. But if the land they cultivated was clearly waste land, *uparis* ceased to be tenants of the village and became—like the *mirasdars* and *chali ryots* around them—tenants of the government. Or if the fields that they were cultivating at the commencement of the survey were those of extinct *mirasdar* families, no owner other than government would be recognizable.[89] The

[89] For suggestions of what may have happened, see the report of G.S.A. Anderson, Superintendent of the Ahmednagar Survey and Assessment, on the settlement of Ahmednagar, Shevgaon, and Newasa *talukas*: SRGB N.S. No. 123 (1871), p. 270. Anderson presents an example of a village book in which three kinds of tenure are distinguished—*miras, inam,* and *gatkuli*. The third type is defined as the lands of extinct families, in Fukazawa, "Lands and Peasants," p. 13; and in Wilson, *Glossary,* p. 169, as "Property, lands, houses and c., the proprietors of which are extinct; unclaimed inheritance; lands of village uncultivated, or without owners, considered in some respects as village property, so that they may be disposed of, sold or leased by the community. . . ." In Anderson's example, *miras* and *inam* lands are listed as owned by the *mirasdars* and *inamdars*. *Gatkul* land is listed as owned by the government.

uparis (or other cultivators of that field) would henceforth have occupancy rights. They would cease to be classed as tenants and would become holders (owners) of those fields so long as the government land revenue was paid. This would have increased the legal security with which the *upari* held the land, although its impact in the setting of a face-to-face village community might not have been great. If the classificatory process described above was common (and only research into the detailed papers of the first settlement can determine that), *uparis* should have moved from the category of tenants of the village to that of holders of government land.

To the extent that *uparis* practiced cultivation as a complement to some other profession, such as cattle raising, several factors may have been at work during the first 30-year settlement to encourage them to become permanent cultivators. As suggested above, access to land on a permanent basis may have become easier. But in addition, the increases in cultivation over the period reduced the volume of lands to be taken up on an occasional basis and the amount of lands on which animals could be freely pastured. The result would have been to make the former occupational patterns of the *uparis* increasingly difficult to maintain. At the same time, decreased rates of land tax, rising prices, and increased trade would have made settled agriculture more attractive. The likely response would have been a shift from occasional cultivation and herding to permanent cultivation.

Finally, to the extent that *uparis* were displaced cultivators, the causes of displacement diminished with the coming of British rule and further declined with the introduction of the Bombay Survey and Settlement. Law and order were restored in the region quite quickly after 1818. High and irregular rates of revenue continued for two to three decades and may have driven some *ryots* to seek other villages in which to cultivate, where the vagaries of the revenue system made rates lower. But *ad hoc* downward revisions of the rates of assessment and the introduction of the Bombay Survey and Settlement would have lured these displaced cultivators back to their own villages. Again, some percent of *uparis* would have become holders.

The Balutedars and Other Artisans

The traditional historiography of the agrarian systems of India has stressed that artisans generally suffered from competition by foreign-produced wares that replaced their more traditional goods.[90] This analysis has tended to assume that the total demand for all such products was constant and that the demonstration of some amount of imports meant a corresponding fall in the demand for traditional, village-produced goods. The preceding pages should have convinced the reader that the agrarian system, at least in the Karnatak and the Deccan, did not have a constant output, or a constant surplus, or a constant demand for goods, but rather that all three variables were rising. As an example, the tiles on all of the houses with tiled roofs built between the beginning and end of the first settlement period had to be produced locally. Either they were produced by local artisans like the potter, or their production demanded the appearance of a rural, nonagricultural activity, i.e., the making of roof tiles.

The prosperity of the *balutedars* must have increased along with that of the village in which they resided so long as the old forms of relationships were maintained. Gooddine, in a rare study of their remuneration in the first half of the nineteenth century, states that the *balutedars* received as their major payment "a tithe of everything grown." Gooddine's report details the shares of grain and other crops and the size of the payment to each of the artisans.[91] What this means is that with every increase in the cultivated area of the village, as long as shares remained fixed, the amount of grain and other crops collected by the *balutedars* would have increased.

Increased cultivation in villages was accompanied by certain increases in the capital stock. Most notable were increases in the number of carts and wells and in the number of superior houses. All of these added to the demand for artisans' labor. The carpenter and the blacksmith both had a share in the construction of new carts. The construction of wells would have generated an increase in the demand for the services of carpenters, blacksmiths, and leatherworkers, as well as the general demand for labor for the digging and lining of the well. The services of the carpenter and blacksmith would be needed for the construction of devices to lift water, while the leatherworkers' services were required to fit these devices with buckets or *mots*. Finally, the need for door and window frames meant that new houses also added to the demand for the carpenter's services, as well as to the general demand for construction labor.

The point to be stressed is this: Increases in the income of cul-

[90] Morris, "Economic Change," pp. 185-195.
[91] SRGB No. 4 (1852), pp. 18-25.

tivators and increases in their numbers increased the demand for a wide range of artisan-produced goods. The process of capital formation also generated increased needs for labor. *Balutedars* shared in the growing prosperity of the villages they served. Other artisans also shared in that prosperity wherever they produced a good for which demand was increasing. The gains from agricultural prosperity during this 30-year period were not confined to a narrow group of people.

5. *Economic Change in Western India, 1860-1920*

Chapter 4 focussed rather narrowly on a small number of changes in the rural sector of the economy, primarily those concerned with land revenue and land tenure. So narrow a focus precluded most discussion of the changing economic environment in which the agriculturists of Bombay Presidency made decisions about what to produce and how much to produce. It is the purpose of this chapter to examine cultivation patterns in the Presidency, especially as they may have been affected by increased trade; to examine the changing patterns of trade in foodgrains and pulses; and finally, to examine the nonagricultural portions of the economy to see how they may have changed the options available to agriculturists.

I. The Agricultural Sector

The literature on Indian agriculture has tended to stress increasing "commercialization" in the second half of the nineteenth century, resulting, the argument runs, in declining food supplies as less land was planted with foodgrains and increasing amounts of wheat were exported. As a result of these changes in cultivation and trade patterns, food supplies and carryover stocks were reduced to dangerously low levels and famine ensued. The end of the nineteenth century witnessed more famines, closer together in time and more widespread in space, than any other period for which equally full records are available.

The evidence which has been presented to support this line of reasoning leaves much to be desired. In general, the occurrence of famines has been used to argue that the amounts of foodgrains farmers were planting must have been decreasing and that commercialization must have been the cause. Statistics on famines, not on crops planted, have been used as the main evidence for the argument. For instance, in his study of famines between 1860 and 1965, B. M. Bhatia has not included *any* statistics on cultivation patterns. He occasionally refers to changes in cultivation patterns, but using only secondary sources.[1]

When we do turn to an examination of the crop statistics, we find that they will not support the view that farmers in western India were planting fewer acres of foodgrains before 1900 or, generally, even that they were planting a smaller percentage of their lands with jowar and bajra, the chief foodgrains eaten by all but the wealthy in western India. Figure 5.1 gives the percentages of land planted with jowar, bajra, wheat, other foodgrains and pulses, cotton, and other crops for the total of the three famine-prone divisions of Bombay Presidency. Using this figure we can trace some of the major events in the Presidency between 1860 and 1920.[2]

The first period of interest is the quinquennium 1861-1865. This period has long been acknowledged as a boom time for the Presidency, as the American Civil War shut England off from supplies of American cotton and created a major speculative boom in cotton in India. There was indeed an increase in the percentage of land planted with cotton. In absolute terms—terms which must be treated with caution given the underlying statistics—cotton cultivation in-

[1] For two expositions of the deterioration of food supplies in South Asia during the latter part of the nineteenth century, see Bhatia, *Famines in India*, and Elizabeth Whitcombe, *Agrarian Conditions in Northern India, vol. 1: The United Provinces under British Rule, 1860-1900* (Berkeley and Los Angeles: University of California Press, 1972). For an early partial refutation of these theses for the period of the American Civil War, see Peter Harnetty, "Cotton Exports and Indian Agriculture, 1861-1870," *Economic History Review* (series 2) 24 (August 1971):414-429. For work on the entire period, see McAlpin, "Railroads, Cultivation Patterns, and Foodgrain Availability."

[2] While Appendix D discusses the flaws in these data in considerable detail, two cautions seem needed here. First, the data increase in both reliability and coverage over time. Before 1870, the data were collected for the information of the government but not published. The methods of collection and reporting were not standardized across districts. The biggest problem that lack of standardization creates is in categories like "other foodgrains" and "other pulses," both of which are needed to determine total foodgrains and pulses. If they were lumped with "other crops," the percentage of land planted with "total foodgrains and pulses" is understated. Second, until the mid-1880s, crops grown on *inamdari* land were not reported. After that, to the extent possible, they were. Data before the mid-1880s thus suffer from two defects that affect total cultivated area—a gradual increase in areas reporting on crops and the non-inclusion of *inamdari* lands. An attempt has been made to correct the latter flaw by increasing all figures before the mid-1880s by a proportion determined individually for each district. These two flaws mean that the crop data must be used with care, but they need not detract seriously from estimates of the percentages of land planted with different crops.

FIGURE 5.1 Percentage of Land Planted with Various Crops, Bombay Presidency, 1855-1920

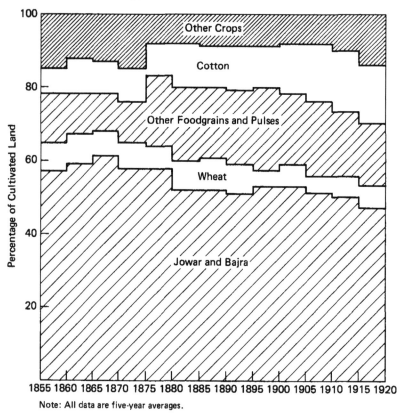

Note: All data are five-year averages.

SOURCE: Appendix D.

creased from 1,092 thousand acres to 1,993 thousand acres.[3] At the same time, the percentage of land planted with jowar and bajra rose—in absolute terms by 2,020 thousand acres. Both of these absolute figures are probably overstated given the increases in coverage of agricultural statistics that were occurring. The absolute and percentage figures, however, do indicate that cotton was not being grown at the expense of jowar and bajra. In the quinquennium 1876-1880 there was a fairly sharp rise in the percentage of land planted with all foodgrains and pulses. Given that there was widespread drought and famine in the first two years of this period,

---

[3] All specific acreage figures are calculated from data in Appendix D.

this increase probably reflects a diminution in the plantings of all other crops as farmers tried to survive and then to restore their depleted grain stocks.

During the remainder of the period until 1900, there was some decline in the proportion of land planted with jowar and bajra (from 58 percent to 53 percent). However, the proportion of land planted with all foodgrains and pulses remained at 80 percent in the final quinquennium of the century. If this is not a statistical artifact, it represents a nearly constant percentage of land devoted to food-grains and pulses over the entire period from 1856-1860 to 1895-1900. This stability does not appear to have come at the expense of foodgrains not grown for export markets (i.e., all the millets, rice, and pulses), since there was no significant rise in the percentage of lands planted with wheat. Cotton cultivation oscillated from period to period but was not much higher at any time than during the boom of the American Civil War.

In the first twenty years of the twentieth century there was a noticeable decline in both the proportion of land planted with jowar and bajra and that planted with all foodgrains and pulses. At the same time, the percentage of land planted with cotton began to increase to levels well above that of the period 1861-1865.

In addition to knowing how much land was planted and how that land was distributed among crops, it is desirable to have some es-timates of how the land/person ratio changed. Table 5.1 contains the figures on per capita plantings for each of the three divisions and for their total. The population of the census is compared against

TABLE 5.1. Gross Sown Acreage per Capita

Year	Gujarat	Deccan	Karnatak	All Three Divisions
1871-1880	1.00	2.24	2.02	1.89
1881-1890	1.17	2.48	2.65	2.16
1891-1900	1.08	2.13	2.20	1.88
1901-1910	1.13	2.16	2.28	1.96
1911-1920	1.25 (1.20)[a]	2.15	2.36	1.99

[a]During this decade, there was a change in the classification of grasslands in Gujarat that resulted in an increase in gross sown area. The figure in parentheses shows what the gross sown acreage per capita would have been in the absence of the reclassification.

SOURCE: Calculated from Appendix B, Table B-1, and Appendix D.

the average acreage for the following ten years, e.g., the 1881 population against average cultivation in 1881-1885 and 1886-1890.

The decade 1881-1890 was a high point in cultivated acreage per capita, although in Gujarat the final period exceeded this one. In the Deccan, cultivation per person declined after 1881-1890. Comparing these figures for the Deccan with the figures on gross sown acreage in Appendix D, Table D-2, it becomes clear that this decline was due to a virtual cessation in the expansion of cultivation while population growth continued. In the Karnatak the real growth of acreage came closer than in the Deccan to keeping pace with population change between 1881-1890 and 1911-1920. The low figures in all three divisions for the decade 1891-1900 were due to the decline in planting that was caused by the several years of drought near the end of the century, although population also declined in that decade.

Reductions in the gross sown acreage per person are scarcely cause for alarm in and of themselves. There is evidence that early in the period (1860s and 1870s), labor was a major bottleneck in the growing of cotton, a crop that is much more labor-intensive than the grain crops with which it was competing for acreage.[4] In addition, there was some growth in productivity through increases in irrigated areas (particularly in Poona), through the use of improved varieties of seed, and probably through the increase in labor per acre of land. Data in Chapter 4 also indicate growth in the capital stock used in agriculture, such as wells, cattle, and carts, which should also have helped to increase productivity. And last but not least, prices for agricultural goods were generally rising (for reasons discussed below), thereby reducing the portion of the crop that had to be sold to pay the land taxes. In other words, while we lack hard evidence, there are some reasons to think that productivity increases (particularly from more intensive farming) could have kept physical output per capita constant even while sown acreage per capita was declining. In addition, falling real tax rates left a larger share of total output inside the agricultural sectors.

Prices and Markets

In India before the second half of the nineteenth century, land transport for bulk commodities was both very expensive and very limited. As a result, those parts of South Asia without access to

---

[4] For a discussion of labor scarcity for harvesting cotton, see McAlpin, "Effects of Markets," pp. 294-298.

water transport were divided into many small markets for foodgrains and other bulky commodities. Only goods that were high in value and low in bulk—spices, fine cloth, dyes, salt, and metal—moved in widespread interregional trade. For agriculturists, the smallness of markets imposed two constraints on prosperity. First, they were compelled to self-insure against crop failures by storing grain (see Chapter 2 for more detail). Second, they had very limited outlets for their surplus produce. Over the course of the second half of the nineteenth century, both of these constraints were removed, with the second disappearing gradually and earlier than the first.

Railroads were first constructed in Bombay Presidency in the 1850s. The three main lines were the Bombay, Baroda, and Central India line north out of Bombay City towards Gujarat, and the two branches of the Great India Peninsular that left Bombay City and went northeast towards the Gangetic Plain at Allahabad and southeast towards Madras. These lines were largely completed by the 1870s. During the late 1870s and the 1880s, the gaps left in these lines were filled. The Dhond-Manmad cutoff was constructed to permit traffic from North India to go to South India without going all the way to Bombay City. The Southern Maratha Railway, built on the recommendation of the Famine Commission of 1880, served the southern districts of Bombay Presidency. As lines spread into the interior of India they first provided farmers with an outlet for surplus produce. Farmers had already needed to sell some crops in order to raise cash to meet the land tax. Railroads provided access to an alternate market in which such sales could be made. While there are not enough data to allow careful study of how prices paid to farmers changed, it is reasonable to expect that as transport costs fell, the prices paid to farmers rose.[5]

In addition, larger amounts of various products could be marketed at constant prices than when demand was confined to the small, local market. As interactions with nonlocal markets developed, some

[5] We expect this primarily because we assume that falling transport costs will permit more arbitrage between spatially separate markets. If, for instance, the price of wheat for export from the Port of Bombay is Rs. 3 per maund, and the price in Nagpur is Rs.1, and transport cost from Bombay to Nagpur is Rs.2.5, Bombay Port prices will have no effect on Nagpur prices unless the latter fall below Rs.0.5 or the port price rises above Rs.3.5. But if transport costs fall to Rs.1 per maund, more Nagpur wheat will be demanded and the price of wheat in Nagpur will rise. Depending upon the relative strength of demand and the extent of Nagpur supplies, the port price of wheat may fall somewhat. The reduction in transport costs will be shared among (1) farmers who sell wheat, (2) traders in wheat, and (3) consumers of exported wheat.

farmers began to grow certain crops specifically for the export market. By choosing crops with high market prices, they could minimize the real burden of land taxes, all other things being equal, and increase their net incomes. For example, after the construction of the Southern Maratha Railway, farmers in Kod *taluka* in Dharwar district began to grow large amounts of chilis for export to Bombay City.[6] Kod was reasonably well endowed with land that could grow this crop, but before the construction of the railway its farmers had lacked a market that could absorb (at prices above costs) all of the chilis they could grow.

Before 1900, farmers did not reduce the proportion of land planted with foodgrains and pulses. Instead, land that was not planted with foodgrains and pulses was shifted among other crops as the market prices of those other crops changed. While it is impossible to tell if farmers stopped storing grain to insure themselves against bad seasons, there is no doubt that they were still growing as large a proportion of grain and pulses as in any period for which there are good records. Railroads, however, freed them from one of the constraints on real income: By 1900 they no longer lacked wide markets for their surplus produce.

In the twenty years after 1900, the second constraint also appears to have been removed. Table 5.2 shows the price of jowar in 12 *talukas* of the Presidency from 1856-1860 through 1911-1915. In the context of changes in agriculture in Bombay Presidency, the sharp convergence of prices after 1890—measured by the decline in the coefficient of variation—supports the argument that farmers could increasingly rely on the market to provide them with grain when their own harvests failed. As farmers were able to give up growing and storing grain for self-insurance against crop failures, they reaped an increase in real income as the land from this use could subsequently be used to grow crops for sale. It is to this phenomenon that the post-1900 increases in the amount of land planted with cotton in the three famine-prone divisions of Bombay Presidency, as well as declines in the proportion of land planted with foodgrains and pulses, can best be attributed. This change in the degree to which farmers shifted land among crops in response to price changes was possible only because the rail network had become sufficiently dense and sufficiently cheap to encourage farmers to accumulate and store assets other than grain with confidence

[6] SRGB N.S. No. 515 (1912), p. 8.

TABLE 5.2. Average, Coefficient of Variation, and Index of Jowar Prices
in Twelve *Talukas* of Bombay Presidency, 1856-1860 to 1911-1915

Quinquennium	Quinquennial Average Price[a]	Coefficient of Variation	Index of Average Price[b]
1856-1860	.94	.27	66
1861-1865	1.57	.21	110
1866-1870	1.57	.19	110
1871-1875	1.56	18	109
1876-1880	2.27	.16	159
1881-1885	1.43	.19	100
1886-1890	1.82	.18	127
1891-1895	1.86	.13	130
1896-1900	2.23	.13	156
1901-1905	2.21	10	155
1906-1910	2.67	.08	187
1911-1915	2.99	.10	209

[a]Rupees per maund.
[b]1881-1885 = 100.
SOURCE: Calculated from data in Appendix C.

that these assets could be turned back into grain at predictable prices
if local or even regional crop failures created a need to do so.[7]

Consistent series on railborne trade in grain would also be helpful
in confirming that interregional grain shipments did play this role.
Unfortunately, the blocks from which data on exports and imports
of grain were gathered changed in 1900. Nonetheless, the available
data on the grain trade of Bombay Presidency before and after 1900
have been assembled in Table 5.3. The first three columns show
the trade of Bombay Port with the rest of the Presidency, the rest
of India, and the total of the two. During the ten years of bad harvests
with which the twentieth century began, imports to the port from
the Presidency did not just decrease—they became negative, as
grain from other parts of India was sent into the Presidency along
the rail lines out of Bombay City. The fifteen years from 1896 through
1910 show a marked drop in grain movements from the interior to
the port as a response to bad harvests in various parts of the interior.

For the rest of the Presidency, the registration blocks of "Gujarat
and Kathiawar" and "South of the Narbudda and below the Ghats"

[7] For a discussion of the difference in patterns of price responsiveness before and
after 1900, see McAlpin, "Railroads, Prices, and Peasant Rationality," pp. 666-669.

TABLE 5.3. Railborne Foodgrain Trade of Bombay Presidency, 1886-1920 (5-year averages in thousands of maunds)[a]

Quinquennium	Bombay Port with the:			Parts of Bombay Presidency with All Other Areas				
	Presidency	Rest of India	Total	Gujarat and Kathiawar	South of the Narbudda and below the Ghats	Khandesh, Nasik, and Ahmednagar	Poona and Sholapur	Southern Maratha Railway
1886-1890	+3,395	+13,469	+16,863	+581	+517	-1,540	-220	-1,279
1891-1895	+2,908	+12,637	+15,545	+581	+219	-2,194	-27	-259
1896-1900	+960	+5,310	+6,270	+879	+575	-75	+911	+85

Quinquennium	Presidency	Rest of India	Total	Gujarat and Kathiawar	Konkan	Khandesh and Nasik	Ahmednagar, Sholapur, Bijapur	Poona and Satara	Belgaum and Dharwar
1901-1905	-2,669	+6,246	+3,577	+5,124	-85	+1,005	+296	+1,969	+939
1906-1910	-257	+5,093	+4,836	+2,829	-262	+633	-1,372	+1,153	+1,020
1911-1915	71	+11,947	+12,017	+5,698	-305	+1,194	-609	+1,584	+878
1916-1920	-2,873	+14,409	+11,536	+8,670	+28	+1,824	-939	+1,645	+1,624

[a] + = net imports; - = net exports.

SOURCE: Calculated from Quarterly Returns of the Railborne Trade of Bombay Presidency.

effectively included the Gujarat and the Konkan, with Surat district included in "South of the Narbudda and below the Ghats." Both of these regions were consistent importers of foodgrains. This was not a recent phenomenon; Gujarat had been importing some grain for several centuries.[8] The other three regions (essentially the Deccan and the Karnatak) were exporters of foodgrains until the bad harvests of the last quinquennium of the nineteenth century, when they became importers.

After 1900, the five reporting blocks were regrouped into six that accord quite well with the natural regions of the Presidency. Surat was moved into the "Gujarat and Kathiawar" block. As a result, the remainder of the old "South of the Narbudda and below the Ghats" block became the new "Konkan" block. Imports of foodgrains into Gujarat increased enormously over the pre-1900 period (only a relatively small part of this increase was due to the inclusion of Surat), and the Konkan shows up as a small net exporter of foodgrains in most periods. This rice-growing region was probably shipping some rice into the Bombay urban market. For the remainder of the Presidency, only the "East Deccan" block, comprised of Ahmednagar, Sholapur, and Bijapur, remained a net exporter of foodgrains. The three blocks comprising the rest of the Deccan and the Karnatak (Khandesh and Nasik, Poona and Satara, and Belgaum and Dharwar) all become consistent net importers of food.

While the peak years of imports are clearly due to poor harvests, the background level of imports must also be explained. Since imports have to be paid for, those regions importing foodgrains must have been exporting some other products. These products could have been some of those produced in the urban sector. For instance, Gujarat exported cloth manufactured at the cotton mills in Ahmedabad City and imported food to feed the workers in those mills. The city of Poona exported some amount of government services to the rest of the Presidency, imported food, and paid for it with part of the tax revenues. Alternatively, other agricultural products could have been exported by the agricultural sector in exchange for imports of foodgrains. As an example, Khandesh exported cotton and could have used the proceeds to pay for imported grain. Since aggregate data are insufficient to tell who consumed imported grain, we must depend on the logical probabilities.

For farmers who consume foods that they grow, and consume it

---

[8] Michael N. Pearson, *Merchants and Rulers in Gujarat* (Berkeley and Los Angeles: University of California Press, 1976), p. 13.

in relatively unprocessed form, growing their own food is generally the lowest-cost way of getting fed. They avoid transport and transaction costs on the food they consume as well as the risk that for some reason food prices may suddenly rise. Their chief cost is the opportunity cost of growing some other crop on their land and selling it. When farmers are very far from markets, the transport and transaction costs are high and the opportunity cost is low, and so they grow their own food. As markets are made accessible to them by falling transport costs, the opportunity cost of growing their own food rises if their land is suited for growing crops with higher values. For instance, land that can grow jowra and bajra can also frequently grow cotton. Further, as markets widen, the profitability of producing goods for the limited local market (e.g., grain for the district headquarters town) may decline relative to the profitability of producing other goods for a more distant market (e.g., cotton for the textile mills in Bombay and Ahmedabad). While a very large comparative advantage in growing nonfood crops may be necessary to persuade farmers to give up growing their own food, a much smaller change in relative prices may result in a switch from production of a crop for the local market to production for a more distant market. As a transitional step, farmers may have grown grain for storage in the late nineteenth century, but sold part of it when harvests were good. After 1900, farmers in regions of Bombay Presidency who could grow crops other than grain, finding themselves freed from the need to store grain as insurance against famines, chose to allocate more land to crops other than grain that could be sold in distant markets. Cotton was clearly one of those crops; oilseeds may have been another. This left the urban populations in areas suitable for crops other than foodgrains without the supplies of the countryside and forced them to import foodgrains.

Table 5.4 gives the number of people who could be fed for a year on the imports of grain into the various regions of the Presidency, the percentage of the population that could be fed, and the percentage of population that was urban.[9] The estimates of how many could be fed are probably upper-bound ones, because lower-bound estimates of foodgrain consumption (1 pound per day, or 4.5 maunds per year, per person) have been used to determine the number. When we compare the urban portion of the population at the 1901,

---

[9] Urban areas were generally defined by the census as those "towns" with over 5,000 population and with some urban characteristics that distinguished them from mere large villages. *Census of India*, 1891, vol. 8, pt. 1, p. 12; 1921, vol. 8, pt. 2, p. 1.

TABLE 5.4. Grain Imports in Relation to Urban Population,
1901-1905 to 1916-1920 and 1921

Years	Gujarat and Kathiawar	Khandesh and Nasik	Poona and Satara	Belgaum and Dharwar
A. Number of people that could be fed by grain imports				
1901-1905	1,139,000	223,000	438,000	209,000
1906-1910	629,000	141,000	256,000	227,000
1911-1915	1,288,000	265,000	352,000	195,000
1916-1920	1,928,000	405,000	366,000	361,000
B. Percent of population that could be fed by grain imports				
1901-1905	42	10	20	10
1906-1910	23	6	12	11
1911-1915	46	11	16	10
1916-1920	69	16	17	18
C. Percent of population in urban areas				
1901	26	17	15	15
1911	26	16	15	15
1921	26	18	18	17

SOURCES· A – Calculated from Table 5.3, on the assumption that foodgrain consumption
was one pound per day (4.5 maunds per year) per person.

B – Calculated from A and Appendix B, Table B-1.

C – *Census of India,* 1901, vol. 9A, p. 3, 1911, vol. 7, pt. 2, p. 2; 1921, vol. 8,
pt. 2, p. 2.

1911, and 1921 census dates with the portion of the population that
could be fed by imported grain, we can see that in Khandesh and
Nasik and in Belgaum and Dharwar railborne imports were *less*
than would have been needed just to feed urban populations. For
Poona and Satara, with between 15 and 18 percent of population
in urban areas and imports to feed 12 to 20 percent of the population,
it appears that imports supplied most of the urban demand.

Only for the Gujarat and Kathiawar block does it appear that
imports of grain greatly exceeded the amount needed to feed the
urban population. This block, however, is more difficult to interpret
than the others because princely state territory formed a larger share
in it than in the others. Since some grain imported into this region
certainly was shipped to these princely states, the figures are biased
upward when we use them to indicate the number of people in
British Gujarat who could be fed. Further, the first twenty years of
the twentieth century saw an unusually high number of years of
bad rainfall in the Gujarat districts. The resultant crop failures (see

Appendix A, Tables A-1 to A-3, for rainfall, condition factors, and the Index of Quality of the Agricultural Season) were met with massive imports of grain. The years with the largest net imports were 1900-1901, 1911-1912, and 1918-1919—all years of crop failure and declaration of famine.[10] If we eliminate just those three years from our calculations, the proportion of the population that could be fed by grain imports falls to 29 percent in 1901-1905, to 26 percent in 1911-1915, and to 60 percent in 1916-1920. While we could continue this exercise, it seems sufficient to say that agriculturists in Gujarat were certainly not growing much grain for the urban areas of the division and that they had in general reduced their grain output to such a level that some imports to the rural sector were necessary every year and that any reduction of "normal" yields would result in large imports.[11]

The data on grain trade, besides suggesting that most of the imports in normal years were used to feed urban populations, also indicate that probably by the end of the nineteenth century and certainly by the beginning of the twentieth century, the movement of grain into regions with harvest shortfalls was a routine process. By the twentieth century, farmers in western India had been freed of the two constraints on prosperity imposed by spatial isolation: They had good markets for their products and they could expect to exchange assets such as money for grain at predictable prices in years when their own crops were short.

The improvements in the environment in which the agriculturists of western India operated went beyond mere removal of constraints, however. The reduction in transport costs that permitted the increase in the size of markets also tied western India into the world markets. One effect of this was the persistent rise of all agricultural prices from 1881-1885 through the 1920s. The causes of the rise in prices were the fall in the value of silver (to which the rupee was tied) and increasing integration into world markets.[12] Since farmers had fixed obligations to the government for the payment of land

[10] Bombay Presidency, *Quarterly Returns of Railborne Trade of Bombay Presidency.*

[11] Statistics for station-by-station rail trade in Bombay Presidency are available for 1884-1885 through 1921-1922. Analysis of these data is an enormous task which, for obvious reasons, has not been undertaken as part of this study. It could be done, however, and used to confront the hypotheses advanced here.

[12] For a more extended discussion, see Michelle Burge McAlpin, "Price Movements and Fluctuations in Economic Activity, 1860-1947," in *The Cambridge Economic History of India*, vol. 2, ed. Dharma Kumar (Cambridge: Cambridge University Press, 1982).

revenue, rising prices benefited them by reducing the real value of their taxes. Between 1881-1885 and 1911-1915, the average price of jowar in the twelve *talukas* of the Deccan and Karnatak examined in Chapter 4 rose by more than 100 percent. In the first revision settlements of these *talukas*, done in the late 1870s and the 1880s, revenue collections per acre increased by an average of 26 percent. This increase in nominal collections was, however, eroded by the continual rise in prices. To the extent that farmers were in debt (as farmers often are), inflation further increased their well-being by reducing the value of the rupees in which they repaid their creditors. Rising prices for agricultural goods benefited all those with surplus produce to sell. Producers of other goods and services may or may not have shared in the prosperity of the agricultural classes, depending on the prices of and demand for those other goods and services. In Chapter 4, arguments were advanced that all groups in the rural community probably benefited from the expansion of agriculture.

To some extent, increased prosperity in the agricultural sector may have increased the demand for agricultural laborers and, if the supply of laborers was constant or falling, their wages. Expanded cultivation of crops like cotton that had high labor inputs relative to the grain crops they replaced would have led to some increase, as would expansions in total cultivation in periods when they occurred.[13] A third source of increased demand could have been the withdrawal of some agriculturists from the labor force to manage their lands and live off of the increasing share of output left to them by declining real taxes. The extent to which this occurred is impossible to tell from aggregate data, but some answers might be procured through village-level studies.

Summary of Changes in the Agricultural Sector

In the agricultural sector of Bombay Presidency between 1860 and 1920, prosperity was generally increasing with some setbacks caused by bad monsoons and attendant bad harvests. The sources of increased incomes for the agricultural sector were: better markets for surplus produce brought about by falling transport costs as railroads were built; rising prices for exported products; reductions in the amount of land used to grow grain for insurance against crop failures; and shifts among crops to those with higher values and

[13] Michelle Burge McAlpin, "The Impact of Railroads on Agriculture in India, 1860-1900: A Case Study of Cotton Cultivation" (Ph.D. dissertation, University of Wisconsin-Madison, 1973), pp. 125-127.

higher profits. Given a relatively equal distribution of land in most parts of the Presidency and relatively little tenancy in the period 1876-1889 (as shown in Table 4.3 of Chapter 4), these gains in prosperity were probably widely distributed through the agricultural community. Increasing cultivation of labor-intensive crops, among other factors, probably increased the demand for agricultural laborers, insuring that they also shared in the gains of the sector.

II. The Urban and Industrial Sectors

This is a book about the agricultural sector, so any excursion into the urban and industrial sectors must necessarily be brief. The purpose of such an excursion is merely to ascertain to what extent changes in these sectors may have worked to reinforce or negate changes in the agricultural sector, particularly by providing employment on a full-time or seasonal basis for some labor from that sector.

The Bombay Presidency was more urban and more industrial from the 1860s on than most of the other parts of India. In 1881 the Presidency was already 14 percent urban, excluding Bombay City, and 19 percent urban including it. By 1921 these percentages had risen to 18 and 24, respectively. Bombay City was the largest or second largest city in South Asia from 1891 on. While its absolute rate of growth was high (see the figures in Table 5.5), the city of Ahmedabad grew much faster, being the fourteenth largest city in

TABLE 5.5. Population of Bombay City and Environs, 1872-1931

Year	Bombay City	Index[a]	Bombay Suburban District	Index[a]	Total	Index[a]
1872	644,000		b			
1881	773,000	100	85,000	100	858,000	100
1891	822,000	106	96,000	113	918,000	107
1901	776,000	100	95,000	112	871,000	102
1911	979,000	127	103,000	121	1,082,000	126
1921	1,176,000	152	155,000	182	1,331,000	155
1931	1,161,000	150	180,000	212	1,341,000	156

[a]1881 = 100.
[b]Not yet created in 1872.
SOURCE: Appendix B, Table B-1, and Census of India, 1931, vol. 8, pt. 2, Imperial Table II.

India in 1891 and the sixth largest in 1921. By 1921, the Presidency had three of the fifteen largest cities in India, Poona having grown to be fourteenth largest.[14]

One of the sources of growth for the region was the cotton textile-mill industry in Bombay City and Ahmedabad. Table 5.6 gives figures on employment in these mills in Bombay City and the rest of the Presidency. From 7,000 employees in 1865, employment in the mills of Bombay City had grown to 127,000 by 1916-1920 and to 204,000 in the Presidency as a whole.

While the cotton textile mills were certainly a force in the growth of these cities, they were not the only force. Both cities served as entrepôts for trade in all manner of goods. Bombay was a major terminus for both shipping and railways, while Ahmedabad served as a collection and dispersal point for many goods flowing out of

TABLE 5.6. Average Number of Mill Hands Employed Daily in Bombay Cotton Textile Mills, 1865-1920

Years	Bombay City	Year	All Bombay Presidency[a]
1865	7,000		
1866-1870	8,000		
1871-1875	11,000		
1876-1880	24,000	1879	35,000
1881-1885	35,000	1884	45,000
1886-1890	49,000	1889	66,000
1891-1895	68,000	1894	89,000
1896-1900	74,000	1899	110,000
1901-1905	88,000	1904	128,000
1906-1910	102,000	1919	162,000
1911-1915	109,000	1914	178,000
1916-1920	127,000	1919	204,000

[a]There were no textile mills outside of Bombay City until the late 1870s.

SOURCES: Bombay City – Calculated from Morris, *Emergence of Industrial Labor*, pp. 213-14.
Bombay Presidency – Calculated from Morris, "Development of Modern Industry."

[14] Only the United Provinces had more cities among the fifteen largest—Lucknow, Benares, Kanpur, Allahabad, and Agra. These cities did not, however, manifest the dynamic growth of Ahmedabad. All of them fell in rank over the period of 1891 to 1921—Lucknow from fifth to eighth, Benares from sixth to eleventh, Kanpur from seventh to ninth (and that was an improvement, for in 1911 it had dropped to twelfth), Allahabad from tenth out of the top fifteen altogether, and Agra from eleventh to thirteenth. Davis, *Population*, p. 131.

and into the regions northwards. In addition, some portion of the factory employment for most kinds of manufactures, with the exceptions of jute and iron and steel, was generated in this region with its rapidly growing urban markets. If a conservative estimate is used that 40 percent of all nontextile factory employment in 1913-1914 was in Bombay Presidency, the total number of factory jobs in the region was 420,000 (made up of 204,000 in cotton textiles and 216,000 in all other industries). There was one factory job for every ten or eleven males between the ages of 15 and 60.[15] Given that factory employment has been estimated to be less than two percent of the total Indian labor force as late as Independence (1947), these figures suggest that Bombay Presidency was unusually well-endowed with such employment by the decade 1911-1921. Of course, some of those jobs were filled by in-migrants from regions outside the Presidency. In his study of the cotton textile mill labor force in Bombay City, Morris found that in 1911 the six districts of the Presidency that supplied the most workers supplied 73 percent of the work force, a figure that had declined by 1921 to 58 percent.[16]

All of the evidence on the growth of the urban and industrial sectors suggests that trends there would have reinforced those in agriculture rather than running counter to them. These sectors were providing agriculturists in need of seasonal or longer employment outside agriculture with increasing opportunities and were simultaneously increasing the demand for agricultural products.[17]

[15] The all-India average daily factory employment in 1913-1914, exclusive of textiles, was 539,000. Morris David Morris, "Development of Modern Industry to 1947," in *The Cambridge Economic History of India*, vol. 2, ed. Dharma Kumar (Cambridge: Cambridge University Press, 1982).

[16] Morris David Morris, *The Emergence of an Industrial Labor Force in India: A Study of the Bombay Cotton Mills, 1854-1947* (Berkeley and Los Angeles: University of California Press, 1965), p. 63.

[17] The most likely objection to this conclusion is that handicrafts were being destroyed at a greater rate than factory employment was expanding. This case has never been buttressed with convincing evidence. However, as late as the revision surveys done in the 1870s and 1880s in the Presidency, there was little evidence that handloom weavers, a group commonly advanced to be among the most affected, had in fact been annihilated by the competition of the mills in Bombay. SRGB N.S. No. 172 (1885), pp. 4-5; SRGB N.S. No. 472 (1908), p. 4; SRGB N.S. No. 553 (1917), p. 3; SRGB N.S. No. 560 (1919), p. 13. As was pointed out in Chapter 4, the assumption necessary to the proposition that handicrafts were eradicated by factory or imported production is that demand for these goods was constant. To the extent that agricultural incomes were rising in Bombay Presidency, the demand for cloth would also have been rising.

6. Changes in the Consequences of Instability: Famines and Famine Relief Under the Raj, 1860-1920

The crop failures and resultant famines that troubled South Asia during the end of the nineteenth century were unparalleled in the distress they created. In Bombay Presidency there were no famines with comparable records where mortality had been nearly so great. The famines became a focus for Romesh Chander Dutt's critique of British rule in India. And yet, as D. R. Gadgil said in his introduction to a reissue of Dutt's work, "Dutt wrote at the end of an era."[1] In terms of the study of famines, the period around the turn of the century certainly does mark a radical change. Before 1902 extensive crop failures meant marked rises in the death rate despite substantial relief efforts to provide people with food and with employment to gain money to buy food. After that time, *even with declining percentages of land planted with foodgrains and pulses in this region*, mortality in periods of declared famines was much lower. This raises the most interesting of questions: How is it that in some periods a crop failure produced widespread death and disruption of the agricultural system and in others a crop failure produced little or no elevation of mortality and minimal disruption of the ongoing agricultural processes?

In seeking to answer this question, this chapter first uses the Index of Quality of the Agricultural Season to explore the relative magnitude of crop failures between 1886-1887 and 1919-1920, and compares these with declarations of famine and elevations of mortality. The remainder of the chapter assesses the changes that combined to alter the consequences of instability.

[1] D. R. Gadgil, "Critical Introduction" to Romesh Dutt, *The Economic History of India*, 2 vols. (Delhi: Publications Division, Ministry of Information and Broadcasting, Government of India, 1960), 1:vii-xxiii.

I. Crop Failures, Declarations of Famine, and Mortality

The decline in mortality in periods of declared famines could have been the result of an actual decline in the severity of crop failures, or it could have resulted from changes in administration policy that led to the declaration of famine in years of relatively slight crop failures. As the discussion in Chapter 2 made clear, the construction of a measure of the quality of the agricultural season that can be used to test these two possibilities is difficult. No meaningful estimates of tonnage of foodgrains produced each year seem possible. Instead, an index, the IQAS, has been constructed that incorporates the condition factors for major food crops and the amount of land planted with all foodgrains and pulses.[2] It is this index which will be used to assess both the actual severity of crop failures and the correspondence between severe crop failures and declarations of famine. The annual values of the index for selected districts are graphed in Figure 6.1.

For the period 1886-1887 through 1919-1920, all the years in which the IQAS is at least one standard deviation below the average for the entire period have been compiled in Table 6.1.[3] Because of the way the IQAS was constructed, the average for each district is 100. The variability of the rainfall and hence of the crops in the various districts is reflected in their different standard deviations. For instance, the standard deviation of the IQAS in Khandesh is 31 while in Poona it is 44. Thus, the years that are listed in Table 6.1 for Khandesh are years when the IQAS was 69 or below, while for Poona only years when the index was 56 or below are listed. This procedure has been used because the absolute values of the IQAS are not comparable across districts and because it takes account of both the average and the dispersion of the quality of the season.

The index indicates very few years more than one standard deviation below normal before 1899-1900. Those years that do appear are confined to 1891-1892 (Bijapur and Dharwar), when there was a more widespread crop failure. Beginning with 1899-1900 there are a number of years with IQAS values more than one standard deviation below the mean in every district. It is possible to argue that the frequent occurrence of such years after 1900 reflects the declining area planted with all foodgrains and pulses—and so it does

[2] See Chapter 2 for the details of construction of this index.

[3] Unfortunately, the index does not stretch back before 1886-1887 to enable us to measure the degree of crop failures that precipitated the famine of 1876-1878.

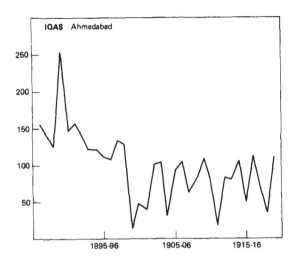

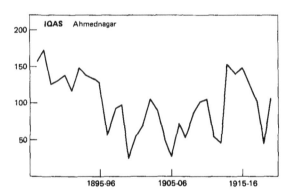

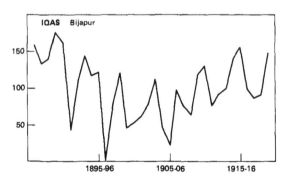

FIGURE 6.1 Annual IQAS in Selected Famine-Prone Districts of
Bombay Presidency, 1886-1887 to 1919-1920

SOURCE: Appendix A, Table A-3.

TABLE 6.1. Years between 1886-1887 and 1919-1920 When IQAS Was At Least One Standard Deviation below District Average for the Period

District	1891-1892	1896-1897	1899-1900	1900-1901	1901-1902	1904-1905	1905-1906	1907-1908	1908-1909	1911-1912	1912-1913	1913-1914	1915-1916	1918-1919
Ahmedabad			x	x	x	x				x			x	x
Kaira		x	x	x	x	x		x		x			x	x
Broach			x*		x	x				x				x
Surat			x*		x	x	x			x				x
Khandesh		x	x*		x			x		x				x
Nasik		x	x		x	x	x	x	x	x				x
Ahmednagar		x	x	x		x	x	x		x	x			x
Poona		x	x	x		x	x	x		x				x
Sholapur		x	x	x			x	x		x		x		x
Satara			x			x	x							x
Belgaum		x	x	x		x	x			x				x
Bijapur	x	x*	x	x		x	x							
Dharwar	x	x	x				x*		x	x*		x		x

*Indicates more than two standard deviations below average.

SOURCE: Appendix A, Table A-3, and Chapter 2, Table 2.3.

for some districts. But it is irrelevant that this is so, since the argument concerns the decline in famine *mortality* after 1900. If absolute production and availability of locally grown food were the key determinants of such mortality before 1900, anything—the weather, the pattern of plantings, or a plague of locusts—that reduced food supplies after 1900 should have exacerbated famine mortality, not diminished it.

It is also possible to argue that the low condition factors that combine with plantings to yield an IQAS more than one standard deviation below the mean reflect not low crop yields in this period, but a change in the reporting methods resulting in a downward bias after 1896-1897.[4] In Chapter 2 it was assumed that this change in reporting had no effect on the comparability of condition factors before and after it occurred. If that is true, then the declines in condition factors that occurred after 1896 were real. This conclusion is supported by an examination of the rainfall data for 1886 through 1920.

In Table 6.2, the first four columns give the average annual rainfall from 1886 to 1920 for thirteen districts in Gujarat, the Deccan, and the Karnatak, while the last three columns give the percentage difference in rainfall between 1886-1895 and the later periods of 1896-1905, 1906-1915, and 1915-1920. With the exception of the districts of Belgaum and Dharwar, average rainfall for the decade 1896-1905 was substantially (11.7 percent to 36.6 percent) below that for the previous decade. While rainfall increased somewhat during the decade 1906-1915, Bijapur still had rainfall more than 30 percent below that of 1886-1895, two other districts had rainfall more than 20 percent less, and four others more than 10 percent less. In the final quinquennium shown in the table, the overall rainfall again declined somewhat. For these thirteen districts taken together, average rainfall was 20.9 percent less in 1896-1905 than in 1886-1895, 12.5 percent less in 1906-1915, and 14.3 percent less in 1915-1920. Averages, of course, can conceal as much as they reveal. But an examination of the yearly data presented in Appendix A that underlie this table will show that while there are other years as wet as those between 1886 and 1895, there are no others as dry or as consistently dry as those between 1896 and 1920.

The data in Table 6.2 strongly support the view that declines in the reported condition factors indicate a real phenomenon and not just a change in the way the statistics were processed. The years

[4] Heston, "Official Yields."

TABLE 6.2. Average Annual Rainfall, 1886-1920, and Differences between 1886-1895 and Later Periods

Division and District	Average Annual Rainfall (inches)				Percent of Difference from 1886-1895		
	1886-1895	1896-1905	1906-1915	1916-1920	1896-1905	1906-1915	1915-1920
Gujarat							
Ahmedabad	32.6	24.6	29.6	27.3	−24.5	− 9.2	−16.3
Kaira	38.8	24.6	30.2	29.7	−36.6	−22.2	−23.5
Broach	40.2	35.5	37.3	37.2	−11.7	− 7.2	− 7.5
Surat	47.4	31.6	40.7	40.9	−33.3	−14.1	−13.7
Deccan							
Khandesh	32.7	25.8	27.7	27.3	−21.1	−15.3	−16.5
Nasik	30.2	25.4	30.5	26.3	−22.3	− 6.7	−19.6
Ahmednagar	26.6	19.3	22.9	25.2	−27.4	−13.9	− 5.3
Poona	34.1	26.9	27.6	26.3	−21.1	−19.1	−22.9
Sholapur	31.2	24.2	24.8	28.1	−22.4	−20.5	− 9.9
Satara	43.2	36.0	39.4	32.9	−16.7	− 8.8	−23.8
Karnatak							
Belgaum	51.8	49.1	54.4	44.6	− 5.2	+ 5.0	−13.9
Bijapur	27.4	19.1	19.1	22.8	−30.3	−30.3	−16.8
Dharwar	32.2	32.5	32.3	33.5	+ 0.9	+ 0.3	+ 4.0
Average percent of difference from 1886-1895					−20.9	−12.5	−14.3

SOURCE: Calculated from Appendix A, Table A-1.

of low rainfall and the years when the IQAS was more than one standard deviation below average (Table 6.1) coincide almost completely. The agrarian system definitely was not subject to less disruption after the turn of the century because of a reduction in crop failures due to improvements in the weather. Quite to the contrary, crop failures became less disruptive for the system in a period when the weather was worsening.[5]

The possibility remains that the administrative structure was creating "paper famines" by declaring famines in years when the extent of crop failure was minimal. To examine that possibility, Table 6.3 has been prepared, showing what percentage of the people in each district were declared to be affected by the famine of a given year whether or not that was a year in which the IQAS was more than one standard deviation below normal. This table shows that the years when a district was declared to have been at least partly affected by famine were also generally years when the IQAS for that district was at least one standard deviation below normal. Of 77 cases where the IQAS for a district is available and where famine was declared, in 64 percent (49 cases) the IQAS for that year was at least one standard deviation below average. The major exceptions to this pattern came in 1900-1901 and 1901-1902, when seven and five districts, respectively, were declared to be affected by famine even though their IQAS values were less than one standard deviation below the average. Presumably most of these districts were so declared because they had not yet recovered from the very severe crop failure of 1899-1900, when three districts had IQAS values more than *two* standard deviations below average.[6]

The other occurrences of famine declaration when the IQAS value does not show the district to have had severe crop failure were in

---

[5] Reid Bryson's work appears to support the conclusion that the decades after 1900 were periods of low rainfall. The years of scanty rainfall in interior western India are due to the same weather pattern that reduces rainfall in northwestern India (Sind, Punjab, and Rajasthan). Bryson has shown that the rainfall in this region was much more deficient between 1900 and 1930 than between 1930 and 1960. U.S. Congress, Senate, *U.S. and World Food Situation, Hearings before the Subcommittee on Agricultural Production, Marketing, and Stabilization of Prices and Subcommittee on Foreign Agricultural Policy of the Committee on Agriculture and Forestry*, 93rd Cong., 1st sess., 1973, p. 140.

[6] Among the effects of the crop failure in 1899-1900 was enough migration to force declaration of famine in Thana, a secure Konkan district, because only after such a declaration could help be provided for in-migrants seeking work and food. The declaration of famine in a small part of Dharwar district in 1900-1901 may have had a similar origin.

TABLE 6.3. Percentages of District Population Declared Affected in Famines, 1876-1877 to 1918-1919[a]

District	1876-1877[b]	1896-1897	1899-1900	1900-1901	1901-1902	1905-1906	1911-1912	1912-1913	1918-1919
Ahmedabad	—	—*	100	100	100	—*	93	—*	100
Panch Mahals[c]	—	—	100	100	100	—	100	—	100
Kaira	—	—*	100	100*	100	—*	84	—*	100
Broach	—	—*	100	15*	29	—*	49	—*	41
Surat	—	—*	75	38*	10	—	—	—*	—*
Khandesh	63	100	100	22*	22	—*	—	—*	12
Nasik	34	100	95	52*	—	16	17	—*	100
Ahmednagar	87	100	100	100	81*	39	100	79	100
Poona	35	46	78	84	17*	35	31	29*	100
Sholapur	100	100	100	100	52*	66	44	45*	21
Satara	43	95	89	95*	—*	33	—*	6*	72
Belgaum	53	35	35	36	16*	42	22	—*	30
Dharwar	64	—*	—	4*	—*	69	34	—*	—
Bijapur	100	100	51	64	62*	100	49*	60*	100
Total for these 14 districts	46	55	78	62	35	29	38	18	60

a Each figure is the percentage of population in the district that lived in *talukas* declared to be suffering from famine; a dash indicates that no famine was declared in any part of the district. When a figure or a dash is not followed by any symbol, it indicates that the IQAS was at least one standard deviation below average. When a figure or a dash is followed by *, it means that the IQAS was *not* at least one standard deviation below average.

b No IQAS figures are available before 1886-1887.

c No IQAS figures are available for Panch Mahals at any time.

SOURCES: 1876-1877 – *Report of the Indian Famine Commission of 1898*, Appendix, vol. 3, p. 200.

1896-1897 – *Narrative of the Famine in India in 1896-1897*, Appendix, p. 2 (affected area and population as of 31 May 1897).

1899-1900 – *Bombay Revenue Proceedings, Famine* (P/5987), No. 2727 of 1900, Monthly Report for May 1900 (p. 4146).

1900-1901, 1901-1902 – *Report on the Famine in Bombay Presidency*, 1899-1902, Appendix 1.

1905-1906 – *Report on the Famine in Bombay Presidency*, 1905-1906, p. 3.

1911-1912 – *Report on the Famine in Bombay Presidency*, 1911-1912, p. 2.

1912-1913 – *Report on the Famine in Bombay Presidency*, 1912-1913, p. 2.

1918-1919 – *Review of Famine Administration in Bombay Presidency*, 1918-1919, p. 3.

1912-1913. In those cases, the occurrence of crop shortages and famine declarations in some of the districts the previous year may have been responsible for creating a situation in which a shortage less than that required to produce an IQAS more than one standard deviation below the mean was still sufficient to cause a need for famine relief operations.[7] These data suggest that famines were not being declared by the administration without cause.

Further support for this view can be drawn from the number of occasions on which a district did have an IQAS at least one standard deviation below the mean and famine was *not* declared. The most conspicuous ocurrence was in 1904-1905, when ten districts had IQAS values more than one standard deviation below average (see Table 6.1) and no famine was declared. In 1907-1908, there were five such districts and in 1908-1909, two. In all three of these years no famine was declared anywhere in the Presidency and the years do not appear in Table 6.3. There are also six cases in Table 6.3 where, even though the IQAS was at least one standard deviation below average, no famine was declared in the district.

These data, showing as they do a less than perfect correspondence between years when districts were declared to be suffering from famine and years when the IQAS was at least one standard deviation less than the average, suggest that there may be considerable truth in the oft-repeated statement that a bad crop did not create famine unless it came close upon the heels of another bad crop. The problem (which appears insoluble at the present level of information and analysis) is to determine how bad a crop failure had to be to produce distress by itself and how close together successive bad seasons had to be to produce a situation of famine by their combined losses. What the data do show is that neither crop failures nor declarations of famine vanished after the beginning of the twentieth century.

Table 6.4 recapitulates the levels of mortality attributed to successive famines from 1876-1878 through 1918-1919. For all except the first famine, the number of districts that had IQAS values more than one standard deviation below the mean has also been given. This comparison reinforces the conclusion that a decline in mortality from famines had occurred even when crop failures were widespread and serious. For instance, in 1905-1906 the mortality attributable to famine is only 2.4 deaths per thousand of population even though nine districts that year had IQAS values (i.e., foodgrain

[7] There are also two cases, one in 1891-1892 and one in 1913-1914, not shown in the table, when famine was declared in a district and the IQAS was not more than one standard deviation below the mean.

TABLE 6.4. Famine Mortality and Crop Failures, 1876-1878 to 1918-1919

Years	Deaths per 1,000 Population Due to Famine	Number of Districts with IQAS 1 or More S.D. below Mean
1876-1878	20.0	(No information on IQAS; famine declared in 9 districts.)
1896-1897	11.5	7
1899-1900	37.9	12
1900-1901	9.0	6
1901-1902	1.3	6
1905-1906	2.4	9
1911-1912	6.0	11
1912-1913	0.2	1
1918-1919	2.5	12

SOURCES· Column 1, Table 3.13, Column 2, Table 6.2 or Table 6.3.

harvests) at least one standard deviation below the mean. This is especially remarkable in view of the fact that there had been ten districts with IQAS values at these levels in 1904-1905. In 1911-1912, even though there were eleven districts with IQAS values at least one standard deviation below the mean, the death rate from famine was only a little more than half of what it had been in 1896-1897, when six districts had IQAS values at least one standard deviation below average. What had happened to reduce mortality from famines?

II. Changes in Risk, 1860-1920

In determining what changes led to a decline in the mortality from famines, it is necessary to return to a discussion of the risk in the agrarian system and to attempt to see how the amount, distribution, and consequences of risk may have altered between 1860 and 1920. This section focuses on two factors: the evolution of famine relief policy under the British and changes in the environment in which agricultural decisions were made.

In thinking about how the risks that individuals and communities engaged in agriculture faced altered as the administrative structure of the British Raj became effective in western India, it may be helpful to consider first how the capabilities and ideology of the Raj differed, at least in western India, from those of its predecessors. There seems no doubt that the Maratha rulers who preceded the British in much of western India were concerned about famines and the attendant dislocation of the agricultural economy. Those of their records that have been examined with these questions in mind show that there were a variety of procedures for remitting revenue and advancing *takavi* (either grants or low-interest loans) in regions where crop failures had been severe.[8]

But however great their concern, the opportunities available to the Marathas either to prevent or to relieve famines were sharply limited. Over most of western India the combination of topography and rainfall meant that irrigation potential was very small, particularly for works that could be relied upon in a year of severe drought. The rivers failed to provide good natural highways for the economical movement of bulky commodities, and overland transport in the black-soil region was prohibitively expensive. The Maratha rulers therefore had neither the chance to build major irrigation works that would prevent crop failures nor the transport capacity to move grain into a region of crop failure in quantities sufficient to avert famine. In addition, the percentage of the income of the region that passed through government hands must have been small relative to the size of the disasters that could visit the region. Even if all the resources of the public fisc could be suddenly shifted to famine relief, how large a dent would these resources have made in the need?

Along with these severe physical limitations on their abilities to prevent or alleviate famines—limitations shared in various ways by rulers in pre-modern western Europe, Russia, and China—the Hindu rulers had an ideology that tended to encourage them to regard the occurrence of drought and famine as the result of human actions— lapses by the ruler or his subjects from the rule of *dharma*. In this view, avoidance of future catastrophe might best be achieved by adherence to the rule of *dharma* (i.e., by right living) rather than by specific policies aimed at increasing the security of cultivators. Of course, the *dharma* of a ruler could be and often was defined to include actions that, if successfully carried out, would have lessened the probability of destructive famines: Cultivators should not be overtaxed, law and order should be maintained, tanks and wells should be built, markets should be well regulated, and so on.

Both capability and ideology could be compromised by the general political instability of the region. An otherwise just and effective ruler could, in times when he was defending his kingdom against attack, find himself compelled to press too hard upon the cultivators

---

[8] Gordon, "Recovery from Adversity," pp. 66-72.

for tax revenue. When drought did occur, a public fisc drained by military expenditure might not contain adequate resources to assist in the rehabilitation of the drought-stricken areas.

The administrators of the British Raj, at least from the 1840s on, had both a different ideology and increasingly different capabilities from their Maratha predecessors. These men were imbued with European notions of progress, conquest of nature, and the perfectibility of solutions. As we saw in the discussion of the Bombay Survey and Settlement system, they were convinced that ways could be found to raise revenue from the land tax and at the same time encourage agricultural development. In like fashion, they were convinced that solutions existed which would permit prevention of deaths during famines, minimize disruption to the agricultural economy, avoid demoralizing the population, and place minimal strain on the public treasury. They were prepared to try out policies, to review them, and to discard those that failed to meet one or more of their objectives. The British administrators were able to create an institutional memory of their efforts that facilitated policy formation (not to mention what the voluminous papers that constituted this memory have done for our ability to study the Raj's administration).

But the development of capabilities for dealing increasingly effectively with food crises was a long and, by a modern scale of time, a slow process. The East India Company officials who took over from the Marathas in 1818 did not have capacities for actions that differed very greatly from those of their predecessors. To the extent that they did, it was because the British officers could call on resources from a much greater area (i.e., Madras or Bengal or Delhi). But in the absence of any transformation of transport capacity, the resources that could be called upon were largely military. They could be used to conquer western India but not, in general, to govern it.

To govern effectively the British needed to mobilize information about agricultural production and its fluctuations and to organize resources to enable them to make decisions and to implement famine policies. It took the British several decades to learn to distinguish between information that was sufficiently accurate for making decisions and that which was not. While some improvements in information-gathering were made under the Company before 1858— including the first twenty years of implementation of the Bombay Survey and Settlement—major bureaucratic improvements for systematizing the collection and use of information date from the beginning of the 1870s, with successive reforms of agricultural statistics and formulation of complex codes for both routine and exceptional events.

Chief among the infrastructures that the British either brought with them or created and that aided their capacity to govern were the mail service, the telegraph, the printing press, and the railways. The first three of these enabled different parts of the administration to communicate both quickly and voluminously. They enabled administrators to create uniform categories for the collection and reporting of information over wide areas.[9] While this kind of information was a key element in allowing them to know where resources were needed, in the absence of the railroad actual transfers of resources would have been very limited. For those parts of India that lacked good water transport, the railroad brought a staggering reduction in transport costs and an equally startling expansion in capacity.

The combination of railroads and information on crops made it possible for even rather massive shortfalls in harvest in several regions of the subcontinent to be mitigated by the surpluses of the remaining regions. The pre-nineteenth-century regimes in India never had available any transport technology that could permit rapid transfers of grain overland in quantities large enough to succor a population facing famine. Guided by their ideology and aided by their abilities to channel information and organize resource flows, the administration of Bombay Presidency (and to a large extent of the rest of India as well) gradually evolved a set of policies for "administering" or "working" famines. By the time of the report of the Indian Famine Commission of 1880, the policies had evolved to the general form they retained until the end of British rule.

Educated in the tradition of Adam Smith, members of the Indian

[9] As an example of a simple matter where it took the administration quite some time to become efficient, consider the names of agricultural crops. The Bombay Presidency included regions where Gujarati, Marathi, and Kannada were spoken. After the administration began to try to compile agricultural statistics for the entire Presidency (1871), they gradually worked to provide fairly disaggregated statistics on minor crops—to stop lumping them all together under "other," "other foodgrains," or "other pulses." For several years the Presidency statistics offer an interesting picture in which some crops appear to be grown only in Marathi-speaking areas, others only in Gujarati-speaking areas, and so on. At last the commissioners of the northern, central, and southern divisions, along with some other officials and some learned native speakers, were assembled one year during the rains and ordered to produce a comprehensive crop list for the Presidency giving the scientific, English, and three vernacular terms for each crop. As soon as this list came into general use, the strange pattern of crops grown only in a single language area disappeared.

Civil Service generally held tightly to the belief that intervention of the government in the daily operation of the economy was to be avoided whenever possible. While all intervention in the economy was viewed as regrettable, types which held out the promise of occurring only once and of yielding revenues adequate to pay for themselves (or reducing the costs of other operations) were viewed as preferable to kinds of intervention which could not be defined within the administration as "productive." Accordingly, the administration tended to favor policies that held out some hope of *preventing* famines—specifically, the construction of railroads and the improvement and extension of irrigation works.

For reasons which have not yet been adequately studied, the British gave priority to the extension of railways.[10] After the report of the Indian Famine Commission of 1880, certain railway lines were constructed specifically to make it possible to move grain quickly and relatively cheaply from areas of surplus production to areas affected by crop failure. These lines were not necessarily expected to show a profit, although some of them did. Of these lines, the one of most concern in western India was the Southern Maratha Railway, which was constructed by a private company under a guarantee by the Government of India that it would earn a specific rate on capital invested.[11] But the lines which were designed, as the Southern Maratha Railway was, mainly to permit grain to be imported into famine-prone regions would have been worthless without the larger network of lines which tied more prosperous regions to the ports and eventually to other parts of the interior.

The volume of railborne trade in grains and pulses increased enormously between 1880 and 1920. As Table 6.5 shows, the increase was far larger than the rather limited increases in the exports of wheat and rice. The shipments of wheat and rice in excess of those bound for the ports moved within India in response to food shortages and price differentials among regions. Data in Chapter 5

[10] However, in western India irrigation possibilities appear to have been very limited with nineteenth-century technology. Rivers in the Karnatak and the Deccan were few, and many of them impractical. That is, the only lands which could be commanded by such canals were lands already in the river bottoms and not in need of irrigation waters. In most parts of the Southern Maratha Country and the Deccan, ground water was too far down for successful construction and operation of wells on a regular basis. SRGB Irrigation Series, No. 5 (1866); and *A Statement and remarks relating to the expenses of irrigation from wells in the Deccan, Khandesh, &c.* by Meadows Taylor [Philip Meadows] (Bombay: Education Society's Press, 1856).

[11] Nalinaksha Sanyal, *Development of Indian Railways* (Calcutta: University of Calcutta Press, 1930), pp. 30-34, 112-114.

TABLE 6.5. Indices of Rail Shipments of Grain and Pulses and Exports of Wheat and Rice, 1881-1920

Years	Index of Rail Shipments of Grain and Pulses [a]	Index of Export of [b]	
		Wheat	Rice and Paddy
1881-1885	100	100	100
1886-1890	112	127	98
1891-1895	155	100	114
1896-1900	196	56	118
1901-1905	220	110	152
1906-1910	260	100	139
1911-1915	337	158	173
1916-1920	365	110	132

[a]1881-1885 average = 100. Absolute value of 1881-1885 average, 3,550 thousand tons.

[b]1881-1885 average = 100. Absolute values of 1881-1885 averages: wheat, 783.9 thousand tons, rice and paddy, 1,365 thousand tons.

SOURCES Column 1, calculated from data in Morris and Dudley, "Selected Railway Statistics." Columns 2 and 3 – McAlpin, "Impact of Trade."

on railborne grain trade for the blocks into which Bombay Presidency was divided for the collection of rail statistics show increasing trade in grain over the entire period. There were large fluctuations in net imports from year to year in response to the robustness of the harvest.

Railroads, of course, could not prevent crop failures or prevent people from dying during such failures. Although they could perform the crucial task of moving grain from one part of India to another, they could not assure that hungry people would have the money to buy that grain. So in addition to railroads and irrigation works, the government of India and its constituent parts attempted to guarantee subsistence levels of living via a set of famine relief policies. The famine relief policies were designed, in general, not only to enable people to survive the current crop failure, but also to permit them to resume normal agricultural operations at the commencement of the next monsoon.

In Bombay Presidency there were four major components of famine relief policy.[12] The first of these was the provision of employment on "relief works" to persons whose normal agricultural employments had been made unavailable by failure of the rains, so that they could

[12] This discussion of famine relief policy is drawn from Bombay Presidency, *Famine Relief Code* (Bombay, 1885), and from discussions in *Proceedings* and *Famine Reports* during and after successive famines.

earn money to buy grain. From the initial establishment of such works on a large scale—in the famine of 1876-1877—debate between the center and the different provinces and presidencies over the appropriate organization and running of relief works continued for a quarter of a century. The major issues were these:

(1) Who was to be admitted to the relief work? Were all comers to be admitted, or only persons who had exhausted their own resources and could no longer survive except by gaining employment at the relief work? In Bombay this issue was generally resolved in favor of excluding those who visibly still had resources of their own. However, no very stringent tests could be applied, and one rather suspects that farmers quickly learned not to appear at relief works looking too prosperous.[13] Since it was deemed essential to persuade those who did need relief to go to the works before they had become too run down to be able to work, administrators were faced with something of a dilemma, and generally seem to have favored people coming to the works with some of their own resources left rather than too weak to work.

(2) How much were workers to be paid and how much were they to be expected to work? Workers commonly came to the works in whole families—man, woman, children, and babes. Most famine codes prescribed different rates of pay for men and women, based partly on the different amounts of work they might do but also on the different amounts of food they might need to maintain their condition. Working children were paid at a lower rate than women, and nonworking children were either fed in kitchens or provided for by additional payments to their parents. Special provisions were also made for nursing mothers and for children who did not yet have teeth in both jaws.[14] Payments were supposed to be based on the local price of the staple grain and to fluctuate with its price, to enable workers to get a constant diet. More or less continual debates raged over the level of payments, with the main controversy precipitated by the conflicting desires to "maintain the people in good condition" and to avoid making the works attractive to those not

[13] "On some few works the difficulty has arisen that persons resorting to them do not appear as yet in urgent need of relief, for they actually bring carts and cattle with them." Letter from Collector of Khandesh to Monteath (Chief Secretary to Government), *Revenue Proceedings, Famine*, P/5985, no. 760 of 1900, India Office Library.

[14] "Nursing mothers, if not required to work, shall get grain equivalent of 2-1/8 lbs. and 1 pie for the child." Milk was to be provided "for children of very tender age who are unable to eat." Bombay Presidency, *Famine Relief Code*, 1900, pp. 20-26.

actually in need of relief (and hence increasing the costs of relief and fostering "a bad spirit" among the people).

In any given famine, some works were judged to have been run too leniently and others too harshly. Among the ways used in Bombay Presidency to separate persons really in need from those who were merely amenable to earning some extra income if conditions were not too difficult were the concentration of workers on big projects (requiring them to come some distance from their homes) and enforced residence on the work site. Both of these policies, it was argued, would not be objected to by those really in need but would discourage those not so needy. However, these policies often had to be modified because of the unavailability of suitable works, the need for agriculturists to be near their farms at the start of the rains, and the refusal of some peoples, particularly tribals, to go far from their homes even if the alternative was starvation.[15]

The second component of famine relief was the provision of "gratuitous relief" or "village dole" to those persons unable to work. Administration of the village dole was the responsibility of the *patel* and *kulkarni* of the village. In the words of a circular from the Collector of Ahmednagar to all village officers during the famine of 1899-1900:

> The Patil Kulkarnis of the villages are in the first place responsible for famine relief administration in the villages. They are not relieved of their ordinary duties but must discharge them as usual; and in addition must discharge their famine duties.
>
> They must bear this well in mind, that it is their duty to see that relief of the proper kind is given to every man, woman, and child in the village who is in need of relief; and that if any person whatever dies in the village through not receiving relief, the Patil Kulkarnis are responsible for his death; and his death is at their doors, and they must answer for it both before the Sarkar and before God.[16]

The remainder of the circular goes on to point out that the "patil kulkarnis" must live in their villages, must not be absent without leave, must visit as far as possible each house daily, must send distressed villagers to the works, and must put others onto the "dole register." Those who were to be placed on the dole register were

[15] Bombay Presidency, *Famine Relief Code*, 1896, pp. 21-23.

[16] "Circular from Collector of Ahmednagar to all Patil Kulkarnis," *Famine Proceedings*, P/5985, p. 331.

persons "*ashakt*" (unable to work) and "*nirashrit*" (without supporters). All others were to be sent to the nearest work and not to
be put onto the dole register.

Dole could be given in two or three ways. If there were many in
the village who needed this kind of relief, a kitchen might be established and cooked food given out. If numbers were insufficient
to justify the expense of a kitchen, dole was to be given in grain
wherever possible. Only if grain dole was for some reason not feasible were doles to be given in cash. Regular checks of the dole
registers by higher officers were supposed to be made, and at least
spot checks were in fact made. Village officers suffered equally for
admitting persons not in need of dole to the registers and for failing
to admit those who were in need.[17] Any substantial rise in the death
rate in a village was held to indicate that the village officers had
been lax in their duties, unless cholera or some other major outbreak
of disease could be proven.

Table 6.6 shows the numbers of persons provided with relief either
through work or by a village dole during the period from 1876-1877
to 1918-1919. "Relief workers" are all those at relief works who were
considered old enough to do some work (generally children from
10 up, although from 7 up was sometimes the case). "Dependents"
are the nonworking children who came to the works with their
parents. Those listed as "gratuitously relieved" are the indigent,
unable to work and without supporters, whom the "patil kulkarnis"
placed on the dole registers.

In the second panel of Table 6.6., the percentages of those relieved
who received each kind of relief are given. We can note a steady
rise until the very last years in the percentage receiving dole in their
villages, while the percentage on relief works declines. These changes
could have come about from a number of causes—changes in famine policy that made village dole easier to obtain, a reduction in the
attractiveness of relief works, changes in classification of persons
receiving relief, or a change in the general economy that altered
the population that sought relief. The argument here is that expansion of *takavi*, the third pillar of famine relief in Bombay Presidency, and increased employment opportunities in nearby rural and
urban areas were largely responsible for the shift.

This third technique of providing famine relief relied upon state
assistance to the private sector to generate employment for some of
those whose normal agricultural occupations had been disrupted

[17] Bombay Presidency, *Famine Relief Code*, 1885, pp. 21-23.

TABLE 6.6. Statistics on Government-Administered Famine Relief, 1876-1877 to 1918-1919

Category	1876-1877[a]	1896-1897[a]	1899-1900[b]	1900-1901[b]	1901-1902[b]	1905-1906[c]	1911-1912[d]	1918-1919[e]
A. Number in Each Category (thousands)								
Relief workers	247	219	540	183	121	18	20	39
Their dependents	53	67	134	33	13	3	—	19
Gratuitously relieved by village dole	33	36	172	76	58	26	26	47
Total daily average	333	322	846	291	192	47	46	105
B. Percentage of Total Daily Average								
Relief workers	74	68	64	63	63	38	43	37
Their dependents	16	21	16	11	7	6	—	18
Gratuitously relieved by village dole	10	11	20	26	30	55	56	45

[a] *Report of the Indian Famine Commission, 1898*, Appendix, vol. 3, p. 206.

[b] *Report on the Famine in Bombay Presidency, 1899-1902*, Appendices 10 and 11. Thar and Parkar eliminated from totals.

[c] *Report on the Famine in Bombay Presidency, 1905-1906*, p. 7

[c] *Report on the Famine in Bombay Presidency, 1911-1912*, p. 7. No statistics are given for the famine of 1912-1913 because no relief works were opened.

[e] Calculated from *Review of the Famine Administration in Bombay Presidency, 1918-1919*, Appendix 3.

by the failure of rains. *Takavi*, or loans to agriculturists to effect improvements on their farms, were made under the Land Improvement Loans Act IX of 1883, although loans of the same kind had been made preceding the passage of the act. These loans—low-interest, rapidly dispensed, and with slow repayment schemes— could be made, and were made, in all years. However, in years of famine, the amount so loaned swelled enormously. The loans could be issued fairly early in the season for work that was expected to last most of the season, like well-building, leveling and bunding of fields, and clearing fields of *nutt* grass. The loans were used to pay wages to labor employed in effecting the improvements, and to maintain the agriculturist, his family, and livestock. The government of Bombay used *takavi* as widely as possible and tried to make it a major source of employment in preference to relief works, which were costly in terms of the personnel needed to administer them and in the questionable value of much of the "work" done. In addition to being cheaper than large works, *takavi* enabled villagers to stay on their own lands and thus reduced the likelihood that the villagers would run into cholera epidemics (almost always a major cause of famine-related deaths) and made it possible for them to be on hand to resume agricultural operations as soon as the rains were favorable. In contrast to relief works, *takavi* provided employment at lower administrative cost, on works which were more often thought to be productive for the agricultural system, and with less disruption to the ongoing functioning of the system.

The fourth pillar of famine relief in Bombay Presidency could be called "reconstruction." Under the Agriculturists' Loans Act XIX of 1884, farmers could be advanced *takavi* loans to enable them to get the seed and cattle necessary to restart agricultural operations after a famine, i.e., to rebuild the working capital which had been depleted. These loans were generally confined to cultivators who had enough land to allow an expectation in the minds of the *taluka* staff that repayment of the loan was possible. For other cultivators who were viewed as too poor to be able to repay such loans but were nonetheless in need of help, help was usually available from the "Charitable Endowments" funds from private sources administered through the collector's office in the district.

In Table 6.7, some data on the amounts loaned under these two acts are presented. Several patterns in the table seem noteworthy. First, the amount of *takavi* increased sharply, even in nonfamine years, from 1890-1891 on. The reasons for this are not now clear, but increased familiarity with the program and a general rise in

TABLE 6.7. Takavi Loans, 1876-1919

| Year | Land Improvement Loans Act, XIX of 1883 | | Agriculturists' Loans Act, XII of 1884 | | Total |
	Rupees (thousands)	Percent of Total	Rupees (thousands)	Percent of Total	Rupees (thousands)
1876-1877	154	62	94	38	249
1877-1878	15	5	279	95	294
1878-1879	8	9	81	91	89
1879-1880	9	10	77	90	86
1880-1881	4	10	35	90	39
1881-1882	16	22	56	79	71
1882-1883	6	18	28	82	76[a]
1883-1884	9	11	72	89	81
1884-1885	31	42	42	58	73
1885-1886	29	41	42	59	71
1886-1887	67	74	23	26	90
1887-1888	32	78	9	22	41
1888-1889	52	63	31	37	83
1889-1890	76	61	48	39	124
1890-1891	175	71	71	29	246
1891-1892	988	82	220	18	1,208
1892-1893	319	65	168	34	487
1893-1894	496	81	113	19	609

1894-1895	760	83	158	17	918
1895-1896	831	76	259	24	1,090
1896-1897	3,835	80	960	20	4,795
1897-1898	750	35	1,422	65	2,172
1898-1899	—[c]		—[c]		—
1899-1900	2,084[c]	66	1,090[c]	34	4,031[a,c]
1900-1901	1,338	15	7,687	85	9,445[a]
1901-1902	1,009	19	4,278	81	6,163[a]
1902-1903	342	12	2,535	88	2,877
1905-1906	1,099	38	1,793	62	2,892[b]
1911-1912	1,251	22	4,410	78	5,661[b]
1912-1913	330	38	530	62	861[b]
1913-1914	168	37	287	63	455[b]
1918-1919	3,436	27	9,343	73	16,075[a,b]

[a]Columns do not sum to total because amounts advanced under the two acts were not reported separately for all districts. Percents calculated on sum of columns in these cases.

[b]Includes only those districts where famine was declared.

[c]1898-1899 may be included in 1899-1900.

SOURCES: 1876-1877 through 1896-1897 — Report of the Indian Famine Commission, 1898, Appendix, vol. 3, p. 210. Covers all of Presidency, including Sind.

1897-1898 through 1918-1919 — Appropriate famine reports.

agricultural prices may have stimulated farmers to use this method of financing improvements on their lands. This is consistent with the second tendency—that of the percentage of *takavi* taken for land improvements to rise from 1877-1878 through 1896-1897. Third, in the years of famine up to 1900 (i.e., 1876-1877, 1896-1897, 1899-1900), there is a tendency toward heavy borrowing for land improvements, while for the year following a famine (1877-1878, 1897-1898, 1900-1901, 1901-1902, 1902-1903) the heavier borrowings are to replenish working capital. It is possible that this is just a function of the accounting year (April 1—March 31), so that advances for seed and cattle come in a second accounting year to be available in time for the onset of the monsoon in June. In any case, Tables 6.6 and 6.7 together make it clear that the enormous increases in *takavi* must have been partly responsible for reducing the numbers seeking employment on the relief works. But only partly. In addition to changes in famine relief policy and the efficiency with which that policy was implemented, changes in the economy in general must be considered.

By the first decade of the twentieth century there had been three major changes in the economic environment of agriculturists that helped to mitigate the effects of a major crop failure. The first of these was the expansion of markets in which agricultural produce could be sold. This tended to stabilize prices as the produce of many local markets was pooled to create a more stable supply curve. Demands from outside India tended to maintain the price of grains grown for export even in years when local good harvests would formerly have driven prices down. Second, the development of reliable trade in grains among the parts of the subcontinent minimized the *local* rise in price resulting from a *local* crop failure. A century earlier, in the almost total absence of economical transport for bulk commodities and hence of regular large-scale grain trade, local crop failures could drive prices toward infinity as grain ceased to be available locally at any price. Together these two changes permitted greater asset accumulation (i.e., the profits from selling agricultural produce in expanded markets) and guaranteed the fungibility of these assets with grain even in years when local crops were short. This guarantee encouraged farmers to give up growing grain for storage, resulting in a further increase in real incomes as farmers grew other products and simultaneously stored a nondeteriorating asset. Third, the overall demand for agricultural and nonagricultural labor increased, making available to farmers in even the most drought-prone areas alternative sources of employment in years when the failure of the rains curtailed their farming. These three changes raised the income of some farmers, lowered the risks of growing crops for the market, and provided new alternatives to self-employment in agriculture. As a result, the probability that a drought would reduce them and their families to starvation was reduced.

III. The Interaction of Farmers, Famine Relief Policy, and Economic Change

In Chapter 2 a model was developed for discussing the options that farmers may use to try to avoid disaster (defined as net income below some specified level) and to minimize the size of shortfalls in net income. The level of net income specified as the disaster level could be either that at which the continuance of agricultural operations in future years is endangered (as when the farmer's capital, including livestock, is wiped out) or that below which some or all of the members of the family are threatened with death due to complications of malnutrition. In the context of localized markets for bulk commodities like grain, these two levels of disaster would probably be quite close together, if only because there would be little possibility that capital could be converted into food to help the family survive.

While the British were certainly aware of the destruction of agricultural capital that could occur because of a drought, their initial efforts at relief seem to have been limited to the preservation of life. They concentrated on building railroads to make it both easy and cheap to move grain into regions with major crop failures. While the absolute supply of food was still a problem in the Karnatak in the famine of 1876-1878, the construction of the Southern Maratha Railway had eliminated this problem by the time of the crop failure of 1891-1892. G. W. Vidal, acting chief secretary to government, wrote:

> A legitimate conclusion to be drawn from the experience of the scarcity in the three districts notified is that in the future a true famine, that is an absence of foodstuffs, is scarcely possible in an area so well served by railways as this was. The reports show that sufficient food for the population was easily transferable thither from parts of the country more favored by nature.[18]

[18] G. W. Vidal, Acting Chief Secretary to Government, "Resolution of Government" of July 26, 1893, in Bombay Presidency, *Report on the History of the Late Famine in the Southern Division* (1891-1892), p. 6.

While providing opportunities to work in return for food or money to buy food had been an integral part of famine policy in earlier famines, Vidal suggested in his summary that

> [l]abourers without means of earning wages are practically subject to the very hardship which a true famine imposes; and what the authorities have to concern themselves about now is to determine how labour can most easily, advantageously, and economically be supplied to those who are able and willing to work. But this problem is easy compared with that which the authorities had to face in 1876-77.[19]

The overall shifts in the methods by which employment was provided have been indicated in the previous section. In general, the movement was from large government-administered relief works (like excavation or the construction of railway roadbeds) to smaller works (like deepening or repair of tanks) and to *takavi*, where farmers determined what work would be done. A further shift occurred as expanding employment opportunities encouraged both rural-to-rural migration and rural-to-urban migration. As workers from drought-stricken regions increasingly found their own seasonal employment, the need for work relief declined.

Although a concern for cattle mortality during drought had been present since the 1870s, it was only during the famine of 1899-1902 that significant attention was devoted to the problem of providing "relief" for cattle (other than allowing shipments of fodder at concessional rates). During that famine, particularly in Gujarat, camps were opened for cattle, attempts were made to move some cattle into regions where grass was available, and experiments with different kinds of fodder were made. Along with the concern for the preservation of working cattle, government policy also placed increased emphasis on reconstruction of depleted working capital.

Over time the emphasis of "famine relief" evolved from the provision of adequate food supplies to the generation of employment to the preservation and reconstruction of working capital. For farmers in drought-prone regions, these different policies would have been roughly congruent with their own orderings. They too were concerned with getting food in years when their own crops failed. They were concerned with the preservation of their working cattle. And the popularity of *takavi* suggests that many farmers were willing to use cheap loans to make capital improvements on their land,

[19] Vidal, "Resolution of Government."

especially when prices for agricultural products were rising. Where British policy and the desires of farmers appear to have been least congruent was in the nature and conditions for admission to relief works and the form in which dole or gratuitous relief was to be given. As with modern welfare systems, potential recipients of relief objected to having to prove that they were destitute by, for instance, going some distance to relief works or being forced to reside at the works. Administrators of the system, as with their modern analogs, found it difficult to combine their humanitarian impulses with the need to contain costs.

The strengthening of the ability of both farmers and administrators to deal successfully with crop failures (i.e., to minimize both loss of life and disruption to ongoing agricultural operations) was due in significant part to the changes in the economy explored in Chapter 5 and summarized above. If all of these changes in the economy were to be subsumed into one, it would probably be that the factors of production (land, labor, even capital with the government as lender of choice in bad crop years) had increasing numbers of alternative uses and were increasingly mobile among these uses. So long as the covariance among different sources of income for the population of rural areas was not strongly positive (i.e., their own crops, labor paid for with government loans for capital improvements, harvest work in nearby regions, and various kinds of nonagricultural labor did not all diminish in the same year), these alternative income opportunities mitigated the distress a crop failure caused. Famine reports written after 1899-1902 provide supporting evidence that it was new alternatives that played a major role in the prevention and alleviation of disaster. Expansion of opportunities for seasonal labor led some district collectors to argue that seasonal migration either to other rural places or to urban areas had become a way of life for communities where agricultural conditions did not provide an adequate living.[20] The collector of Ahmednagar is quoted in the 1912-1913 famine report:

> Emigration was encouraged in every possible way and saved the situation. I have never seen so severe a famine attended with so little human distress. Though reliable figures are not available the total (emigrants) of a little over a lakh officially reported is probably well under the mark. Villages were almost deserted in the worst tracts, only the village servants and a few bagayat cultivators remaining. Thus in Mahalaxmi-Hiware there were only

[20] Bombay Presidency, *Report on the Famine*, 1911-1912, p. 6.

219 persons found in February out of the 1000 odd who were present at the last census. Fattehpur inhabitants were reduced from 127 to 19. Most emigrants returned with the rains. The commonest labour connections are with the Berars and Khandesh, but Lonavla [a Bombay suburb] attracted a certain number, who are going there this year as soon as they have harvested their few crops. To these classes of petty cultivators, a bad season only means an earlier exodus.[21]

These reports also indicate that agriculturists did not respond passively to the existence of job alternatives. Unlike the aimless wandering of agriculturists whose own resources had run out that characterized crop failures in the nineteenth century, the increasing reliance on migration in regions where major harvest shortfalls were common was well organized.[22] When the lack of early rains made it clear that the harvest was going to be drastically short, one or two men would be sent out from a village to see what work was available and where. As soon as the short harvest was collected (and perhaps before for some men, if the limited harvest did not require all hands for completion), the men of the village would leave for work elsewhere. Villages are reported to have housed only women, children, and old men in some years of crop failure. Those left behind could tend the livestock, live off of the short harvest, and expect that the government would step in to provide relief—including grain sales or gratuitous relief—if necessary. With the beginning of the next agricultural season, the men would return to the village with some earnings from their outside employment which could be used to resume agricultural operations. In most cases, the livestock would also have been preserved through the actions of the women and children. In the words of the famine report of 1905-1906:

[21] Bombay Presidency, *Report on the Famine*, 1912-1913, p. 6.

[22] The mortality associated with wandering appears to have been high. First, the act of wandering about tended to produce exhaustion and further strain on malnourished individuals. Second, wanderers frequently came in contact with diseases which they might have escaped had they remained in their own villages. The British were not unaware of these problems, and they attempted to stem wandering by judicious placement of relief works and requirements of residence on relief works. And yet relief works themselves sometimes contributed to famine-related deaths because makeshift sanitary arrangements and conglomeration of people provided ideal conditions for the spread of cholera. Since panic usually followed an outbreak of cholera, those who survived or who had not been stricken fled back to their villages or out onto the roads, taking the infections with them. In Bombay Presidency elaborate regulations for the construction of famine camps gradually eliminated outbreaks of cholera in the camps.

There is from the affected districts an annual exodus to the neighboring territories and districts varying in degree according to the nature of the season. . . . In Khandesh alone, owing to the good harvests and industrial development as shown by the increase in ginning factories, the demand for labour was so great that in spite of the unprecedented immigration into the district the wages of unskilled labour rose by half. . . . On this occasion the people did not wander forth aimlessly in search of work, but knew exactly where they were going. Men were sent out in advance from the different villages as soon as signs of trouble arose, and on receipt of definite news from them as to the prospects of work elsewhere, the general exodus commenced.

This extensive exodus proved to be of great service. Although the distress was severe, the numbers on relief were very low and a great saving in expenditure to the State resulted. The emigrants left their dependents behind them and a large portion of these, who were helpless, had to be brought on the dole lists and relieved gratuitously. On the other hand, the returning emigrants brought back with them savings sufficient to carry them on till normal times returned.[23]

In the first decade of the twentieth century, the interaction of the general expansion of the economy, the increasingly diverse options available to agriculturists, and the famine relief policies of Bombay Presidency combined to prevent crop failures from becoming major demographic and economic catastrophes. The life-threatening risk associated with agriculture in western India had been significantly reduced and redistributed. Railroads reduced the probability of failure of food supplies by connecting regions with different weather patterns. Increased employment opportunities reduced the risk that drought would leave laborers and small cultivators without work and income. The government took over some of the burden of caring for dependents during periods of shortfall through the village dole. It also helped to preserve working capital and to create more capital stock by lending large amounts to farmers at rates which, given the rise in prices, were probably negative. Of these three factors, the general expansion of the economy—including new employment opportunities and regular large-scale trade in commodities—was definitely the most important one in mitigating the effects of crop failures. British famine policy became increasingly successful over

[23] Bombay Presidency, *Report on the Famine*, 1905-1906, p. 11.

time in part because the growth of the economy meant that fewer and fewer people needed to turn to the government for total relief. Nonetheless, the absorption of risk by the government—both by providing care for dependents on the village dole and by large disbursements of *takavi*—was important both in creating an environment in which organized migration in search of employment was possible and in directly expanding one alternative source of employment.[24] It was the combined impact of all these changes that reduced the mortality associated with crop failures.

[24] After 1906 the government absorbed an additional (albeit small) proportion of the risk associated with agriculture by a regular policy of suspension and remission of revenue demands when crops were bad. (Heston, "Official Yields," pp. 319-321.) However politically popular this policy may have been, the figures in Table 4.2 suggest that the economic impact could not have been large.

7. A Reinterpretation of a Century of Change

As noted in the introduction, the famines that occurred in India at the end of the nineteenth century were and have remained a touchstone both for anti-imperialist rhetoric and for interpretations of the economic history of the nineteenth century. Thus far in this book I have focussed on providing a lengthy case study of the famines that occurred in western India in the nineteenth century and the beginning of the twentieth century. Such a case study has considerable merit because of the unique kinds of data available for studying both the demographic effects of severe food crises and the evolution of the impact of these food crises from the times when they caused major elevations of mortality to later times when their demographic impact was minimal. But because of the importance of these famines in the interpretations of the economic history of India, it is now necessary to examine in some detail the analyses of Dutt and others of the causes of these famines and to see how the data presented in this volume confirm or contradict them. The final section of this chapter attempts a new synthesis, reinterpreting the experience of the economy of western India from 1818 to 1920.

I. The Analysis of the Causes of Famines

There were two major strands in Dutt's analysis of the causes of Indian famines. The first of these began with the land revenue systems in the parts of British India that were not covered by the permanent settlement of 1793. The second strand emphasized the drain from India to England of resources to cover part of the costs of governing India. While each of these lines of argument has been treated by authors other than Dutt, his formulation has been and remains a highly influential one. It will therefore be used here with only occasional references to other writers to show how widely accepted Dutt's view has been.

From his experience in Bengal, Dutt was convinced that a permanent settlement of land revenues—fixing once and for all, with no escape clauses for the government, the amount of land revenue to be demanded from a province—was the only way to end the poverty of Indian cultivators and to permit the development of agriculture. Dutt contrasted land revenue policy and practice in Bengal, which had an old permanent settlement, with those in the rest of British India, where land revenue was fixed for a term of years, most commonly 30 years. In this contrast the systems in the Presidencies of Madras and Bombay were seen to be the worst. Dutt concluded, "The accumulation of agricultural wealth was impossible so long as Settlement Officers retained the power of varying the Land Tax at each recurring settlement according to their own judgement. And any permanent improvement in the condition of the peasantry was impossible when the peasantry possessed no security against arbitrary enhancements of the State-demand."[1]

Implicitly in this passage and explicitly elsewhere,[2] Dutt argued that in any province with a varying land tax (though it should be borne in mind that it varied in any locale only at 30-year intervals), land taxes were raised to absorb all or more than all of the economic rent accruing to agricultural lands. Again quoting Dutt, "A nation of cultivators can never permanently improve their own condition if the State is ever ready to screw up its demands with the first signs of prosperity."[3] To support his position Dutt cited two kinds of evidence: first, aggregate figures on the revenue collections in various districts; and second, the occurrence of famines. While Dutt realized that increases in aggregate collections alone did not prove that the burden on agriculture was increasing, he maintained that increases in cultivation could not have offset increases in collections. He wrote: "It is sometimes forgotten that the lands last taken up are inferior in productive powers; and increase in Land Revenue in proportion to the cultivated area is an increase out of proportion to the produce."[4]

While this thesis has a pleasing logic to it, it is flawed in two ways. It ignores (as does the work of Ricardo from which it derives in part) the possibility that circumstances of location, technology, security, etc., often prevent a neat sequence of cultivation expanding from the very best to the very worst lands; and it fails in any case to offer us any statistics on cultivation that would permit us to know whether or not land revenue increased as fast as or faster or slower than cultivation expanded. When he used the occurrence of famines

---

[1] Dutt, *Economic History of India*, vol. 2, p. 36.

[2] Dutt, *Economic History of India*, vol. 2, pp. 45-46, 238-239, 253.

[3] Dutt, *Economic History of India*, vol. 2, p. 252.

[4] Dutt, *Economic History of India*, vol. 2, p. 253.

as support for his conclusions, Dutt's reasoning was essentially circular. Famines ("the most intense and the most widely extended yet, known")[5] occurred at the end of the nineteenth century. They must be due to the poverty of the Indian people. The poverty of the Indian people was due in large part to the constant increases in land revenue, which prevented them from becoming any less poor or perhaps made them even poorer. Except for the economic drain (of which more later), Dutt considered no other possible causes of these famines.

Without exploring the nature or magnitude of the economic drain from India to Great Britain, let us examine Dutt's argument about its effect on India's food supplies and hence its role in precipitating famines. Dutt wrote that "India had to meet a heavy drain . . . she was unable to meet this demand by manufactured articles; and she met it therefore with the food supply of the people to a larger extent than she would otherwise have exported."[6] Dutt inferred that the agriculturists raised cash to pay their land revenue by selling foodgrains. These foodgrains were quickly transported by the railroads to the seaports and exported to Europe. These exports formed part of a long-term excess of exports over imports that financed the transfer of tribute from India to Great Britain but "the brisk grain trade . . . concealed the fact that the homes and villages of a cultivating nation are denuded of their food to a fatal extent. . . ."[7] Dutt realized that increased demand for Indian agricultural products encouraged expansion of cultivation and raised prices, but the gains from these processes that might be expected to accrue to agriculturists, he argued, were swallowed up by increases in land revenue in the areas that were not permanently settled. As cultivation expanded, land taxes were demanded on newly cultivated fields, and as prices rose, each resettlement brought an increase in the level of land taxes.[8] Already-poor Indians were brought even closer to famine by the export of foodgrains. Dutt did give figures on the value of grain exported, but he did not examine the quantity of grain exported in relation to the volume of grain produced in the subcontinent or to the per capita needs of the population.

While several modern writers on the same period that Dutt so forcefully handled have a somewhat different emphasis—tending to stress, more than Dutt did, the destruction of corporate village

[5] Dutt, *Economic History of India*, vol. p. v.
[6] Dutt, *Economic History of India*, vol. 2, p. 262.
[7] Dutt, *Economic History of India*, vol. 2, pp. 252-253.
[8] Dutt, *Economic History of India*, vol. 2, p. 253.

responsibility for land revenue, particularly in Bombay Presidency, and the increasing economic differentiation of the peasantry[9]—their analysis of the causes of famines has not changed. For instance, Irfan Habib wrote in an article published in 1975:

> This vast change in Indian agriculture (sometimes called 'commercialization') had a polarizing effect on the rural population. As the quantity of food available for the home market declined— and it declined as fast as the railway network extended—famines repeatedly ensued. It had been the expectation of the proponents of the railways that these would help to banish famines by bringing in supplies. But the very opposite took place: the supplies went out! This is not the place to chronicle the famines, which has in any case been done often. Suffice it to say that they steadily increased in frequency and scale, culminating in the great famines of 1896-97 and 1899-1900, when millions perished.[10]

It is worth noting that neither Habib nor the sources he cites for this paragraph have presented any new evidence about the period.

The arguments advanced by Dutt and taken up by other writers raise a number of questions that can be answered by data generated in the course of this study of famines in western India. The answers are necessarily most clearly applicable to the parts of Bombay Presidency studied in detail. But since Dutt tended to regard the Bombay Survey and Settlement system as one of the worst from the point of view of the peasantry, this limitation loses some of its force.

II. Questions and Answers

There are several questions that flow from Dutt's work and cover most of his argument. First, were the famines of 1896-1897 and 1899-1900 the worst ever? Second, was the land revenue between 1837 and 1900 increasing as rapidly as cultivation was extended during the course of a settlement and, at the time of resettlement, was the land revenue increase in excess of the rise in prices during the previous 30 years? If we can find the answers to this two-part question we shall be well along towards knowing whether the share of produce left to agriculturists for their own use was rising or falling over this period. Finally, how large were exports relative to outputs,

[9] R. Kumar, "Rise of Rich Peasants."
[10] Irfan Habib, "Colonization of the Indian Economy, 1757-1900," *Social Scientist* 3 (March 1975):43.

and would their retention within India have prevented famines? The last part of this question is particularly difficult to answer because of the complexity of the variables that might be considered.

Depending on the answers to this first set of questions, there are two others that logically emerge. First, if British policies on land revenue and trade in foodgrains were not the cause of the famines at the end of the nineteenth century, then what were the causes? Second, what changes in policy or economy after 1900 so sharply reduced the incidence and/or importance of famines? The remainder of this section of the chapter discusses these questions in the order that they have been asked.

Severity of Famines

In part, disputation over the severity of famines is somewhat like the question about whether or not there is a "noise" if a tree falls in the middle of a forest and there is no human nearby to "hear" it fall. We know from a variety of sources—records of the East India Company, records of the Mughal Empire, records of regional kingdoms, religious literature—that famines occurred over much of South Asia for as much of its history as we can examine. Some of these famines have been attributed to the ravages of wars, others to floods or drought. But only for famines that occurred *after* the government of Great Britain became directly responsible for the governance of India (1858) do we have any very full or complete evidence of the *severity* (defined here as the elevation of mortality) of famines. Evidence from earlier periods is, at best, fragmentary not only on the mortality caused by famines, but also on the frequency of their occurrence. Thus, to say that famines in the latter half of the nineteenth century were unprecedented in frequency and severity is to do what any excellent politician (and Dutt and his colleagues in the Nationalist movement were among the best) might wisely do—to make political use of crises.

However, the absence of data to confirm Dutt's statement makes it not wrong, but merely unsupported. It is necessary to take at least a cursory glance at one earlier period to see if it seems likely that Dutt's position can be upheld. Consider the latter half of the sixteenth and the first half of the seventeenth century. Habib has furnished us with an account of both the frequency and the severity of some of the famines in this period. With respect to the great famine of 1630-1632 which occurred in both Gujarat and the Deccan, he has written:

The most harrowing scenes were witnessed. Parents sold their children so that they might live. There was wholesale migration in the direction of the less affected lands, but few could even complete the first stages of the journey before death overtook them; and the dead blocked the roads ... ultimately cases of cannibalism became common.... Of all the provinces affected Gujarat suffered the most heavily. Three million of its inhabitants are said to have died during the ten months preceding October 1631; while a million reputedly perished in the country of Ahmednagar. The cities of Gujarat were, by death or flight, reduced to almost one-tenth of their former state. The villages could hardly have fared much better.[11]

Habib went on to cite sources that reported that fifteen years later, the revenue collections from this area had not yet recovered their former levels, nor had cultivation.[12]

It seems likely that the estimates of mortality that Habib gave are too high for Gujarat, unless *nine-tenths* of the population was actually removed. After all, the population of the parts of Gujarat included in the Bombay Presidency was only 3.1 million in 1891, which was surely more than it had been in 1631. However, the death of a quarter or a third of the population of Gujarat does seem possible. Habib argued that import of grain into the region was hampered in the first year of the famine because the transport capacity of the *banjaras* was largely utilized in supplying Shahjahan's army at Burhanpur.[13] He also noted that two contemporary sources reported that, while it was mainly the poor who perished in the first year of the famine, by the second year the rich also began to succumb.[14]

The mortality experienced in Gujarat in the famine of 1899-1901 is the worst on record for western India in the British period. Total registered death rates were 36 per thousand for 1899, 157 per thousand for 1900, and 45 per thousand for 1901.[15] Of these total death rates, 93.3 per thousand were attributed to famine in 1899-1900 and 34 per thousand in 1900-1901.[16] These figures indicate that in

[11] Irfan Habib, *The Agrarian System of Mughal India (1556-1707)* (New York: Asia Publishing House, 1963), pp. 103-104.

[12] Habib, *Agrarian System*, p. 105.

[13] Habib, *Agrarian System*, p. 104.

[14] Habib, *Agrarian System*, p. 103.

[15] See Appendix B, Table B-6.

[16] Chapter 3, Table 3.13. Deaths from famines were estimated for agricultural years (April 1 to March 31) while general demographic statistics were compiled for

the worst portion of this two-year famine, about fifteen to sixteen percent of the population died, and that about three-fourths of those deaths were caused by famine. Terrible as these levels of deaths in 1899-1901 were, they do not approach either the levels Habib cites or even the much more modest levels to which it seems reasonable to reduce the estimates of mortality for 1630-1631.

When we turn to the study of the frequency of famines, our problems are no less substantial than when we study their severity. A key part of the problem is almost certainly a change in the use of the word "famine." As Moreland, writing in the 1920s, noted: "It is . . . impossible to compare the frequency of famines in the two periods [sixteenth and seventeenth vs. nineteenth and twentieth centuries] because the significance of the word has altered in the interval: a famine is now a period when distress is such as to require the intervention of the State, but if we were to rely upon the chronicles of the sixteenth century, we should define it as a period when men and women were driven by hunger to eat human flesh."[17] Whatever the problems of shifting definitions, Habib cited famines or severe scarcities in the Mughal Empire in 1554-1556, the mid-1560s, 1572-1573, 1574-1575, 1578-1579, 1587, 1588, 1589-1590, 1596, 1613-1615, 1630-1632, 1636-1637, 1640, 1642, 1644, 1646, 1647, 1648, 1650, 1651, 1658-1660, 1662-1663, 1670, 1682, 1685, 1691, 1694-1695, 1696-1697, and 1702-1704.[18] Using the commercial records of the Dutch and English trading companies, Moreland constructed a partial list of scarcities that includes the years 1618-1619, 1630, 1635, 1640, 1642-1643, 1645-1647, 1648, 1650, 1658, and 1659-1660.[19] While these lists of the frequency of severe scarcity and famines are, as Moreland has pointed out, not directly comparable to lists from the second half of the nineteenth century, it would be clearly unwise to accept at face value statements that famines were more frequent and severe in this latter period than at any earlier one. As Habib has written: "The famines thus, from time to time, introduced into the stolid isolation of agricultural production, a terrible element of fluidity and confusion. If there had been

---

calendar years. Therefore the data on total death rates and those on estimates of deaths from famine do not cover exactly the same periods, although they do overlap.

[17] W. H. Moreland, *India at the Death of Akbar* (Delhi: Atma Ram & Sons, 1962), p. 119.

[18] Habib, *Agrarian System*, pp. 101-109.

[19] W. H. Moreland, *From Akbar to Aurangzeb: A Study in Indian Economic History* (first published 1923; reprinted ed. New Delhi: Oriental Books Reprint Corporation, 1972), pp. 207-209.

nothing else, this alone would have sufficed to explain the migratory characteristics of the medieval peasantry."[20]

Share of Land Revenue in Agricultural Output

Dutt argued that in the Bombay Presidency, revenue collections during the 30-year settlement increased as rapidly as cultivation and that this tended to increase the burden of this tax because land brought into cultivation in the course of the settlement period could be expected to be of lower productivity than that already under cultivation. He further argued that at the time of resettlement, the level of land revenue was raised, thereby taking an even larger share of the harvest from cultivators.[21] The government of Bombay, Dutt argued, saw these increases as justified by rising prices and improved access to markets.

A challenge to this argument hinges on two key variables. The first of these is the amount of rupees of land revenue collected per acre (nominal value of collections) and the second is the number of *maunds* of jowar that had to be sold at prevailing prices to pay this rupee amount (real value of collections or real collections). Tables 7.1 and 7.2 summarize for the twelve *talukas* of Bombay Presidency that were studied intensively in Chapter 4 the course of these two variables from the quinquennium before the introduction of the Bombay Survey and Settlement system to that after the first resettlement. (For the intervening quinquennia and the precise years when settlements went into effect, see Appendix C.)

From Table 7.1 it is clear that at the time of the first settlements, nominal collections per acre were reduced (by widely varying amounts in different *talukas*). It is also clear that they continued to fall during the term of the first settlement and that they rose with the intro-

---

[20] Habib, *Agrarian Systems*, p. 110.

[21] Dutt commonly used the share of produce taken by the government as his measure of the land revenue burden and I have also done so. Some may think that it would be better to attempt to use the share of the *economic rent* collected in taxes instead. This has not been done for two reasons. First, no one, either in the Bombay Survey and Settlement system or in the cadre of scholars who work on Indian economic history, has been able to separate the economic rent from returns to labor and capital. Second, could we do so we would succeed in imposing a very western category on agriculturists without being at all confident that this category had any relevance to the ways they made decisions about holding and cultivating land. When the dominant mode of agriculture is owner cultivation, the separation of family maintenance from the operation of the farm is difficult both conceptually and empirically. In these contexts, the share of total output that must be surrendered to the government has the advantage of being reasonably simple to estimate and, I argue, more relevant to the farm family's perception of its well-being than the more abstract, if more elegant, concept of the share of economic rent.

TABLE 7.1. Nominal Values of Revenue Collections in 12 *Talukas* of
Bombay Presidency Before, During, and After First 30-Year Settlement[a]

Division, District, and Taluka	Collections in Quinquennium (rupees per acre)				Column 4 as Percent of Column 1
	(1) Before First Settlement	(2) After First Settlement	(3) Before First Resettlement	(4) After First Resettlement	
DECCAN					
Khandesh					
Amalner	1.75	1.43	1.03	1.35	77
Erandol	1.69	1.35	1.03	1.16	69
Ahmednagar					
Ahmednagar	.82	.62	.54	.70	85
Shevgaon	.75	63	.48	.65	87
Satara					
Khatav	.79	.64	.51	.61	77
Man	.37	.30	27	.31	84
KARNATAK					
Belgaum					
Sampgaon	1.58	1.39	1.22	1.53	97
Athni	.49	.46	.41	.59	120
Bijapur					
Bagalkot	79	.60	.59	.66	84
Badami	.78	.56	.55	.60	77
Dharwar					
Kod	1.43	.99	.96	1.11	78
Ron	.92	.62	.65	.86	93

[a]Because all of the data underlying this table have been reduced to five-year averages, the exact year of settlement falls sometimes at the beginning, sometimes in the middle, and sometimes at the end of a quinquennium. Where the actual date was at the beginning or end, I have selected quinquennia for this table designed to contrast as effectively as possible the status before and after settlement. The settlement years are given in Appendix C.

SOURCE: Appendix C.

duction of the first resettlement. However, a glance at the last column of the table, which gives nominal collections in the quinquennium after the first resettlement as a percentage of nominal collections in the quinquennium before the first settlement, shows that in every *taluka* except one (Athni in Belgaum), nominal collections per acre were smaller at the end of the period than they had been at the beginning of the period. This does not mean that the government of Bombay was collecting less revenue at the end of the period than at the beginning, but rather that it was, in most cases and on the average, collecting less revenue from each of a much larger number of acres occupied for cultivation.

During the course of the first settlement, as can be seen by comparing columns 2 and 3 in Table 7.1, average nominal collections per acre declined in eleven of twelve *talukas*. This is what we would expect, since the Bombay Survey and Settlement system assessed lower taxes on lands of lower quality, and as these lands were taken up in the term of the first settlement they pulled down the average payments per acre for the *taluka*. Dutt was clearly wrong, then, when he argued that revenue collections in the Presidency increased in proportion to the increase in cultivation. However, since the declines in nominal collections are in many cases quite small, it is possible that, had prices been constant, the share of produce that had to be sold from all fields to pay this average land revenue per acre might have risen. That is, the productivity of new lands might have been proportionately lower than the taxes on them. Given the state of our figures on productivity, we may never know whether that would have been the case.

However, the issue is irrelevant, since prices during this period were not constant but had a strong upward trend. In Table 7.2, where real values of collections per acre are given, we can see that these values fell much more rapidly during the course of the first settlement than nominal collections did. That is, even though the average number of rupees that had to be paid in land tax for each acre in, say, Badami *taluka* of Bijapur district declined only from .56 to .55, the number of *maunds* of jowar that had to be sold to get that many rupees declined by almost 40 percent.[22] In the historical case as it actually occurred, nominal collections per acre declined slightly during the first settlement in eleven of these *talukas*, but the real value of collections per acre fell much more due to rising prices. The inevitable result was that more produce was left in the hands of the cultivators—although there may have been other factors at work in the agricultural sector to remove some of this produce from them.

In the last column of Table 7.2, where the real value of collections per acre in the quinquennium after the first resettlement is given as a percentage of the real value per acre in the quinquennium before the first settlement, we can see that real collections per acre

[22] Obviously, it would be more satisfactory to use a weighted price index for all commodities commonly grown for sale in these regions to determine changes in the real value of collections per acre. Lack of adequate price data for long series of years makes this alternative not feasible. The use of jowar prices only probably does not impart a systematic bias to changes over time, although it may well tend to bias upwards at a point in time the share of produce that was needed to pay the land revenue. It may have this effect because alternate crops were higher in value.

TABLE 7.2. Real Values of Revenue Collections in 12 *Talukas* of
Bombay Presidency Before, During and After First 30-Year Settlement[a]

Division, District, and Taluka	Value of Collections (maunds of jowar per acre)				Column 4 as Percent of Column 1
	(1) Before First Settlement	(2) After First Settlement	(3) Before First Resettlement	(4) After First Resettlement	
DECCAN					
Khandesh					
Amalner	2.73	1.72	.56	.81	30
Erandol	2.41	1 69	.52	.64	27
Ahmednagar					
Ahmednagar	.77	.67	.24	.35	45
Shevgaon	1.09	.83	.35	.32	29
Satara					
Khatav	1.36	.90	.23	.26	19
Man	.47	.28	.12	.14	30
KARNATAK					
Belgaum					
Sampgaon	1.41	1.25	.73	.82	58
Athni	__b	.43	.29	30	70[c]
Bijapur					
Bagalkot	__b	.92	.45	.36	39[c]
Badami	1.24	.70	.43	.40	32
Dharwar					
Kod	5.50	3.81	.60	1.22	22
Ron	1 10	.89	63	.57	52

[a]See note to Table 7 1.

[b]Jowar prices not available.

[c]Column 4 as percent of column 2.

SOURCE· Appendix C.

fell in all *talukas*. Experience, however, was varied: In Khatav *taluka* of Satara district, the real value of average collections per acre had fallen to only 19 percent of its original value, while in Sampgaon *taluka* of Belgaum district, the real value of collections per acre remained at 58 percent of its initial value. Nevertheless, is it possible, given these figures, to argue that land revenue collections were maintained at such a pitch as to leave the cultivator no larger a share of his produce at the end of the period than at the beginning? If the relative shares of government and cultivator were to be constant in the face of these kinds of declines in the value of real collections per acre, average productivity per acre must also have dropped dramatically. For instance, if the government's share of the produce from a set of fields in the *taluka* of Amalner in Khandesh district were to have remained constant while the real value of collections per acre for these fields fell from 2.73 *maunds* of jowar per acre to 0.81 *maunds* of jowar per acre, average productivity per acre must have undergone a like decline—to have dropped in the quinquennium after the first resettlement to 30 percent of what it had been in the quinquennium before the first settlement. The argument is the same for any other of these *talukas*. Productivity of newly cultivated fields low enough to reduce average productivity even to 60 or 70 percent of its initial figure seems extremely unlikely. Dutt's argument that government took a constant or increasing share of produce in Bombay Presidency during the second half of the nineteenth century cannot be confirmed using these *taluka*-level data. Because the decline in real value of collections per acre is so much more important than the change in nominal collections per acre, and because this decline is due to rising prices, it seems very likely that detailed studies in other regions of India will also show a decline in the real value of collections per acre—a decline that will almost certainly outpace any decline in average productivity per acre.

One final note to this section: Dutt has repeatedly stated that no capital accumulation could take place in Bombay Presidency because of the constant increases in land revenue. It may therefore be worthwhile to recall Table 4.2 from Chapter 4, where substantial increases in carts, wells, agricultural cattle, and superior houses are recorded. These increases in capital during the first 30-year settlement were possible because cultivators kept an increasing share of their output.

Export Trade in Foodgrains

We turn next to the argument that high and rising land revenue demands forced grain into the market—grain that was then exported to leave the country particularly liable to famine. The finding that the real burden of land revenue as a share of output was falling in western India in the second half of the nineteenth century certainly suggests that increased sales of grain were voluntary rather than forced by the need to meet rising real values of revenue collections. However, particularly in regions where the distribution of claims to agricultural produce was very uneven, it is still possible that the rich sold for export the grain that the poor needed to eat.

Table 7.3 gives the annual tonnage of wheat and rice exports from India between 1871 and 1919 as well as estimates of these exports

TABLE 7.3. Total and Per Capita Exports of Wheat and Rice
from India, 1871-1919

Years	Average Yearly Total Exports of Wheat and Rice (thousand tons)	Exports Per Capita (pounds)
1871-1875	984.4	8.6
1876-1880	1,200.3	10.5
1881-1885	2,149.0	18.7
1886-1890	2,330.7	19.4
1891-1895	2,339.0	18.6
1896-1900	2,041.3	16.1
1901-1905	2,949.2	23.2
1906-1910	2,679.6	20.4
1911-1915	3,599.0	26.6
1916-1919	2,656.2	19.6

SOURCES. Exports calculated from McAlpin, "Impact of Trade," p. 28. Population figures used as divisors, from Davis, *Population*, p. 27 (with, e.g., the 1872 population figure used as the divisor for the 1871-1875 exports, and the average of the 1872 and 1881 population figures used as the divisor for the 1876-1880 exports).

in per capita terms.[23] Before discussing the substantive meaning of this table, a word on the statistics themselves is needed. The per capita exports are overstatements. The population divisors for particular periods (1876-1880, 1896-1900, 1916-1919) are too low because the divisors are a simple average of beginning and ending population. While this process biases all of the estimates up somewhat, its effect is greater in those periods when the second half of a decade witnessed unusually high mortality. Per capita exports are nevertheless preferred to exports as a share of output because the latter series would have even more serious flaws. First, exports include all of India while output figures include only British India and ignore princely India. A series of exports as a share of output would therefore have an unknown and probably unknowable upward bias. Second, for reasons elaborated at length in Chapter 2, any and all output series can be constructed only by the most daring leaps of faith because of the frailty of the underlying yield data.

Exports per capita fluctuated around a rising trend over the period 1871-1919, with the peak involving the export of little more than 26 pounds of grain per person per year in the quinquennium 1911-1915. If exports of foodgrains had, in general, been prohibited, would

[23] No grains other than wheat and rice were exported from India in significant volume.

the famines at the end of the nineteenth century have been prevented? It is tempting at first to answer "yes." For instance, if grain exports had been forbidden between 1891 and 1895, then, we might reason, at the beginning of the crop failure of 1896-1897 there would have been 93 pounds (18.6 lbs./year x 5 years) more stored grain available for each person in India (assuming that there were no losses in storage). That amount is about one-fourth of the yearly grain requirement of an adult. So large a stock could not but have helped to keep grain prices down, even if it could not have done anything to help those thrown out of work by the drought find money to buy food. Yet the answer, however plausible it may seem, is far too simplistic. To be precise, it assumes that nothing in the relations of production, distribution, or consumption would have been changed by a prohibition of foodgrain exports *except* that grain that would have been exported would instead have been stored in India.

While this is clearly not the place to examine all of the changes in the Indian economy that might have been brought about by a prohibition of foodgrain exports, consider only the following three. First, if exports of foodgrains had been forbidden, prices for foodgrains probably would have been lower. If this were the case, would as many acres have been planted with wheat and rice, or would these acres have been planted instead with cotton, sugar cane, and jute? In other words, if foodgrain exports had been forbidden, would the same amount of foodgrains still have been produced? Possibly not. Second, if foodgrain prices were lower, how would this affect the share of produce that had to be sold to pay the land revenue? If some land was shifted to cotton, sugar cane, and jute, tending to increase supplies of those goods and lower their prices, then agriculturists could find themselves confronting generally lower agricultural prices and having to sell more of their output to pay the land revenue. Their incomes would fall. Third, if agricultural incomes fell, how would this have affected the growth of sectors that sold to agriculture? Could the cotton textile industry, for instance, have grown as fast as it did?

This line of questioning could be continued. What is clear from even this much analysis, however, is that additional foodgrains would not necessarily have existed to be utilized within the economy if their export had been forbidden. How large any changes in prices and output might have been can be determined only by empirical work to estimate the relevant supply and demand relationships. In any case, exports of foodgrains in the second half of the nineteenth century do not seem to have been caused by the pressure of in-

creasing real land revenue collections, nor is it clear that the prohibition of these exports would have increased the supply of food
available to the Indian economy. It does not appear that exports of
foodgrain can have been a major cause of the famines at the end
of the nineteenth century.

Causes of Famines

There is a complex social and economic matrix through which
an initial decline in available food supplies is distributed among the
population.[24] If that social and economic matrix can distribute the
initial shortage very equally across the population, then there is a
range of declines in food supplies that can be dealt with in the
society without any starvation. Very large shortages may exceed the
ability of even the most equitable and efficient systems to avoid all
starvation. It should be noted that the controlling groups within a
society may well place different values on different lives and seek
not to prevent deaths but to assure the survival of some segment
of the population that they deem to be most important. The elaborate
social system of the Tuareg was designed precisely to *avoid* an equal
distribution of access to scarce resources in times of drought. The
Tuareg's system was intended to preserve the upper level of society
first and then as many more people as possible—but not necessarily
all of the people. In contrast, most modern governments have been
committed, at least on paper, to the general preservation of life. The
success of their efforts, rightly or wrongly, has been judged by how
many people died and only secondarily by how many people were
left without resources to resume their normal lives at the end of a
famine.

Since the elevation of mortality has been used as the measure of
the severity of famine in this book (and by the government of India
and its critics), a recapitulation of the causes of the famines at the

---

[24] A. K. Sen, "Starvation and Exchange," has argued that it is misleading to attribute famines to declines in the availability of food. Rather, he argues, famines
result when a share of the population is deprived, for whatever reason, of its enti-
tlement to exchange some service (most often its labor) or good for food at the price
that usually prevails in the economy. I tend to see Sen's "failure of exchange enti-
tlement" as just one special case of all those possible ways that a society can, through
its social and economic matrix, distribute the effects of some initial decline in food
supplies or rise in the prices of food across the population. There are some levels of
shortage so severe that even if food could be very evenly distributed, some starvation
would still result. Unjust as it seems to us, few societies where famines have been
studied seem to have had indigenous mechanisms for coping with food shortfalls
that encouraged equal distribution of food.

end of the nineteenth century necessarily focuses on the cause and size of the decline in food supplies and on the way the society and economy distributed those shortages across the population. As Chapter 2 and Chapter 6 have shown, the period from 1896 to 1905 was an unusually dry one in Bombay Presidency. The Index of the Quality of the Agricultural Season (IQAS) generally shows its lowest single-year values in 1899-1900 and its lowest five-year averages in one of the quinquennia from 1896 through 1910. Both the rainfall and the crops that depended upon the rainfall were bad during this period—worse, in fact, than in any of the preceding or following periods for which we have the same kinds of data available. The episodic declines of food production at the end of the nineteenth and the beginning of the twentieth centuries were large absolutely and large in relation to other such declines, at least for the area included in Bombay Presidency.

If we were considering a time before, say, 1850, it would be enough for most regions of South Asia to note that food production had declined very sharply to explain a famine. For parts of India largely dependent on overland trade, the costs and the physical limits of this trade made it impossible to move so bulky a commodity as grain in amounts large enough to relieve a widespread crop failure. But by the end of the nineteenth century a large trade in grain and pulses was being carried by the railroads. This trade was not by any means all used up in carrying exports to the port cities; a considerable proportion remained as grain carried from one part of the interior to another.[25] As a result, even rather large declines in food production could be compensated for by imports from other regions of India. We need, therefore, to seek further to see why elevations of mortality should nonetheless have occurred as a result of these particular crop failures.

If food supplies were adequate (and there is not much dispute that they were sufficient for the subcontinent as a whole), then we must ask why some or all of the population did not consume enough of these supplies to avert elevations of mortality. In any rural community the incomes of a number of persons who earn a living by activities other than the cultivation of their own lands are determined by (1) the amount of agricultural work available and (2) the disposable income of the agriculturists. But when there is a drought, the amount of agricultural work for which labor is hired can fall

[25] Michelle Burge McAlpin, "The Impact of Trade on Agricultural Development: Bombay Presidency 1855-1920," *Explorations in Economic History* 17 (January 1980):28-30, and Table 6.5 above.

towards zero. Dry fields cannot be plowed and sown, unsown fields do not have to be weeded, and poor crops take little labor to harvest. The income of all but the wealthiest cultivators may be too much reduced to permit the purchase of any nonessential items—new clothing is not bought and the weavers suffer, new houses are not built and carpenters and associated craftsmen have smaller incomes. The *balutedars* of the village, even in a year of drought, receive their share of the output, but when that output is dramatically reduced, so are their incomes. The cultivators themselves may still have enough to eat—from stored grain from previous harvests or, by the late nineteenth century, because they have assets and credit to enable them to buy grain imported into the region. But unless other members of the rural community can find alternative sources of employment to enable them to earn income, the mere fact that railroads can bring in food will not avert their suffering. Most, though not all, of these noncultivating members of the rural community are unlikely to have many stored assets to be converted into grain; they must have employment as the drought progresses if they are to have money to buy food.

Sources of employment and income from activities other than the normal yearly work of local agriculture are essential, then, to the prevention of distress—leading perhaps to mortality—among those sections of the rural community with few if any stored assets and little credit. The fewer and smaller such alternate sources of employment and income are, the more likely that a severe drought will cause elevations of mortality even though the transport capacity exists to alleviate any aggregate shortage of food in the region.[26]

During the famines of the nineteenth and early twentieth centuries the government of India focused its efforts on generating employment for those people whose normal work was unavailable (or unremunerative, like that of weavers) during the drought. Efforts to give people food directly, as charity, took second place. While both railway construction after 1880 and railway rates in times of declared famine were formed with the ability to move grain into a drought-stricken region as an explicit consideration, the govern-

[26] Even with alternate employment available, weaker sections of the society that exist in all times at least partly on charity may suffer high rates of mortality. One of the authors of the text of the 1901 census for Bombay reported the almost total disappearance from the Bombay Presidency since the 1891 census of the blind, the insane, and lepers. As he noted, these people could not make use of available relief, either works or charity, when their usual sources of support were withdrawn. *Census of India*, 1901, vol. 9, pt. 1.

ment of India did not generally permit its constituent parts to import grain into a region on government account, nor did it practice the distribution of free food to the population at large. In Bombay Presidency the government fed people who were confined in poor houses (usually those judged too old, ill, or weak to work) and assisted some people in their villages with free food, but most charity was left to private individuals or groups of individuals.

The famine of 1896-1897 in Bombay Presidency was certainly severe, particularly in the Deccan, but it caused less than 60 percent as much mortality as the famine of 1876-1878. Neither of these periods of drought, it should be noted, resulted in a declaration of famine in Gujarat (see Table 3.13). It was in the droughts of 1899-1900 and 1900-1901 that mortality in both Gujarat and the Deccan reached its highest levels, with Gujarat recording higher mortality from famine than any other part of Bombay Presidency ever had. Since we have found Dutt's explanations of the causes of famines unconvincing, we need to come to some other conclusions to explain the extraordinary mortality in this famine.

In part, the severity of the drought and the resulting almost total cessation of agricultural operations were responsible for these elevations of mortality. A larger proportion of the rural population was necessarily affected by a severe drought than by a mild one—perhaps including even cultivators in the Deccan who had used up a major portion of their stored assets in surviving the drought of 1896-1897. Because of the severity of the drought and because of the closeness with which it followed that of 1896-1897, the need of the population for alternate sources of employment and income was unusually great.

Basically, five sources of alternative employment in a drought year were available in Bombay Presidency near the end of the nineteenth century. The first was agricultural work in adjacent regions where drought had not curtailed agricultural operations. But this drought was a widespread one in Gujarat and the Deccan and their adjacent regions, so that relative to need, agricultural work in nearby regions was probably also scarce. Second, work might be available on construction projects in rural areas—railroad embankments, irrigation canals, roads, and the like. We do not know the extent of such employment in 1899-1901 in the Deccan and Gujarat. A third source of employment was in making capital improvements to land, financed either by individuals or by the government through *takavi* loans. This method of financing land improvements and incidentally generating employment was widely used in the Karnatak and the

Deccan, but there is no evidence that it had become common in Gujarat before 1899. Fourth, labor might migrate to urban areas in the hope of finding employment there. However, the chances of factory employment for large numbers of agricultural workers in a year of drought were small. Factory employment could help a family, a village, or a *taluka* to survive a drought, but only if some members of the group were regularly employed in a factory and had earnings that could be used to supplement lean agricultural incomes. While for all of Bombay Presidency, average daily employment of mill hands in the cotton textile industry was 110,000 in 1899, almost 70 percent of these were employed in Bombay City, where Gujaratis formed an insignificant part of the labor force.[27] In the absence of contrary evidence, it may be assumed that most of the cotton textile mill jobs in Ahmedabad were filled by Gujaratis, but the total number of jobs was not large relative to the distressed population in 1899-1901.

Fifth and finally, government relief works could provide employment at wages that were set to enable workers to buy specific amounts of grain and other foodstuffs. Because no famine had been declared in Gujarat in 1876-1878 or 1896-1897, the majority of civil servants in that division had had no experience with setting up or running relief works. Nor had the laboring population or the smaller cultivators become accustomed to seeking work from the government in years of drought. As Table 7.4 shows, a slightly larger proportion of the population of Gujarat received some form of relief than in the Deccan. But it also shows that, compared to what was usual, the average IQAS was much worse in the districts of Gujarat in 1899-1900. In addition, the composition of relief efforts was different in the Gujarat from what it was in the Deccan: a smaller percentage of those receiving government relief were workers or their dependents and a much larger percent were gratuitously relieved.

While this might at first glance make it appear that in Gujarat, government officials offered more humane relief—that is, they did not require people to work to earn money to buy food—it may also have other interpretations that are more consistent with the much higher death rates experienced in Gujarat than in the Deccan. The first of these is that relief works adequate to the demand for work were not organized and rules about allowing dependents to stay with workers at the works were very tight. As a result, more of those relieved may have *had* to be relieved gratuitously because of the

[27] Table 5.6, and Morris, *Emergence of Industrial Labor*, p. 63.

TABLE 7.4. Death Rates, IQAS, and Percentage and Composition of
Relieved Population in Famine of 1899-1900

	Gujarat	Deccan
Excess death rate per thousand population 1899-1900	93.3	26.7
Average IQAS, 1899-1900	14	42
Total daily average number relieved as a percent of 1891 population	9.6	8.8
Composition of relieved (percent):		
Relief workers	56	68
Their dependents	9	19
Gratuitously relieved	35	12

SOURCES: Excess death rate – Table 3.13. Average IQAS – Calculated from Appendix A,
Table A-3. Relief statistics – Calculated from *Report on the Famine in Bombay
Presidency*, 1899-1902, Appendix 10.

unavailability of work for them. A second possibility is that works
were opened late, after part of the population needing relief had
become to weak to work—and after their dependents had already
perished—and that these remaining individuals were therefore relieved gratuitously. A third possibility is that the presence of large
numbers of tribals required larger amounts of gratuitous relief because no works could be organized for them that were close enough
to their homes that they could be persuaded to go to the works.
Detailed studies of Gujarat before and during this famine are needed
to determine precisely which alternate sources of income and employment were particularly lacking or underutilized in Gujarat compared to the Deccan. However, it seems possible to suggest already
that the very high death rates in Gujarat resulted from (1) the
severity of the drought and the harvest failure, (2) an unfamiliarity
on the part of both the people and the civil servants with coping
with such severe drought and crop failure, and (3) a shortage of
alternative sources of income and employment for the distressed
population resulting in part from (2) but also partly from longer-
term phenomena.

III. Towards a New Synthesis on Agrarian Change in Western India

Both D. R. Gadgil and B. M. Bhatia have noted and explained the
declining political concern with drought and famines in the decades

after 1900. They attributed some of the change to various activities by the government—such as irrigation—that decreased the potential for reduced food output and that changed the rules about the collection and suspension of land revenue. Each of them also saw the reforms that moved India towards self-government as important in generating the changes mentioned above as well as others that further reduced the havoc caused by drought and improved relief efforts in times of drought. In addition, Bhatia mentioned increased mobility of labor as lessening the impact of drought by permitting agricultural laborers "to migrate to urban areas for employment,"[28] and he stressed the importance of foodgrain imports after 1921 to help explain why "from 1910 to 1940 there were 18 scarcities but no loss of life due to starvation over the entire period."[29] Bhatia apparently chose to ignore such loss of life as could be attributed to famine conditions in 1911-1912 and 1918-1919.

The explanations that Gadgil and Bhatia offered are only partly consistent with their explanations for the occurrence of famines up to the end of the nineteenth century. Both of them saw the level of land revenue as destructive earlier and viewed changes in the methods of its collection as reducing the likelihood of famine. Both also stressed the increased responsiveness of government, as a result of increasing Indian representation. And each saw some role for economic factors—Gadgil noted rising prices for agricultural goods and Bhatia noted increased mobility of labor into urban areas in years of stress. But their arguments were not well supported with evidence, nor were their underlying premises always consistent with existing data.

Consider land revenue. As has been shown, real value of land revenue collections in one area where detailed data are available had been declining rather steadily (and had reached generally low absolute levels) *before* the end of the nineteenth century. Since the declines were due more to long-term movements of prices than to specific revenue policies, they are likely to have been widespread. While it surely is the case that real value of revenue collections per acre continued to fall as prices rose after 1900, this trend was not new. In the absence of detailed studies, the effects of new policies on suspension and remission of land revenue in years when crops were below normal cannot be determined. It seems unlikely that

[28] Bhatia, *Famines in India*, pp. 282-308; Gadgil, "Introduction" to Dutt, *Economic History of India*, 1:xx.
[29] Bhatia, *Famines in India*, p. 309.

such policies could have offered much help to agriculturists in areas where the real value of collections per acre was already low.

Explanations that attribute change in the serious effects of droughts to increased Indian representation in government suffer from a similar lack of detailed research that would permit us to determine what changes came about as "popular ministers in the provinces, industry, agriculture, forestry, etc. began to receive closer and more active governmental attention and assistance."[30] Such research as there is on industrial policy between 1900 and 1925 does not offer much support for Gadgil's position.[31]

In preference to the explanations offered by Gadgil and Bhatia, I want to outline and provide some support for an alternative set. This set stresses, to the exclusion of political factors, changes in the economic environment and behavioral responses to those changes. Essentially, India was going through changes and gaining the ability to contain shortfalls in harvest that many European states had completed by the early decades of the nineteenth century. As with these European states, a key element in the ability to withstand harvest shortfalls was the improved transport network and the greater penetration of the market into rural areas. These changes had several effects. First, they tended to raise rural incomes by providing higher prices for farm goods that were sold, thereby increasing the chances of agriculturists to accumulate assets. Second, after 1900, when large flows of grain among regions became common (see Table 5.3), agriculturists could more safely give up growing grain to insure themselves against drought. This form of self-insurance had been a very expensive one, requiring storage each year of perhaps twenty percent of a year's consumption needs to be effective. This represented grain that might otherwise have been sold or land that might have been used to grow some other crop. Obviously, these stores were very nearly without price in years of severe harvest shortfalls, but in other years they represented a loss to the system of rotting grain and opportunities foregone. After 1900, however, we observe an increased responsiveness of farmers to prices in allocating their lands among food and nonfood crops, as they increasingly gave up self-insurance with grain and instead either stored other assets and relied upon the market to supply them with grain or expected to

[30] Gadgil, "Introduction" to Dutt, *Economic History of India*, 1:xx.

[31] Clive J. Dewey, "The Government of India's 'New Industrial Policy' 1900-1925: Formation and Failure," in *Economy and Society: Essays in Indian Economic and Social History*, ed. K. N. Chaudhuri and Clive J. Dewey (Delhi: Oxford University Press, 1979), pp. 215-257.

earn money in years of bad harvests from some other form of employment.[32] The gains in income from removal of the need to self-insure cannot be closely estimated but there is no doubt that they were *gains*.

In this changed environment, agriculturists made other decisions that affected the ability of the region as a whole to cope with harvest shortfalls. The combination of the removal of the need to self-insure, rising prices for agricultural goods (both absolutely and relative to nonagricultural goods), and better markets encouraged agriculturists to expand production in general and the production of higher-value, more labor-intensive crops in particular. Both of these changes tended to increase the demand for agricultural labor and to encourage seasonal rural-to-rural migration out of areas where opportunities for agricultural expansion were minimal into those where nature and man (in the form of new irrigation projects) provided more generous opportunities. These migrations, which occurred in all years, provided an important source of income in all years, but especially in those when crops in the home districts of the migrants were bad. In these latter years, the wages from migrant labor both helped families survive the drought itself and enabled them to retain the resources they needed to resume agricultural operations when the rains commenced for the next season. Wages earned by migrants to urban areas probably had a similar role in the rural economy. However, urban factory jobs with their special skill requirements probably did not provide temporary employment to agricultural workers but rather provided another source of income to the family if some of its male members could move permanently to such jobs. Associated urban jobs (carting, general labor, etc.) are more likely to have provided whatever urban employment agricultural workers displaced by drought found in the city.

Overall, the economy of western India had become more diversified and better able to survive adversity. Instead of selling agricultural products only in local markets, agriculturists could now sell in local, urban, regional, and international markets. Instead of being able to buy grain only from the local area, they had access to surpluses from the region and from other regions. Instead of relying entirely upon local agricultural employment for an income, small

---

[32] McAlpin, "Railroads, Prices, and Peasant Rationality," pp. 666-669; Raj Krishna, "Farm Supply Response in India-Pakistan: A Case Study of the Punjab Region," *Economic Journal* 63 (September 1963):477-487; Dharm Narain, *Impact of Price Movements on Areas under Selected Crops in India 1900-1939* (Cambridge: Cambridge University Press, 1965).

agriculturists and agricultural workers could now seek work in other districts and regions where agriculture was more expansive. They could also seek work in urban areas and in nonagricultural activities of rural areas. And, as a last resort, the government could provide relief work in years when the rains failed. This diversification of the economy both raised incomes and lowered risks, and it especially lowered the risk of dying in a famine. After 1920 these risks had been so much reduced that for the first time in five decades of recorded population figures, a sustained high rate of population increase became the norm in both Bombay Presidency and the rest of India.

It should be noted, however, that the gains from diversification of the economy were and are reversible. If administrative capacity breaks down and the transport system with it, areas can be thrown back upon their own resources. To the extent that older insurance mechanisms (like the growth and storage of grain, the use of drought-resistant varieties, and cultivating practices designed to reduce variations in output) have been abandoned, a drought in times of such administrative collapse could have more severe consequences than the droughts that occurred when the regions still had a full measure of indigenous insurance mechanisms.

A New Economic History of Western India, 1818-1847

The information and analysis presented in this book suggest that the older formulations about agrarian change in western India and about the course of agricultural incomes stand in need of revision. While to attempt such a revision is necessarily risky, without one we are left with only a set of facts that are out of congruence with the older theory. The interpretation that follows is consistent with this new set of facts.

With some violence to reality, the period from 1818 to 1947 may be divided into four periods for ease of exposition. The first of these is from 1818 to 1840, bounded by the date of the British conquest of much of what became Bombay Presidency and the date when the first of Wingate and Goldsmid's settlements under the new Bombay Survey and Settlement system became effective. This period was clearly a very bad one for most of the Deccan and the Karnatak. While open warfare ceased for the most part, that was the only benefit of British rule in this early period. Relying on incomplete and perhaps misleading information about the taxable capacity of the region, the East India Company tried to collect taxes that in retrospect were clearly above what the country could pay.

The hardship of the agriculturists asked to pay these taxes was increased by the unwillingness of the East India Company to assume the traditional responsibility of rulers for the reconstruction of agricultural regions ravaged by war and by generally falling prices that increased the real value of already heavy revenue collections. The reasons for the price falls and for their subsequent rises are not clear: the same trends can be observed in several other parts of the world but conclusive explanations are still lacking. Sporadic reductions in revenue demands were made and there were several attempts to improve the general system of assessment and collection, but until the efforts of Wingate and Goldsmid these attempts tended to be shortlived. Under these conditions cultivation appears to have been stagnant or perhaps slightly decreasing (the quality of the cultivation statistics before the Bombay Survey and Settlement makes a more precise statement impossible). There was a severe famine in at least part of the area in the early 1830s and, in the absence of contrary evidence, it seems likely that population was fairly constant over the entire period, with the gains in good years wiped out by famine in other years. Further evidence on this point would be welcome. It is not clear that British rule during this initial period had any particular impact on relations within the village among *patels, mirasdars, uparis*, and *balutedars*.

The second period runs from about 1840 to about 1870, the latter date marking the end of the first 30-year settlement in some *talukas* and a break in the upward trend of prices that had been dominant since the 1840s. During this period a cadastral survey was completed for most parts of the Deccan and the Karnatak. This survey had several effects. First, it generally lowered the level of taxes per acre of land. Second, these taxes now bore a general relationship to the inherent productivity of the land, modified somewhat by the advantages or disadvantages of its location. Third, it made individual cultivators directly responsible to the government for the payment of these taxes and it made continued occupation of specific pieces of land contingent upon the payment of its taxes. For land that was not *inamdari* land, there were no distinctions in tenure from one plot to the next. It was with this cadastral survey that the British actually entered the village in ways that had the potential to alter its internal structure. No longer did one group of cultivators have in their hands the disposition of parts of the uncultivated lands of the village. No longer did the *patel* bargain with the government on behalf of the village. No longer were there distinctions between how *mirasdars* and *uparis* held land. But the word "potential" has been used because we lack the detailed studies that would tell us to what degree the internal structure of the village was actually affected. It is certainly possible that the *mirasdars* as a group succeeded in substituting economic power for their quasi-legal customary jurisdiction in the village.

Whatever the effects of the Bombay Survey and Settlement on the internal structure of the village, after its introduction we can observe a rapid general rise in lands occupied and in cultivation. These changes may have been facilitated by the security of tenure and the lowered tax rates that the new settlements provided, but they were also encouraged by the rise in prices that began in the late 1840s. Fragmentary figures indicate that the population grew during this period but not as rapidly as the area under cultivation increased, suggesting that individuals must have been working harder. The most likely incentive for this intensified labor would seem to be improved prices for agricultural goods and lower tax rates. The climax of the period was reached during the American Civil War, when cotton prices rose dramatically and cultivation expanded with corresponding enthusiasm. This period also saw the beginning of serious construction of what we would now call social overhead capital—the expansion of the road network and the commencement of railroad building. This period was clearly one of rising real incomes in agriculture, because of lower nominal and real tax burdens and the increase in markets for surplus produce. Commercialization of agriculture clearly had not occurred, but new opportunities to market nonfood crops and some other surpluses nonetheless increased agricultural incomes.

The third period, from 1870 to 1920, is divided into two subperiods, stretching from 1870 to 1905 and from 1905 to 1920. Increases in cultivated area in this period were at a much lower rate than in the preceding one, though there appears to have been further increase in the intensity of cultivation. In spite of the disastrous weather conditions in the decade from 1896 to 1905, and in spite of the epidemics of plague and influenza that contributed to keeping population growth down, the trend of agricultural income over this period continued to be an upward one. This was made possible by two trends that characterized the whole period and one that became important only in the second sub-period. First, from 1881-1885 on, the terms of trade were increasingly in favor of agriculture.[33] Second, as agricultural prices continued to rise, the real value of tax

[33] McAlpin, "Price Movements."

collections per acre continued to decline. Both of these trends were in some part made possible by the continued expansion of the transport network for carrying goods to market. After 1905 there is evidence of the abandonment of costly mechanisms for self-insurance and increased commercialization of agriculture. Each of these had a one-time effect in raising the level of agricultural incomes. It should be noted that the gains from all of these increases in income may have been widely distributed. Particularly after 1905 real wages in agriculture were rising, but agricultural employment may have been increasing earlier. And while cultivators with different amounts of surplus produce to market certainly derived different amounts of income from this activity, the evidence we have on, for instance, the construction of better houses, suggests that a major proportion of cultivator families participated in the gains in income.

The fourth and final period considered here includes the years from 1920 to 1947. In some senses this period is a very perplexing one. For the first time since 1872, when good population figures became available, there was sustained increase in population over several decades—an increase of about 1.2 percent per year. What is remarkable is that even though many areas had little room for expansion of cultivation, output appears in general to have kept pace with these population increases. In the Deccan and the Karnatak this appears to have been made possible by increasing the intensity of cultivation, including more irrigation and the introduction of deep plowing of the heavy black soils. Because we know so little about this period, it is difficult to determine if agricultural incomes per capita were rising, steady, or falling. It is clear that even with the easy sources of expansion in the agricultural sector almost exhausted, that sector nevertheless continued to grow at rates that nearly enabled it to keep up with high rates of population growth.

IV. Summary

In the introduction to this volume I pointed out that Dutt's theories about the causes of famines at the turn of the century were a part of a much more general interpretation of the economic history of India under British rule. In the course of this study a number of the strands of Dutt's argument have been subjected to the tests of careful logic, of economic theory, and of new data. While the data have been drawn from Bombay Presidency, many of the conclusions are likely to be found to be equally applicable to other parts of India.

What has emerged from this work is a reinterpretation of nine-teenth-century Indian economic history. I want to stress four elements of this reinterpretation. First, there is no evidence that either the initial land revenue assessments or the revisions of these assessments led to the impoverishment of the *ryots*. Data on revenue collections and on prices of jowar suggest instead that real tax rates declined very sharply between the initiation of the Bombay Survey and Settlement system and the end of the century. The decline in real tax rates, since it is in part the result of rising agricultural prices, may be found to be quite widespread in British India. Second, railroads did not precipitate famines at the end of the century. On the contrary, the development of good transport for bulk commodities permitted the import of grain into regions of harvest failure and thus helped to limit the mortality from such disasters. Again, since this result relies on the creation of a rail network, it may be found to apply to several other Indian regions as well.

Third, the severe famines at the end of the nineteenth century were associated with a period of extraordinary dryness in Bombay Presidency. The repeated years of drought appear to have exhausted the resources of cultivators and to have overwhelmed administrative relief efforts, particularly in Gujarat. Finally, the cessation of periods of major famine has been shown to be due to the development of a transport network, the growing economic opportunities in the region, and the efforts of the British administration to provide an effective relief system. Before the end of the first decade of the twentieth century, recurrent famines had ceased to be a social, economic, and demographic nightmare for India. Since that period there has been only one famine with major loss of life—the Bengal famine of 1943-1944—and that one was due in large measure to the destruction of the very systems—transport, economic opportunities, and government relief—that had helped to mitigate earlier crises.

Appendices

TABLE A-1. Annual Rainfall in Inches, 1858-1945[a]

Year	Ahmedabad Observatory	Kaira	Broach	Surat	Khandesh (Erandol)	Nasik	Ahmednagar	Poona	Sholapı Observat
1856									
1857									
1858		22.28						26.30	
1859		34.28						41.93	
1860		31.06							
1861		28.52							
1862		33.12							
1863		28.03							
1864		15.69							
1865		24.36						34.29	
1866		27.32				23.67		23.38	
1867		20.09				27.31		30.98	
1868		38.91				20.25		38.14	
1869	34.30	33.38				28.51	31.86	27.99	
1870	28.16	38.69				33.01	44.62	37.79	
1871	32.01	33.44				21 86	20.15	28.92	
1872	33.24	58.83				25.41	28.71	22.87	
1873	23.50	22.86				22.21	29.98		
1874	40.30	23.22				35.54	29.62		
1875	23.61	35.92				38.02	21.92	33.84	
1876	22.13	30.38				18.14	8.46	15.37	
1877	21.65	26.44		18.57		21.09	26.07	21.69	32.09
1878	47.89	42.18	63.12	84.61		52.86	24.81	32.78	68.13
1879	31.86	26.48	41.29	35.17	44.11	35.08	28.47	33.64	22.70
1880	28.69	59.10	57.93	32.50	25.78	20.02	20.16	22.23	36.07
1881	33.84	47.69	43.83	29.87	16.72	22.44	18.09	24.73	22.80
1882	31.09	40.96	41.29	42.94	28.81	41.52	21.20	36.23	40.57
1883	20.16	29.41	49.63	50.17	52.49	60.62	41.87	47.42	39.93
1884	35.48	57.91	53.42	40.34	36.52	31.15	23.80	38.39	21.79
1885	22.88	27.36	35.57	38.54	28.27	33.81	20.55	37.53	30.69
1886	33.45	39.71	43.16	49.41	36.13	37.28	43.46	35.53	36.87
1887	25.24	48.27	34.21	39.63	36.38	33.40	23.34	32.45	39.41
1888	14.76	20.06	18.96	29.49	23.29	19.99	19.26	34.02	25.81
1889	24.89	41.22	33.73	40.22	26.27	22.93	23.15	37.49	32.82
1890	22.75	27.24	26.98	56.35	37.03	29.37	21.60	39.52	27.59

Satara	Belgaum Observatory	Bijapur	Dharwar	Kolaba (Alibag)	Thana (Bassein)	Ratnagiri Observatory	Kanara Observatory
	47.88						
	59.02						
	38.83						
	50.05						
43.18	38.17						
53.54	57.72						
34.41	50.91						
48.50							
35.90	39.12						
40.00	45.46						
30.70	46.30						
39.66	38.48						
40.95	50.12						
37.44	48.63						
54.49	55.19						
40.90	36.29						
40.86	45.29						
44.48	40.33						
47.85	56.49						
58.08	63.61						
31.16	35.91						
31.26	46.82					89.67	
47.19	53.97	34.94	39.75	145.02	114.90	165.53	
39.99	54.91	37.52	36.53	74.77	73.83	97.43	
28.68	35.17	27.16	37.00	79.67	79.48	100.96	96.50
35.77	44.05	22.77	30.99	77.11	80.94	82.06	96.63
57.12	73.42	38.78	48.33	89.29	73.40	120.03	113.65
47.31	54.12	25.82	28.57	89.09	98.81	110.84	151.49
47.18	50.84	11.01	25.97	84.22	70.23	108.03	93.56
47.36	50.28	30.18	29.25	76.53	54.60	93.18	115.05
38.02	40.92	31.25	31.39	102.14	76.45	125.10	148.04
46.95	54.19	22.43	36.64	113.11	84.67	114.20	144.67
51.82	48.13	21.92	33.34	75.55	50.74	95.18	126.92
46.21	57.60	36.04	38.64	86.01	79.21	111.43	184.39
37.46	52.13	28.56	28.54	95.65	84.95	126.47	125.04

TABLE A-1 (Continued)

Year	Ahmedabad Observatory	Kaira	Broach	Surat	Khandesh (Erandol)	Nasik	Ahmednagar	Poona	Sholapur Observato
1891	25.68	28.27	58.64	63.89	37.49	25.99	16.18	18.68	23.76
1892	51.18	58.45	39.12	55.15	44.19	35.14	42.16	45.19	39.28
1893	43.53	41.17	52.24	45.45	25.10	38.38	25.55	32.06	33.25
1894	51.06	49.55	65.49	65.08	32.29	20.08	25.35	33.59	20.97
1895	33.63	33.71	28.84	29.07	28.25	29.51	25.97	32.48	31.60
1896	32.75	40.28	69.99	42.83	26.22	36.34	19.66	43.31	18.40
1897	31.80	24.07	42.34	39.02	37.18	28.46	18.23	37.18	20.42
1898	34.89	34.63	47.51	32.52	26.20	27.59	14.73	22.12	34.85
1899	4.84	6.05	9.61	18.49	12.26	14.57	12.32	12.37	12.81
1900	16.02	21.98	32.80	34.19	36.78	32.98	17.85	30.56	18.93
1901	19.13	17.75	22.11	18.45	26.57	16.79	17.36	30.18	24.92
1902	28.03	32.38	49.46	55.08	21.81	30.30	30.31	31.12	30.41
1903	26.32	20.75	46.82	40.19	28.38	25.39	33.47	28.48	43.32
1904	9.60	9.84	15.80	14.29	23.17	20.71	15.10	15.75	22.72
1905	42.36	38.08	17.69	20.26	19.09	20.70	13.64	17.34	14.79
1906	37.95	32.41	42.77	29.86	28.00	22.00	22.20	18.52	19.65
1907	33.31	42.86	35.09	38.88	24.78	30.10	17.12	41.47	25.83
1908	32.31	32.72	28.30	47.45	25.66	17.13	21.31	23.32	25.44
1909	29.83	19.57	42.60	53.26	24.55	31.08	22.47	18.30	37.19
1910	25.46	21.72	44.92	36.48	29.75	34.85	37.11	32.47	29.32
1911	9.83	14.98	18.54	19.63	20.62	18.69	17.42	17.34	19.83
1912	38.72	50.43	54.97	57.49	20.08	28.65	10.03	26.69	15.93
1913	35.86	36.38	43.79	37.65	26.60	51.24	23.77	26.85	15.19
1914	40.67	37.77	42.77	58.39	49.52	39.29	19.70	33.73	28.14
1915	12.08	12.30	18.75	27.57	27.16	31.77	38.25	36.81	30.95
1916	25.24	24.20	47.47	57.28	34.94	35.03	47.23	30.07	48.80
1917	49.29	61.47	58.78	59.54	36.29	28.00	30.55	31.97	31.15
1918	8.43	7.28	13.34	16.31	13.87	17.40	14.57	14.58	15.41
1919	29.27	32.21	38.25	40.09	34.58	33.28	21.59	32.42	30.28
1920	24.38	23.15	28.37	31.08	16.89	17.54	12.03	22.31	14.66
1921	40.75	32.89	40.40	53.58	27.10	17.09	18.41	16.15	27.73
1922	37.69	22.27	30.11	40.63	21.79	21.21	22.69	24.93	18.34
1923	14.14	13.26	11.20	27.37	22.17	28.31	18.13	15.56	22.09
1924	25.90	29.08	22.91	43.88	25.98	29.14	21.49	21.10	26.26
1925	22.94	27.52	26.46	27.02	16.90	20.73	25.97	14.14	26.63

Satara	Belgaum Observatory	Bijapur	Dharwar	Kolaba (Alibag)	Thana (Bassein)	Ratnagiri Observatory	Kanara Observatory
36.30	47.36	13.70	27.84	82.05	82.86	91.17	82.28
43.47	64.26	35.37	37.26	117.42	109.83	137.60	154.56
43.96	51.45	28.95	32.34	80.38	86.53	87.99	111.98
50.28	49.66	25.11	25.81	93.30	90.67	96.89	90.66
37.12	52.25	30.28	29.88	81.17	98.48	85.40	102.99
50.83	64.29	11.03	39.64	113.75	129.05	67.78	99.32
46.61	48.12	28.47	41.24	101.02	95.88	136.16	129.75
35 97	55.37	26.09	41.95	101.48	87.68	118.97	133.75
20.34	30.55	19.07	23.26	44.45	30.76	59.21	72.33
43.47	62.74	13.74	31.21	80.01	57.91	95.92	131.17
37.66	58.05	17.84	34.17	83.39	67.95	79.31	134.49
37.45	52.97	19.05	38.46	80.27	64.05	96.62	151.83
35.30	42.79	29.41	27.84	102.64	88.29	105.69	136.10
21.75	47.53	14.19	26.93	59.30	43.06	96.37	113.12
30.47	28.74	11.60	20.17	46.71	33.34	56.19	88.06
34.87	47.56	23.99	36.53	65.93	55.69	92.06	93.94
47.67	57.71	15.07	36.54	95.18	92.16	80.69	101.57
43.68	56.73	15.01	24.74	70.56	56.01	85.54	138.66
33.88	46.03	18.76	28.53	78.20	85.13	99.30	110.22
44.96	41.74	23.85	27.91	90.96	64.31	86.56	113.58
22.54	42.48	13.59	42.97	55.06	67.02	73.42	80.84
52.02	71.81	13.91	23.09	76.12	65.32	99.91	104.65
31.98	40.90	20.22	25.54	87.52	76.34	72.80	104.94
56.68	86.88	17.90	47.77	100.19	85.69	124.33	152.74
48.01	51.25	28.94	28.99	96.36	68.31	101.61	101.08
38.84	54.87	39.03	36.61	119.67	85.53	152.74	145.22
37.43	49.25	29.67	31.89	118.58	104.46	115.95	135.07
17.27	29.91	9.58	29.75	34.71	43.41	67.78	99.49
34.18	43.84	22.03	37.68	79.37	71.10	92.28	116.04
36.56	44.90	13.69	31.64	44.37	43.95	57.63	83.65
25.07	50.93	17.81	26.59	89.29	99.61	102.15	93.45
45.75	45.65	22.46	30.63	76.63	76.38	100.92	113.61
27.60	57.73	12.17	33.36	91.55	66.73	92.83	128.17
33.16	49.84	14.55	32.58	71.65	74.93	99.16	119.30
26.00	50.30	19.96	37.38	60.79	61.20	75.71	121.04

TABLE A-1 (Continued)

Year	Ahmedabad Observatory	Kaira	Broach	Surat	Khandesh (Erandol)	Nasik	Ahmednagar	Poona	Sholapur Observatory
1926	49.63	45.57	44.33	58.91	28.99	26.60	18.41	30.18	26.33
1927	78.64	68.70	34.63	39.35	25.28	31.86	23.56	25.61	25.41
1928	35.00	26.80	34.99	30.44	29.65	22.97	35.44	23.07	33.15
1929	24.58	23.06	35.30	55.45	20.83	26.38	20.68	20.65	23.99
1930	27.53	37.34	33.20	44.10	28.79	36.15	30.23	31.58	22.17
1931	32.17	31.75	34.78	53.27	44.04	39.50	30.62	23.89	26.06
1932	31.37	28.36	27.34	42.93	19.08	42.19	27.95	30.06	31.95
1933	42.99	42.40	26.31	53.36	31.04	53.84	38.70	36.55	28.00
1934	28.59	36.61	31.00	51.13	38.40	24.82	33.54	21.43	30.01
1935	22.97	21.67	20.68	40.47	20.86	21.53	23.42	23.28	29.43
1936	22.17	20.93	25.04	27.55	29.59	23.78	12.43	18.30	22.20
1937	39.61	34.28	28.47	65.22	19 92	36.12	25.73	30.76	26.84
1938	20.66	17.12	29.03	43.85	43 38	37.01	43.94	37.59	43.96
1939	19.89	19.05	38.79	29.30	24.14	20.74	15.05	17.94	13.74
1940	18.05	17.30	30.96	63.47	25.56	22.41	23.05	25.46	30.46
1941	44.50	56.14	28.04	44.98	21.99	21.12	18.18	20.34	24.13
1942	47.72	40.71	56.63	53.52	35.11	20.50	25.41	29.35	17.47
1943	33.78	41.05	35.72	36.08	25.96	26.71	34.19	35.40	32.17
1944	39.88	31.59	33.78	56.99	37.99	32.52	22.23	28.05	23.11
1945	36.76	33.10	53.05	68.83	27.60	19.25	16.05	22.75	

[a]Blank spaces are years for which no rainfall data could be retrieved for specific districts.

SOURCES· Ahmedabad 1869-1920, Belgaum 1856-1920 — Clayton, *World Weather Records.*

Kaira 1858-1877, 1894-1922, Broach 1894-1922, Surat 1894-1922, Nasik 1866-1879, 1894-1921, Satara 1860-1877, 1894-1922; Dharwar 1894-1921 — Gazetteers and supplements for the appropriate districts.

Kaira 1886-1893, Broach 1886-1893, Surat 1886-1893, Nasik 1891-1893, Satara 1891-1893 Dharwar 1891-1893, Kolaba 1891-1902, Thana 1891-1902, Kanara 1891-1902, Ratnagiri 1891-1902 — *Season and Crop Reports* for the appropriate years.

Satara	Belgaum Observatory	Bijapur	Dharwar	Kolaba (Alibaġ)	Thana (Bassein)	Ratnagiri Observatory	Kanara Observatory
39.28	51.20	16.93	26.62	79.32	85.31	112.79	99.43
42.84	43.85	15.17	32.96	86.08	62.17	98.63	115.89
32.40	45.86	27.02	34.19	89.68	88.62	116.37	151.17
44.69	43.90	25.90	32.83	73.63	55.52	91.94	149.53
55.74	45.70	23.47	30.37	93.10	95.45	96.04	109.70
52.13	55.07	22.97	36.83	100.58	130.28	151.92	145.63
62.43	74.91	28.38	47.38	79.59	83.40	111.56	121.79
49 97	66.58	30.39	46.24	88.78	86.08	123.60	169.82
40.91	50.15	21.83	31.72	113.39	86.43	129.45	113.64
28.14	35.27	23.83	29.18	90.03	73.26	99.31	95.65
31.05	42.65	10.61	20.86	76.43	63.58	109.85	124.58
35.57	57.17	12.51	25.33	73.53	88.41	110.25	112.86
40.41	42 05	31.07	24.76	112.22	90.38	141.41	113.57
34.01	64.74	21.48	24.33	60.94	64.49	125.80	
39.70	51.73	17.21	22.31	98.00	83.34	100.93	
36.17	48.97	19.01	21.85	28.37	45.42	55.39	
48.06	63.79	19.38	21.54	90.85	101.80	112.83	
47.61	58.48	31.82	38.85	83.12	92.12	99.88	
68.38	52.09	21.40	42.58	72.23	84.68	104.76	
41.14	44.35	13.42	23.08	87.13	88.35	95.41	

Kaira 1878-1885, Broach 1878-1885, Surat 1877-1885, Nasik 1880-1890, Satara 1878-1890, Dharwar 1878-1890, Kolaba 1878-1890, Thana 1878-1890, Kanara 1880-1890, Ratnagiri 1877-1890 – Bombay Meteorological Department, *Rainfall Previous to 1891.*

Khandesh 1879-1888 – SRGB N.S. No. 239 (1890); 1889-1918 – SRGB N.S. No. 595 (1923).

Ahmednagar 1869-1938, Poona 1857-1938, Sholapur 1877-1938, Bijapur 1878-1938 – Mann, *Rainfall and Famine.*

All districts, last date given above to 1945 – India Meteorological Department, *Monthly and Annual Rainfall and Number of Rainy Days, period 1901-1950.*

TABLE A-2. Weighted Condition Factors for Major Grain Crops,
1886-1887 to 1919-1920

Year	Ahmedabad	Kaira	Broach	Surat	Khandesh	Nasik
1886-1887	87	97	68	100	114	109
1887-1888	85	104	84	97	109	120
1888-1889	73	87	99	78	93	85
1889-1890	145	100	100	98	102	108
1890-1891	88	99	79	100	92	98
1891-1892	91	98	103	105	117	106
1892-1893	71	84	109	97	103	98
1893-1894	65	100	86	96	105	100
1894-1895	66	92	98	89	96	106
1895-1896	73	75	95	91	93	109
1896-1897	77	46	87	74	47	47
1897-1898	86	96	73	81	111	94
1898-1899	88	89	80	82	94	92
1899-1900	28	36	34	15	19	43
1900-1901	39	71	54	80	87	64
1901-1902	34	46	47	58	62	44
1902-1903	73	81	93	92	94	103
1903-1904	83	66	73	92	69	77
1904-1905	31	35	34	57	62	55
1905-1906	78	64	56	52	74	48
1906-1907	81	73	76	90	79	64
1907-1908	54	33	69	73	39	40
1908-1909	62	54	69	90	68	48
1909-1910	78	83	81	112	84	67
1910-1911	71	77	76	77	88	88
1911-1912	31	25	33	58	57	55
1912-1913	70	84	96	94	64	61
1913-1914	74	93	73	95	98	74
1914-1915	79	84	87	89	88	90
1915-1916	43	31	55	74	101	92
1916-1917	73	99	77	95	89	85
1917-1918	47	48	73	77	81	69
1918-1919	58	21	28	57	47	35
1919-1920	81	83	87	86	102	78

Ahmednagar	Poona	Sholapur	Satara	Belgaum	Bijapur	Dharwar
101	115	92	120	84	111	98
110	117	92	114	103	89	90
80	89	79	77	55	88	73
80	105	81	71	94	110	76
85	103	115	83	83	103	85
71	59	62	57	49	24	40
90	109	85	75	93	63	88
90	99	86	90	89	96	81
84	95	86	84	80	75	74
83	94	63	77	115	75	92
46	34	23	54	38	6	60
59	68	45	84	86	50	75
63	80	76	88	75	72	77
19	45	41	48	38	30	43
41	45	42	54	47	32	57
47	59	55	63	59	35	75
68	73	92	79	73	48	74
63	52	48	87	85	76	85
35	29	47	40	44	32	68
22	34	32	31	45	16	33
49	68	60	77	69	59	72
36	39	38	59	56	50	80
53	44	50	67	54	40	51
65	58	76	71	81	76	73
69	77	72	77	93	83	84
38	40	49	56	48	57	42
33	61	51	82	88	60	85
100	78	38	61	69	59	65
96	66	78	75	78	92	71
93	97	86	88	78	92	90
81	96	77	72	63	67	73
67	79	81	73	67	64	78
43	31	57	50	48	66	45
69	78	77	75	71	90	75

TABLE A-2 (Continued)

Year	Ahmedabad	Kaira	Broach	Surat	Khandesh	Nasik
Five-Year Averages						
1887-1890[a]	98	97	88	93	105	106
1891-1895	76	95	95	97	103	102
1896-1900	70	68	74	69	73	77
1901-1905	52	60	58	76	75	69
1906-1910	71	61	70	83	69	53
1911-1915	65	73	73	83	79	74
1916-1920	60	56	64	78	84	72
1887-1920	70	72	74	82	83	78

[a]Four-year average.

Ahmednagar	Poona	Sholapur	Satara	Belgaum	Bijapur	Dharwar
93	107	86	96	84	100	84
84	93	87	78	79	72	74
54	64	50	70	70	47	69
51	52	57	65	62	45	72
45	49	51	61	61	48	62
67	64	58	70	75	70	69
71	76	76	72	65	76	72
66	71	66	72	71	64	71

SOURCE Computed from acreage statistics and anna-valuation of crop statistics in the *Annual Reports of the Department of Land Records and Agriculture, Bombay Presidency* (title varies) by the formula:

$$WCF = \frac{A_W CF_W + A_R CF_R + A_J CF_J + A_B CF_B}{A_W + A_R + A_J + A_B},$$

where A = acreage for wheat, rice, jowar, and bajra, and CF = condition factor.

TABLE A-3. Index of the Quality of the Agricultural Season,
1886-1887 to 1919-1920[a]

Year	Ahmedabad	Kaira	Broach	Surat	Khandesh	Nasik
1886-1887	156	157	109	135	127	136
1887-1888	142	167	116	127	128	155
1888-1889	127	140	132	94	110	108
1889-1890	254	157	144	132	124	147
1890-1891	147	154	94	131	108	135
1891-1892	158	156	152	142	143	144
1892-1893	144	137	170	146	129	135
1893-1894	122	163	114	124	123	125
1894-1895	122	149	162	126	119	141
1895-1896	110	111	125	128	112	135
1896-1897	109	68	133	90	52	48
1897-1898	136	139	112	116	153	122
1898-1899	129	132	137	117	107	115
1899-1900	13	22	6	15	18	34
1900-1901	47	85	75	97	98	74
1901-1902	40	56	46	69	62	52
1902-1903	101	107	138	121	112	138
1903-1904	104	87	102	119	73	91
1904-1905	32	42	40	60	74	66
1905-1906	94	82	66	57	82	55
1906-1907	105	97	99	110	90	82
1907-1908	64	40	82	75	46	50
1908-1909	83	71	90	110	88	63
1909-1910	110	109	103	137	110	92
1910-1911	83	97	91	88	106	117
1911-1912	19	27	35	53	64	65
1912-1913	84	97	120	101	85	83
1913-1914	82	104	91	93	116	94
1914-1915	104	95	125	94	110	120
1915-1916	51	34	75	81	143	128
1916-1917	111	131	98	101	111	119
1917-1918	70	62	89	74	102	97
1918-1919	37	21	24	50	52	36
1919-1920	111	104	103	84	126	100

Ahmednagar	Poona	Sholapur	Satara	Belgaum	Bijapur	Dharwar
159	176	141	189	125	158	142
174	180	145	179	155	134	132
125	135	129	121	85	139	105
130	158	132	113	147	174	109
138	161	188	132	129	164	124
118	90	103	86	74	41	50
146	171	141	115	147	109	136
139	144	135	130	130	147	115
134	139	135	118	118	117	109
128	137	98	108	147	120	135
57	43	24	70	48	3	81
93	95	69	117	132	82	114
98	110	121	121	117	120	120
24	50	66	60	57	46	60
54	51	54	72	65	51	85
70	79	88	86	88	62	113
106	100	149	108	108	80	108
93	70	69	118	119	114	119
52	38	69	50	60	48	90
27	43	42	40	54	22	42
72	93	86	102	94	97	102
53	52	54	76	75	76	105
84	60	74	84	72	66	67
10i	78	115	91	110	118	99
105	107	106	98	123	128	110
53	46	59	70	60	77	44
46	81	77	102	117	92	106
152	105	44	76	97	100	45
140	90	117	93	104	140	101
147	138	135	111	110	154	130
126	138	117	98	84	98	102
104	112	123	99	88	87	99
44	22	78	65	59	91	57
106	108	116	104	101	147	105

TABLE A-3 (Continued)

Year	Ahmedabad	Kaira	Broach	Surat	Khandesh	Nasik
Five-Year Averages						
1887-1890[a]	170	155	125	122	122	137
1891-1895	139	152	138	134	124	136
1896-1900	97	94	103	93	88	91
1901-1905	65	75	80	93	84	68
1906-1910	91	80	88	98	83	102
1911-1915	74	84	92	86	96	96
1916-1920	76	70	78	78	107	96

[a]For method of calculation, see text of Chapter 2.

Ahmednagar	Poona	Sholapur	Satara	Belgaum	Bijapur	Dharwar
147	162	139	151	128	151	122
135	141	140	116	120	116	107
80	87	76	95	100	74	102
75	68	86	87	88	71	103
67	65	74	79	81	76	83
99	86	81	88	100	107	81
105	104	114	95	88	115	99

[b]Four-year average.

TABLE B-1. Total Population of Bombay Presidency
by Districts and Divisions, 1872-1931 (in thousands)

District and Division	1872	1881	1891	1901	1911	1921	1931
Ahmedabad	832	856	922	796	828	891	1,000
Broach	350	327	341	292	307	308	334
Kaira	783	805	872	716	692	711	742
Panch Mahals	241	255	313	261	323	375	455
Surat	608	614	650	637	654	674	694
Gujarat	2,814	2,857	3,098	2,702	2,804	2,959	3,225
Ahmednagar	777	750	889	838	945	732	988
Khandesh	1,032	1,239	1,437	1,429	1,616	1,718	1,978
Nasik	736	779	842	815	905	833	1,000
Poona	922	902	1,068	995	1,072	1,009	1,170
Satara	1,061	1,061	1,225	1,145	1,081	1,025	1,180
Sholapur	721	584	752	722	768	744	878
Deccan	5,249	5,315	6,213	5,944	6,387	6,061	7,194
Belgaum	946	865	1,012	993	944	953	1,077
Bijapur	807	628	798	737	863	797	869
Dharwar	999	893	1,051	1,113	1,026	1,037	1,103
Karnatak	2,752	2,386	2,861	2,843	2,833	2,787	3,049
Thana[a]	674	725	820	811	882	913	1,016
Kanara	398	422	446	454	431	402	418
Kolaba	524	565	595	606	594	563	629
Ratnagiri	1,019	997	1,106	1,168	1,204	1,154	1,303
Konkan	2,615	2,709	2,967	3,039	3,111	3,032	3,366
Total, British districts	13,430	13,267	15,139	14,528	15,135	14,839	16,834
Bombay City	644	773	822	776	979	1,176	1,161
Grand total	14,074	14,040	15,961	15,304	16,114	16,015	17,995

[a]Bombay Suburban District has been added to Thana throughout.

SOURCES: 1872-1911 – *Census of India*, 1911, vol. 8, pt. 2, Imperial Table II.
1921-1931 – *Census of India*, 1931, vol. 8, pt. 2, Imperial Table II.

TABLE B-2. Male Population of Bombay Presidency
by Districts and Divisions, 1872-1931 (in thousands)

District and Division	1872	1881	1891	1901	1911	1921	1931
Ahmedabad	441	439	473	408	432	476	528
Broach	183	168	175	149	158	159	175
Kaira	419	427	461	376	370	380	396
Panch Mahals	126	131	162	132	166	193	237
Surat	305	306	322	318	327	337	348
Gujarat	1,474	1,471	1,593	1,383	1,453	1,545	1,684
Ahmednagar	398	381	452	418	476	370	501
Khandesh	532	633	733	723	815	871	1,004
Nasik	379	397	431	413	456	424	509
Poona	477	456	545	503	543	517	601
Satara	539	532	613	568	539	511	592
Sholapur	371	296	382	363	391	383	454
Deccan	2,696	2,695	3,156	2,988	3,220	3,076	3,661
Belgaum	484	435	511	502	480	487	552
Bijapur	413	312	399	369	434	406	441
Dharwar	512	447	528	561	521	529	566
Karnatak	1,409	1,194	1,438	1,432	1,435	1,422	1,559
Thana[a]	349	374	428	422	457	478	534
Kanara	206	223	234	236	220	204	214
Kolaba	268	286	299	304	295	280	315
Ratnagiri	491	473	514	548	553	525	609
Konkan	1,314	1,356	1,475	1,510	1,525	1,487	1,672
Total, British districts	6,893	6,716	7,662	7,313	7,633	7,530	8,579
Bombay City	400	465	518	480	640	771	747
Grand total	7,293	7,181	8,180	7,793	8,273	8,301	9,323

[a]Bombay Suburban District has been added to Thana throughout.

SOURCES: 1872-1911 – *Census of India*, 1911, vol. 8, pt. 2, Imperial Table II.
1921-1931 – *Census of India*, 1931, vol. 8, pt. 2, Imperial Table II.

TABLE B-3. Female Population of Bombay Presidency
by Districts and Divisions, 1872-1931 (in thousands)

District and Division	1872	1881	1891	1901	1911	1921	1931
Ahmedabad	392	417	448	388	395	415	472
Broach	168	158	167	143	148	149	159
Kaira	364	378	411	341	322	—331	347
Panch Mahals	114	124	151	129	157	181	218
Surat	303	308	328	319	327	337	345
Gujarat	1,341	1,385	1,505	1,320	1,349	1,413	1,541
Ahmednagar	380	369	437	420	469	362	487
Khandesh	499	606	703	706	800	847	973
Nasik	357	383	410	402	449	408	491
Poona	446	446	522	493	529	492	569
Satara	522	530	612	577	542	514	587
Sholapur	350	288	370	359	377	360	424
Deccan	2,554	2,622	3,054	2,957	3,166	2,983	3,531
Belgaum	462	430	501	491	464	466	524
Bijapur	394	316	399	368	429	391	429
Dharwar	487	446	523	552	505	508	537
Karnatak	1,343	1,192	1,423	1,411	1,398	1,365	1,490
Thana[a]	324	351	392	389	425	434	482
Kanara	192	199	212	218	210	198	204
Kolaba	256	279	296	301	299	283	314
Ratnagiri	528	524	592	620	650	629	693
Konkan	1,300	1,353	1,492	1,528	1,584	1,544	1,693
Total, British districts	6,538	6,552	7,474	7,216	7,497	7,305	8,255
Bombay City	245	308	304	296	339	405	414
Grand total	6,783	6,860	7,778	7,512	7,836	7,710	8,669

[a]Bombay Suburban District has been added to Thana throughout.

SOURCES: 1872-1911 — *Census of India*, 1911, vol. 8, pt. 2, Imperial Table II.
1921-1931 — *Census of India*, 1931, vol. 8, pt. 2, Imperial Table II.

TABLE B-4. Divisors for Correcting Birth and Death Rates for
Changes in Population[a]

Years	Gujarat[b]	Deccan	Karnatak	Konkan
1891-1895	0.9733 (1.0164)	0.9913	0.9988	1.0048
1896-1900	0.9089 (1.0539)	0.9696	0.9958	1.0170
1901-1905	1.0074	1.0146	0.9992	1.0046
1906-1910	1.0262	1.0516	0.9972	1.0162
1911-1915	1.0109	0.9895	0.9968	0.9948
1916-1920	1.0385	0.9635	0.9888	0.9820
1921-1925	1.0174	1.0355	1.0182	1.0213
1926-1930	1.0619	1.1282	1.0649	1.0761

[a]Calculated as the average of the population in years zero and four, divided by the population in year zero (for the first half of the decade); and as the average of the population in years five and nine, divided by the population in year zero (for the second half of the decade). Compound annual growth rates from Table 3.2 have been used to produce intercensal populations.

[b]Figures in parentheses for Gujarat were calculated using population growth rates for 1881-1891.

TABLE B-5. Birth Rates by Divisions, 1891-1930
(number of births per 1,000 population)

Year	Gujarat	Deccan	Karnatak	Konkan
1891	39	42	43	30
1892	34	41	39	31
1893	34	43	41	31
1894	34	41	41	31
1895	35	43	42	30
1896	38	43	40	34
1897	38	37	36	33
1898	37	34	32	28
1899	39	43	39	34
1900	22	29	33	28
1901	25	29	27	25
1902	37	42	31	34
1903	31	38	33	30
1904	39	44	33	33
1905	38	38	34	30
1906	37	41	35	33
1907	37	41	33	30
1908	40	43	38	33
1909	41	42	37	36
1910	41	46	38	36
1911	40	45	40	33
1912	40	41	39	35
1913	39	41	40	35
1914	42	45	41	37
1915	42	44	40	36
1916	44	41	39	33
1917	42	41	41	33
1918	38	37	36	31
1919	35	32	32	25
1920	36	35	36	27
1921	36	36	37	33
1922	35	36	37	35
1923	37	44	39	35
1924	41	41	39	36
1925	40	42	37	33

TABLE B-5 (Continued)

Year	Gujarat	Deccan	Karnatak	Konkan
1926	40	44	41	37
1927	40	45	41	34
1928	39	48	40	37
1929	40	47	41	37
1930	40	47	42	35

SOURCES: 1891-1910 – Calculated from *Census of India*, 1911, vol. 7, pt. 1, pp. 109-111.
1911-1920 – Calculated from *Census of India*, 1921, vol. 8, pt. 1, p. 17.
1921-1930 – Calculated from *Census of India*, 1931, vol. 8, pt. 1, pp. 108-109.

TABLE B-6. Death Rates by Divisions, 1891-1930
(number of deaths per 1,000 population)

Year	Gujarat	Deccan	Karnatak	Konkan
1891	32	31	27	22
1892	40	31	34	25
1893	33	31	26	23
1894	42	38	29	28
1895	27	37	28	25
1896	36	36	29	28
1897	31	51	41	35
1898	30	26	44	24
1899	36	40	39	30
1900	157	66	36	48
1901	45	31	60	28
1902	50	42	48	25
1903	46	49	68	27
1904	48	49	57	31
1905	35	35	31	27
1906	38	39	29	30
1907	39	38	29	27
1908	32	27	25	26
1909	30	29	29	27
1910	33	35	28	27
1911	27	27	48	26
1912	39	43	38	27
1913	31	29	29	24
1914	32	36	31	25
1915	26	30	30	25
1916	34	41	36	26
1917	41	48	50	28
1918	80	109	92	67
1919	33	34	27	36
1920	34	28	30	31
1921	26	29	21	25
1922	24	27	26	23
1923	28	29	30	23
1924	27	33	31	25
1925	25	25	26	23

TABLE B-6 (Continued)

Year	Gujarat	Deccan	Karnatak	Konkan
1926	36	30	30	24
1927	28	29	31	25
1928	30	33	28	25
1929	31	35	34	26
1930	33	36	30	36

SOURCES· 1891-1910 – Calculated from *Census of India*, 1911, vol. 7, pt. 1, pp. 109-111.
1911-1920 – Calculated from *Census of India*, 1921, vol. 8, pt. 1, p. 17.
1921-1920 – Calculated from *Census of India*, 1931, vol. 8, pt. 1, pp. 108-109.

TABLE B-7. Life Table for Ages 0-10

	Males	Females	Total	Percent of Total
Births	100,000	100,000	200,000	100
Survive to age:				
1	79,500	83,600	163,100	82
2	75,400	78,900	154,300	77
3	71,500	74,500	146,000	73
4	67,800	70,300	138,100	69
5	64,300	66,400	130,700	65
6	63,500	65,600	129,100	65
7	62,700	64,800	127,500	64
8	61,900	64,000	125,900	63
9	61,200	63,200	124,400	62
10	60,500	62,400	122,900	62
Number of children ages 0-4 at end of 5 years	358,500	373,700	732,200	73
Number of children ages 5-9 at end of 10 years	668,300	693,700	1,362,000	68
Age-specific death rates, average of 1886-1890				
1	205	172		
1-5	52	56		
5-10	12	12		

SOURCE: Calculated from data in 1891 Census, vol. 7, pt. 1, p. 73, on population figures adjusted for growth, 1881-1891, and using percents in age group from 1891 Census.

TABLE B-8. Population of Divisions by Age and Sex, 1881-1931 (in thousands)

Age	1881 M	1881 F	1891 M	1891 F	1901 M	1901 F	1911 M	1911 F	1921 M	1921 F	1931 M	1931 F
					Gujarat							
0-5	177	177	213	218	126	123	209	210	188	191	223	225
5-10	214	196	223	202	185	173	176	159	231	213	219	196
10-15	188	149	179	137	192	154	146	109	195	156	206	176
15-20	131	110	143	119	139	119	131	106	121	99	156	142
20-40	488	462	529	504	488	473	502	479	488	444	526	473
40-60	225	229	249	253	214	227	240	229	263	243	266	232
> 60	49	64	57	72	37	50	49	57	60	67	55	53
Unspec.	—	—	—	—	1	1	—	—	—	—	1	—
Total[a]	1,472	1,386	1,593	1,505	1,382	1,320	1,454	1,349	1,545	1,413	1,652[c]	1,496[c]
					Deccan							
0-5	349	372	474	506	345	368	462	491	379	405	562	580
5-10	397	379	440	415	434	431	419	408	469	461	489	459
10-15	350	282	351	281	410	346	367	305	401	331	435	402
15-20	192	190	238	238	229	225	247	249	217	211	311	328
20-40	865	865	1,003	991	957	967	1,030	1,039	944	936	1,159	1,114
40-60	420	403	516	469	486	470	539	504	504	473	558	506
> 60	119	130	150	168	127	148	157	170	161	166	148	144
Unspec.	—	—	—	—	2	2	—	—	—	—	—	—
Total	2,694	2,621	3,171[b]	3,067[b]	2,988	2,957	3,221	3,166	3,076	2,984	3,661	3,532

TABLE B-8 (Continued)

Age	1881		1891		1901		1911		1921		1931	
	M	F	M	F	M	F	M	F	M	F	M	F
	Total, All Four Divisions of Bombay Presidency											
0-5	836	872	1,127	1,183	841	879	1,074	1,118	931	977	1,261	1,293
5-10	990	935	1,082	1,020	1,065	1,042	978	949	1,133	1,103	1,147	1,070
10-15	872	709	832	670	995	837	873	729	963	803	1,034	936
15-20	527	492	611	583	599	561	633	604	550	516	745	755
20-40	2,192	2,183	2,462	2,453	2,327	2,360	2,453	2,478	2,349	2,320	2,703	2,613
40-60	1,033	1,032	1,234	1,174	1,190	1,176	1,281	1,229	1,241	1,188	1,330	1,212
> 60	267	328	328	405	291	359	344	391	363	399	324	331
Unspec.	—	—	—	—	4	3	—	—	—	—	1	—
Total	6,716	6,551	7,676	7,487	7,311	7,217	7,635	7,499	7,530	7,306	8,545	8,210

aTotals may not add due to rounding.
bThere is a persistent and unexplained discrepancy between the totals of the age/sex table and the district population totals.
cThe totals of the age and sex tables do not equal the totals of district population because no age and sex figures were collected in Ahmedabad City.

SOURCES: Census of India, 1881, Bombay Presidency, vol. II, p. 25.
1891, vol. 8, pt. 2.
1901, vol. IX-A, pp. 72-74.
1911, vol. 7, pt. 2, pp. 78-80.
1921, vol. 8, pt. 2, pp. 71-73.
1931, vol. 8, pt. 2, pp. 103-105.

Karnatak

Age												
0-5	116	118	224	228	176	183	191	196	178	184	223	226
5-10	164	163	199	193	211	209	169	171	199	198	206	200
10-15	179	154	136	115	206	177	180	157	186	160	191	177
15-20	99	88	113	104	108	95	125	114	101	89	141	134
20-40	407	414	473	478	423	434	449	444	459	432	497	470
40-60	186	193	235	222	245	231	252	236	228	221	241	216
> 60	43	61	59	82	62	83	68	79	72	81	60	66
Unspec.	—	—	—	—	—	—	—	—	—	—	—	—
Total	1,194	1,191	1,438	1,423	1,431	1,411	1,434	1,398	1,422	1,365	1,559	1,490

Konkan

Age												
0-5	194	205	217	231	194	205	211	221	186	197	254	262
5-10	214	197	220	209	234	229	214	211	235	231	233	214
10-15	155	125	166	136	187	161	180	158	182	156	202	181
15-20	105	104	118	122	123	122	130	135	111	117	138	151
20-40	431	442	457	480	459	486	472	515	458	508	520	557
40-60	201	207	234	230	247	248	250	260	245	252	265	258
> 60	56	73	64	83	65	78	69	86	70	84	61	69
Unspec.	—	—	—	—	1	1	—	—	—	—	—	—
Total	1,356	1,353	1,475	1,492	1,510	1,529	1,526	1,585	1,488	1,544	1,672	1,693

Appendix C
Data from Settlement Reports

In Anglo-Indian usage, the verb "to settle" acquired the meaning "to decide how much revenue an area will pay and who will pay it." A *Settlement Report* was one of the products of *settling* a group of villages. In addition to recommending rates of land tax, such a report generally described the climate, access to markets, population, and overall level of prosperity. Depending upon the particular concerns of the officer writing the report, various other kinds of information might be included. A Settlement Report recommended rates for various classes of lands. The village papers produced by the survey and classification process contained the area and class of each field as well as the name of its holder. Over the life of the Bombay Survey and Settlement, reports tended to become more uniform in their inclusion and presentation of information. A report from 1920 is typically a much more bureaucratic document than one from 1850.

In the initial settlements under the Bombay Survey and Settlement, reports generally included revenue histories of the groups of villages for as long as they had been under British rule. These revenue histories were intended to show changes in the cultivation of land and in the revenue paid and to help settlement officers determine what rates of taxation should be imposed under the new settlement. While the statistics on these variables had been collected since the beginning of British rule, they were typically still very much the product of earlier Indian systems. The amount of land "rented" from the government for cultivation generally had not been measured in any very precise way. It was often still reported in Indian units (*bighas*) which varied in size from place to place. Figures on revenues collected did not suffer from the same problems, although there may have been some confusion in village-level records between revenue owed and revenue paid. Small fluctuations (up to five percent) in either lands occupied for cultivation or revenue collected (paid) should probably not, in isolation, be regarded as anything more than a reflection of the random errors in the data. When other information is available (like independent reports of a major famine in 1833 or information that the district collector reduced the rates), such fluctuations may be indicative of real changes.

After the introduction of the Bombay Survey and Settlement into a group of villages, the basis for the statistics improved considerably. A reasonably precise measurement of villages and fields had been completed.[1] Conventions for reporting the disposition of revenue not paid on time were developed. The volume of calculations to be done to aggregate field-by-field data to *taluka* data certainly must have introduced errors, but overall the statistics after the first settlement are better than those before. Their error is probably not more than half that of the earlier figures; it might be as little as one-fifth. Thus, fluctuations in these later series of as little as 1 to 2.5 percent may reflect real changes.

There are several problems with using Settlement Reports to reconstruct portions of the agrarian economic history of Bombay Presidency. The most serious problem is the paucity of *talukas* or parts of *talukas* for which exactly the same villages figure in three successive Settlement Reports (original and two revisions). This paucity makes it impossible to take a random sample of some form from all *talukas* and still have long time series. The inability to use such a sample also limits the strength of generalizations that it is wise to make from the *talukas* that have been included.

Even using other criteria to select *talukas* for closer study, it has not always been possible to achieve uniform coverage for three Settlement Reports. For those cases where the coverage between reports differed by a significant amount, information on the adjustments made is provided in Table C-1. Differences of three or fewer villages have been consistently ignored, and some larger differences in numbers of villages have been ignored when the differences were not reflected in totals for government land occupied and revenue collected. My surmise is that the differences in numbers of villages are due to splitting and/or combination of villages.

[1] See discussion by R. B. Pitt, Acting Deputy Superintendent, Deccan Revenue Survey, for a table of errors found when Erandol *taluka*, Khandesh district was resettled in 1889-1890. Of 8,966 "survey numbers" remeasured, 89 percent differed from the first measurement by less than 5 percent. An additional 6 percent differed from the first measurement by 6-10 percent. SRGB N.S. No. 239 (1890), pp. 1-3.

TABLE C-1. Adjustments for Differing Coverage of Settlement Reports[a]

Taluka	Series [b]	Years Adjusted	Adjustment Factor (multiplicative)	Years Derived from
Badami	GLO	1820-1840	.75	1841-1850
	RC	1820-1840	.66	1841-1850
Kod	GLO	1881-1910	1.35	1879-1882
	RC	1881-1910	1.31	1879-1882
Sampgaon		Data for 106 villages available 1826-1827 to 1843-1844. Data for 109 and 31 villages available 1843-1844 on. Data for 31 villages extrapolated back to 1826-1827 at same level as 1843-1844 to 1848-1849.		
Ahmednagar	GLO	1886-1915	.86	No overlap of series, ratio of 82 villages (first report) to 95 villages (second report) used to adjust.
	RC	1886-1915	.86	
Shevgaon	GLO	1886-1915	.5	No overlap of series, ratio of 80 villages (first report) to 160 villages (second report) used to adjust.
	RC	1886-1915	.5	

[a]Calculated from data in Settlement Reports. Author will furnish original data upon request.

[b]GLO = government lands occupied. RC = revenue collections.

TABLE C-2a. Statistics from Settlement Reports on Government Lands Occupied, Revenue Collections, Collections per Occupied Acre, and Jowar Prices (five-year averages)

Division: Deccan
District Khandesh
Taluka: Amalner
No. of villages· 250-276
Dates of settlements. 1857-1858, 1867-1868, 1887-1888, 1917-1918

Quinquennium	Government Land Occupied (acres)	Revenue Collections (rupees)	Collections per Occupied Acre (rupees)	Jowar Price (rupees per maund)
1815-1820	44,000[a]	94,000[a]	2.14[a]	—
1821-1825	45,000	88,000	1.96	—
1826-1830	48,000	88,000	1.83	—
1831-1835	51,000	90,000	1.76	—
1836-1840	62,000	98,000	1.58	—
1841-1845	58,000	108,000	1.86	—
1846-1850	73,000	123,000	1.68	.45[b]
1851-1855	76,000	133,000	1.75	.64
1856-1860	101,000	144,000	1.43	.83
1861-1865	154,000	189,000	1.23	1.48
1866-1870	201,000	226,000	1.12	1.67
1871-1875	200,000	236,000	1.07	1.57
1876-1880	230,000	240,000	1.04	2.04
1881-1885	238,000	249,000	1.05	1.57
1886-1890	244,000[c]	251,000[c]	1.03[c]	1.84
1891-1895	d	d	d	1.67
1896-1900	—	—	—	2.36
1901-1905	—	—	—	2.37
1906-1910	—	—	—	2.84
1911-1915	—	—	—	3.19
1916-1920	—	—	—	3.33[e]

[a]1818-1819, 1819-1820 only.

[b]1847-1848, 1848-1849, 1849-1850 only.

[c]1885-1886, 1886-1887, 1887-1888 only.

[d]Second revision settlement report does not give year-by-year figures because of smallness of variation. Government land occupied averaged 243,000 acres, revenue collections averaged 327,000 rupees, collections per acre averaged 1.35 rupees.

[e]1915, 1916, 1917 only.

SOURCES SRGB N.S. No. 93 (1865); SRGB N.S. No. 229 (1889), SRGB N.S. No. 585 (1921).

NOTE· Quinquennia in Tables C-2a through C-2ℓ are designated by crop years — e.g., 1815-1820 refers to crop years 1814-1815 to 1819-1820.

TABLE C-2b.

Division: Deccan
District: Khandesh
Taluka: Erandol
No. of villages: 229
Dates of settlements: 1857-1858, 1864-1865, 1889-1890, 1919-1920

Quinquennium	Government Land Occupied (acres)	Revenue Collections (rupees)	Collections per Occupied Acre (rupees)	Jowar Price (rupees per maund)
1815-1820	56,000[a]	145,000[a]	2.59[a]	---
1821-1825	41,000	98,000	2.39	—
1826-1830	39,000	91,000	2.33	—
1831-1835	40,000	90,000	2.25	---
1836-1840	61,000	107,000	1.75	—
1841-1845	56,000	111,000	1.98	—
1846-1850	69,000	121,000	1.75	.50[b]
1851-1855	81,000	137,000	1.69	.70
1856-1860	102,000	138,000	1.35	.80
1861-1865	156,000	180,000	1.15	1.65
1866-1870	190,000	210,000	1.11	1.62
1871-1875	205,000	217,000	1.06	1.73
1876-1880	204,000	217,000	1.06	2.32
1881-1885	211,000	220,000	1.04	1.87
1886-1890	214,000[c]	222,000[c]	1.03[c]	1.99
1891-1895	d	e	e	1.80
1896-1900	---	---	---	2.42
1901-1905	---	---	---	2.44
1906-1910	---	—	---	2.94
1911-1915	---	—	---	3.17
1916-1920	---	—	---	3.20

[a]1818-1819, 1819-1820 only.

[b]1848-1849, 1849-1850 only.

[c]1889-1890 missing.

[d]The second revision settlement report gives no statistics on area occupied. At the end of the first settlement (1888-1889), only 11,700 acres of unoccupied land were reported, so GLO cannot have increased by more than that amount.

[e]The average demand after 1889-1890 was about 250,000 rupees. If we assume that an average of 215,000 acres was occupied, average revenue per acre would have been 1.16 rupees.

SOURCES: SRGB N.S. No. 93 (1865), SRGB N.S. No. 239 (1890); SRGB N.S. No. 595 (1923).

TABLE C-2c.

Division: Deccan
District: Ahmednagar
Taluka · Ahmednagar
No. of villages: 82
Dates of settlements: 1851-1852, 1883-1884, 1915-1916

Quinquennium	Government Land Occupied (acres)	Revenue Collections (rupees)	Collections per Occupied Acre (rupees)	Jowar Price (rupees per maund)
1815-1820	86,000[a]	92,000[a]	1.07[a]	--
1821-1825	96,000	93,000	.97	--
1826-1830	75,000	75,000	1.00	--
1831-1835	74,000	65,000	.88	--
1836-1840	98,000	71,000	.72	—
1841-1845	104,000	85,000	.82	.75
1846-1850	98,000	80,000	.82	1.07
1851-1855	117,000	73,000	.62	.92
1856-1860	166,000	90,000	.54	1.08
1861-1865	168,000	91,000	.54	1.76
1866-1870	181,000	96,000	.53	1.75
1871-1875	180,000	96,000	.53	1.57
1876-1880	176,000	95,000	.54	2.23
1881-1885	173,000[b]	94,000[b]	.54[b]	1.53[c]
1886-1890	178,000	125,000	.70	1.89
1891-1895	180,000	127,000	.71	1.91
1896-1900	180,000	128,000	.71	2.27
1901-1905	180,000	80,000	.44	2.14
1906-1910	180,000	84,000	.47	2.62
1911-1915	178,000	108,000	.61	2.95

[a]1819-1820 only.
[b]1883-1884, 1884-1885 missing.
[c]1883-1884 missing.

SOURCES: SRGB N.S. No. 123(1871); SRGB N.S. No. 167(1885), SRGB N.S. No. 175(1886), SRGB N.S. No. 575(1920).

TABLE C-2d.

Division: Deccan
District· Ahmednagar
Taluka: Shevgaon
No. of villages: 79-81
Dates of settlements· 1851-1852, 1852-1853, 1884-1885, 1913-1914

Quinquennium	*Government Land Occupied (acres)*	*Revenue Collections (rupees)*	*Collections per Occupied Acre (rupees)*	*Jowar Price (rupees per maund)*
1815-1820	47,000[a]	38,000[a]	.81[a]	—
1821-1825	46,000	38,000	.83	—
1826-1830	49,000	42,000	.86	—
1831-1835	43,000	37,000	.86	—
1836-1840	66,000	43,000	.65	—
1841-1845	68,000	47,000	.69	.61
1846-1850	64,000	48,000	.75	.69
1851-1855	75,000	47,000	.63	.76
1856-1860	130,000	63,000	.48	.83
1861-1865	127,000	62,000	.49	1.34
1866-1870	133,000	64,000	.48	1.51
1871-1875	137,000	65,000	.47	1.24
1876-1880	135,000	65,000	.48	2.56
1881-1885	135,000[b]	65,000[b]	.48[b]	1.39[b]
1886-1890	133,000	86,000	.65	2.01
1891-1895	135,000	90,000	.67	1.82
1896-1900	138,000	91,000	.66	2.33
1901-1905	137,000	80,000	.58	2.03
1906-1910	138,000	81,000	.59	2.31
1911-1915	139,000[c]	86,000[d]	.62[c,d]	2.76

[a]1818-1819, 1819-1820 only.
[b]1884-1885 missing.
[c]1913-1914, 1914-1915 missing.
[d]1914-1915 missing.

SOURCES: SRGB N.S. No. 167(1885), SRGB N.S. No. 569(1920).

TABLE C-2e.

Division: Deccan
District. Satara
Taluka · Man
No. of villages· 72
Dates of settlements. 1858-1859, 1889-1890, 1921-1922

Quinquennium	Government Land Occupied (acres)	Revenue Collections (rupees)	Collections per Occupied Acre (rupees)	Jowar Price (rupees per maund)
1846-1850	117,000[a]	44,000[a]	.38[a]	—
1851-1855	121,000	45,000	.37	.79
1856-1860	159,000	48,000	.30	1.08
1861-1865	226,000	61,000	.27	1.80
1866-1870	230,000	61,000	.27	1.86
1871-1875	231,000	62,000	.27	1.56
1876-1880	231,000	61,000	.27	2.72
1881-1885	225,000	61,000	.27	1.59
1886-1890[b]	224,000	60,000	.27	2.17
1891-1895	c	69,000	.31	2.23
1896-1900	--	79,000	.35	2.60
1901-1905	--	70,000	.31	2.14
1906-1910	--	67,000	.30	2.80
1911-1915	--	74,000	.33	3.45
1916-1920	--	79,000	.35	3.67
1921-1925	--	78,000[d]	.35	6.27[d]

[a]1848-1849, 1849-1850 only.

[b]1889-1890 missing.

[c]No acreage figures given in the report, apparently because of the smallness of unoccupied government land at the expiration of the first settlement (3,670 acres). During the next 30 years this decreased to 1,780 acres. The report does include collections per acre after 1890.

[d]1920-1921 only.

SOURCES· SRGB N.S. No. 240(1890), SRGB N.S. No. 634(1929).

TABLE C-2f.

Division   Deccan
District: Satara
Taluka : Khatav
No. of villages: 55-56
Dates of settlements: 1858-1859, 1890-1891, 1921-1922

Quinquennium	Government Land Occupied (acres)	Revenue Collections (rupees)	Collections per Occupied Acre (rupees)	Jowar Price (rupees per maund)
1846-1850	85,000[a]	67,000[a]	.79[a]	.69[a]
1851-1855	84,000	66,000	.79	.58
1856-1860	107,000	68,000	.64	.71
1861-1865	151,000	76,000	.50	1.31
1866-1870	150,000	75,000	.50	1.80
1871-1875	150,000	75,000	.50	1.88
1876-1880	148,000	74,000[b]	.50	2.24
1881-1885	141,000	72,000	.51	1.53
1886-1890	142,000[c]	72,000[c]	.51[c]	2.25
1891-1895	— [d]	86,000	.61	2.31
1896-1900	—	100,000	.70	2.70
1901-1905	--	91,000	.64	2.22
1906-1910	--	91,000	.64	2.94
1911-1915	--	103,000	.72	3.29
1916-1920	--	109,000	.77	3.85

[a]1848-1849, 1849-1850 only.

[b]Average uncollected balance at the end of the year of 21,000 rupees.

[c]1889-1890 missing.

[d]No acreage figures given in the report, apparently because of the smallness of unoccupied government land at the expiration of the first settlement (5,000 acres). During the next 30 years this decreased to 1,575 acres. The report gives collections per acre after 1890.

SOURCES: SRGB N.S. No. 241(1891); SRGB N.S. No. 622(1928).

TABLE C-2g.

Division: Karnatak
District: Belgaum
Taluka . Sampgaon
No. of villages: 137-140
Dates of settlements: 1852-1853, 1853-1854, 1883-1884, 1913-1914

Quinquennium	*Government Land Occupied (acres)*	*Revenue Collections (rupees)*	*Collections per Occupied Acre (rupees)*	*Jowar Price (rupees per maund)*
1826-1830	97,000[a]	149,000[a]	1.54[a]	—
1831-1835	98,000	136,000	1.39	—
1836-1840	97,000	142,000	1.46	—
1841-1845	97,000	129,000	1.33	.91[b]
1846-1850	101,000	160,000	1.58	1.12
1851-1855	114,000	158,000	1.39	1.11
1856-1860	141,000	175,000	1.24	1.24
1861-1865	153,000	186,000	1.22	2.35
1866-1870	158,000	191,000	1.21	1.92
1871-1875	160,000	194,000	1.21	2.04
1876-1880	160,000	195,000	1.22	2.70
1881-1885	159,000	194,000	1.22	1.67[c]
1886-1890	160,000	245,000	1.53	1.86
1891-1895	162,000	252,000	1.56	1.95
1896-1900	162,000	252,000	1.56	2.16
1901-1905	162,000	252,000	1.56	2.21
1906-1910	159,000	250,000	1.57	2.79
1911-1915	160,000[d]	250,000[d]	1.56[d]	2.61[d]

[a]1826-1827, 1827-1828, 1828-1829, 1829-1830 only.

[b]1842-1843, 1843-1844, 1844-1845 only.

[c]1880-1881, 1881-1882, 1882-1883 only.

[d]1910-1911, 1911-1912 only.

SOURCES: SRGB N.S. No. 94 (1865); SRGB N.S. No. 172 (1885), SRGB N.S. No. 553 (1917).

TABLE C-2h.

Division: Karnatak
District· Belgaum
Taluka · Athnı
No. of villages: 64-74
Dates of settlements: 1851-1852, 1852-1853, 1885-1886, 1913-1914

Quinquennıum	Government Land Occupied (acres)	Revenue Collections (rupees)	Collections per Occupied Acre (rupees)	Jowar Price (rupees per maund)
1841-1845	157,000[a]	78,000[a]	.50[a]	---
1846-1850	155,000	76,000	.49	---
1851-1855	155,000	72,000	.46	1.07[b]
1856-1860	194,000	86,000	.44	1.18
1861-1865	223,000	93,000	.42	1.90
1866-1870	242,000	97,000	.40	1.83
1871-1875	245,000	97,000	.40	1.75
1876-1880	243,000	97,000	.40	2.35
1881-1885	235,000[c]	97,000[c]	.41[c]	1.41[d]
1886-1890	249,000	147,000	.59	1.94[e]
1891-1895	255,000	150,000	.59	2.06
1896-1900	257,000	150,000	.58	2.26
1901-1905	257,000	136,000	.53	2.06
1906-1910	257,000	147,000	.57	2.66
1911-1915	257,000[f]	149,000[f]	.58[f]	3.09[g]

[a] 1841-1842, 1842-1843, 1843-1844, 1844-1845 only.
[b] 1851-1852, 1852-1853, 1853-1854, 1854-1855 only.
[c] 1880-1881, 1881-1882 only.
[d] 1880-1881, 1881-1882, 1882-1883 only.
[e] 1889-1890 only
[f] 1910-1911, 1911-1912, 1912-1913 only.
[g] 1910, 1911, 1912, 1913 only.

SOURCES SRGB N.S. No. 181 (1886), SRGB N.S. No. 552 (1917).

TABLE C-2i.

Division: Karnatak
District: Bijapur/Kaladgi
Taluka: Bagalkot
No. of villages: 123-126
Dates of settlements: 1850-1851, 1884-1885, 1913-1914

Quinquennium	Government Land Occupied (acres)	Revenue Collections (rupees)	Collections per Occupied Acre (rupees)	Jowar Price (rupees per maund)
1820[a]	---	99,000	--	--
1821-1825	77,000[b]	99,000	1.29	—
1826-1830	77,000	62,000	.81	—
1831-1835	68,000	58,000	.85	--
1836-1840	69,000	65,000	.94	--
1841-1845	67,000	59,000	.88	—
1846-1850	66,000	52,000	.79	--
1851-1855	77,000	46,000	.60	.65
1856-1860	106,000	63,000	.59	1.03
1861-1865	133,000	77,000	.58	1.42
1866-1870	144,000	81,000	.56	1.45
1871-1875	146,000	82,000	.56	1.41
1876-1880	147,000	82,000[c]	.56	2.65
1881-1885	140,000[d]	82,000[d]	.59[d]	1.32
1886-1890	146,000	97,000	.66	1.81
1891-1895	151,000	103,000	.68	1.80
1896-1900	153,000	103,000	.67	2.00
1901-1905	153,000	103,000	.67	2.55
1906-1910	153,000	103,000	.67	2.50
1911-1915	154,000[e]	103,000	.67	2.79

[a]1819-1820 only.

[b]1824-1825 only.

[c]Actual collections averaged 10,000 rupees less than this figure.

[d]1880-1881, 1881-1882, 1884-1885 only.

[e]1910-1911, 1911-1912, 1912-1913 only.

SOURCES· SRGB No. 5(1853), SRGB N.S. No. 176(1886), SRGB N.S. No. 564(1920).

TABLE C-2j.

Division· Karnatak
District: Bıjapur/Kaladgı
Taluka: Badami
No. of villages· 129-140
Dates of settlements: 1850-1851, 1885-1886, 1913-1914

Quinquennium	Government Land Occupied (acres)	Revenue Collections (rupees)	Collections per Occupied Acre (rupees)	Jowar Price (rupees per maund)
1815-1820	--	43,000[a]	--	--
1821-1825	55,000[b]	42,000	.76	--
1826-1830	60,000	36,000	.60	--
1831-1835	57,000	38,000	.67	--
1836-1840	59,000	44,000	.75	--
1841-1845	55,000	43,000	.78	--
1846-1850	54,000	42,000	.78	.63
1851-1855	68,000	38,000	.56	.80
1856-1860	88,000	49,000	.56	1.03
1861-1865	105,000	57,000	.54	1.45
1866-1870	111,000	58,000	.52	1.25
1871-1875	111,000	58,000	.52	1.48
1876-1880	105,000	56,000[c]	.53	1.87
1881-1885	85,000[d]	47,000[d]	.55[d]	1.28
1886-1890	108,000	65,000	.60	1.50
1891-1895	116,000	71,000	61	1.63
1896-1900	120,000	72,000	.60	1.92
1901-1905	121,000	62,000	.51	2.13
1906-1910	121,000	69,000	.57	2.56
1911-1915	123,000	72,000	.59	2.58

[a]1818-1819, 1819-1820 only.

[b]1823-1824, 1824-1825 only.

[c]Actual collections averaged 10,000 rupees less than this figure.

[d]1880-1881, 1881-1882, 1882-1883 only.

SOURCES: SRGB NO. 5(1853); SRGB N.S. No. 213(1887); SRGB N.S. No. 179(1886), SRGB N.S. No. 560(1919).

TABLE C-2k.

Division: Karnatak
District: Dharwar
Taluka: Kod
No. of villages: 245
Dates of settlement: 1848-1849, 1879-1880, 1908-1909

Quinquennium	Government Land Occupied (acres)	Revenue Collections (rupees)	Collections per Occupied Acre (rupees)	Jowar Price (rupees per maund)
1821-1825	—	93,000	—	.33
1826-1830	54,000	89,000	1.65	.33
1831-1835	52,000	68,000	1.31	.52
1836-1840	54,000	69,000	1.28	.41
1841-1845	49,000	82,000	1.67	.34
1846-1850	46,000	66,000	1.43	.26
1851-1855	85,000	84,000	.99	.26
1856-1860	120,000	111,000	.93	.35
1861-1865	163,000	143,000	.88	1.27
1866-1870	179,000	155,000	.87	1.12
1871-1875	169,000	149,000	.88	1.03
1876-1880	170,000	163,000	.96	1.61
1881-1885	167,000	185,000	1.11	.91
1886-1890	180,000	199,000	1.11	1.05
1891-1895	183,000	202,000	1.10	1.47
1896-1900	186,000	206,000	1.11	1.71
1901-1905	188,000	207,000	1.10	1.76
1906-1910[a]	189,000	185,000	.98	2.39

[a]1905-1906, 1906-1907, 1907-1908 only.

SOURCES· SRGB No. 12 (1853); SRGB N.S. No. 160 (1883); SRGB N.S. No. 515 (1912).

TABLE C-2ℓ.

Division: Karnatak
District: Dharwar
Taluka· Ron
No. of villages: 20
Dates of settlement· 1850-1851, 1885-1886, 1903-1904

Quinquennium	Government Land Occupied (acres)	Revenue Collections (rupees)	Collections per Occupied Acre (rupees)	Jowar Price (rupees per maund)
1841-1845	25,000	25,000	1.00	.80[a]
1846-1850	24,000	22,000	.92	.84
1851-1855	37,000	23,000	.62	.70
1856-1860	55,000	35,000	.64	1.06
1861-1865	61,000	39,000	.64	1.14
1866-1870	61,000	39,000	.64	1.00
1871-1875	61,000	39,000	.64	1.40
1876-1880	62,000	40,000	.65	1.95
1881-1885	63,000[b]	41,000[b]	.65[b]	1.04
1886-1890	63,000	54,000	.86	1.52[c]
1891-1895	63,000	54,000	.86	1.66
1896-1900	63,000	54,000	.86	1.98
1901-1905[d]	63,000	54,000	.86	2.50

[a]1845 only.
[b]1883-1884, 1884-1885 missing.
[c]1887, 1888 missing.
[d]1900-1901, 1901-1902, 1902-1903, 1903-1904 only.
SOURCES: SRGB N.S. No. 179 (1886); SRGB N.S. No. 213 (1887); SRGB N.S. No. 472 (1908).

Appendix D
Agricultural Statistics

Sources and Quality of Agricultural Statistics

The government of India first began attempting to have its regional administrative units collect and publish agricultural data in 1866. The orders issued that year required the provincial and presidency governments to publish, among other things, tables of area cultivated and uncultivated, crops cultivated, agricultural stock, and prices of produce, as appendices to the annual administrative reports. Two governments (Punjab and Central Provinces) began publishing these tables in 1867-1868; two more (Bombay Presidency and Berar) followed in 1871-1872; Madras Presidency began in 1874-1875. The two other major units (Bengal Presidency and the Northwest Provinces and Oudh) published no statistics until 1893-1894 and 1885-1886, respectively.

In 1884 the government of India modified the tables, introduced a new sub-table on irrigation, compiled the returns of the different administrative units, and began publishing them as *Returns of Agricultural Statistics of British India*. This publication does not include any totals for the administrative units but rather presents their separate figures side by side. In 1891 there was a further revision of the tables so that total acreage, classification of areas (including irrigation), area under crops, and stock all appeared in one table. In 1894-1895 the table on prices of produce was discontinued. The general form of the tables remained unaltered through the 1920s. All of these data were collected for districts (the basic administrative unit) and for a large variety of crops, although the crop list was altered from time to time.

It is not possible to say much about the reliability of these data as a whole. *Returns of Agricultural Statistics of British India* provides no information on how the numbers were collected. For such information it is necessary to consider each province or presidency separately. Because of the early date at which most of Bombay Presidency came under British control (1818), it is possible by using unpublished materials in the India Office Library (London) and the

Secretariat Record Office (Bombay) to extend the agricultural data back at least fifteen years before the published data begin.

1854-1855 to 1870-1871

The statistics for this period are found in the *Annual Reports of Settlement and Survey, Supplementary Statement of Cultivation,* forwarded from the division commissioners to the government of Bombay and then to London. The reports are now bound in *Collections to Revenue Despatches to Bombay.* There are three main problems with these statistics. (1) Many of the districts had been initially settled in the 1820s and some survey work had been done. In the early 1840s a complete cadastral survey of the Presidency was begun. Where that survey was incomplete or not yet begun in 1854-1855, the area, both total and that planted with specific crops, is reported in *bighas* or in *bighas* and acres. As the survey teams progressed from year to year, more and more of the total area was reported in acres. In general, the data in acres should be more reliable than that in *bighas*, since the figures were the product of the survey. *Bighas* were not uniform throughout the Presidency; sometimes there is doubt that they were uniform even throughout a district. (2) This period probably had more boundary changes between administrative units than any other period. These changes make district-level data particularly difficult to retrieve, although they do not generally affect the divisional totals. (3) There does not appear to have been a standard form for reporting areas planted with different crops. As a result, the headings under which crops were reported varied from division to division and from year to year. Most of the time major crops were reported separately, but a wide variety of other uses of land seems to have been episodically lumped into "other." One of the more troublesome "lumpings" includes fallows or occupied waste, making it impossible to get an accurate figure on area *cropped* for some years.

1871-1872 to 1882-1883

Bombay first attempted to publish unified agricultural statistics in 1871-1872. In theory, the village accountant filled out a form (which he had to draw up himself after a model in Hope's *Manual of Revenue Accounts*) giving for each field the acreage planted to different crops and the yield in *maunds* (1 *maund* = 82 pounds). He tallied the acreage over all fields, subtracted double-cropped land, and reported on a host of other variables. The accountant had available to him, wherever the survey had been completed, a register of fields giving the area of each. The accountant's reports were sent to *taluka* headquarters, where the *taluka* report was compiled and forwarded to district headquarters. From the district level, reports were assembled into divisional reports titled Huzoor Form 17-H (from 1876-1877 on). This form was printed as part of the *Annual Report on the Revenue Settlement of the Collectorates of the Northern (Southern, Central) Division.* The figures published in *Bombay Administration Reports* (from 1876-1877 on) were drawn from Huzoor Form 17-H.

From 1871-1872 through 1875-1876 the data contained in the *Bombay Administrative Reports* vary from year to year with respect to crops listed and the amount of information given on double-cropping and fallows. The assembly of the Presidency report from those of the collectorates was rendered more difficult by the presence at the lower levels of reports in the Gujarati, Marathi, and Kannada languages. As a result, the same crop sometimes appears twice in the published report—once as *ragi* and a second time as *natchni* or *nagli.* The equivalence of the terms went unnoticed in the Bombay office and the published statistics lead the unwary to believe that there are two crops rather strangely present in some districts and not in others. A classification scheme for all agricultural produce was prescribed by the Secretary of State for India in 1875, and this was presumably responsible for the change in the form of statistics in 1875-1876. However, consistency in format did not immediately reach down to the level of the village accountant.

In 1879, in an attempt to achieve greater reliability and uniformity in the village accounts' reports upon which all else rested, the three divisional commissioners and the survey and settlement commissioner proposed some reforms in Village Form #16. They made up a list of all crops grown in the Presidency with English, botanical, Gujarati, Marathi, and Kannada names. This list and the Secretary of State's classification of crops were then used to make up and print forms for the village accountant in which each crop had a place. The commissioners hoped that this would eliminate the "lumping" of a variety of crops under "other" in the interests of saving space and would avoid confusion about what to call a crop. This list was completed and sanctioned for use in the village forms in 1883.

These changes over the period mean that there is an increase in the number of crops (or even groups of crops, like oilseeds and pulses) for which separate data are available. This would seem to be an improvement, but it creates a problem. If one is attempting to use a classification like "foodgrains, pulses, oilseeds, cotton, other," it will appear that the acreage planted with foodgrains, pulses, and oilseeds is increasing over time while the percentage of land planted with "other" declines. One suspects, however, that in fact minor foodgrains, pulses, and oilseeds were being rescued from the oblivion of "other" by improvements in reporting. This occurred even before the improved Village Form #16 was sanctioned and distributed, because district and divisional clerks, who had previously been as inclined as the village accountant to save space by lumping crops into "other," appear to have stopped doing so as demands from above for better agricultural statistics filtered down.

1883-1884 to 1919-1920

The government of Bombay next asked the commissioners to arrange to include "alienated" lands and villages in the annual agricultural reports. Alienated land was land which did not pay full revenue to the government directly, and up to this time it had not been reported in the village accountant's papers. The lands thenceforth to be included fell into three categories: (1) land in government villages which was alienated; (2) land which was alienated but which had been surveyed; and (3) alienated land which had not been surveyed. Inclusion of the first category required only that some additional fields be added to the accountant's roster of fields on which crop statistics were to be compiled. Inclusion of the second class of lands required that some person or persons be found to fulfill the reporting functions of the nonexistent revenue staff. The third class of lands had first to be surveyed before crops could be accurately reported (rather than just estimated).

The inclusion of alienated lands introduces a major discontinuity into the time series one would like to be able to construct. There do not appear to be any published records of the amount of land newly included each year, although there are some reports for 1885-1886 in which land in each district was disaggregated by the form in which a given village was predominantly held (*ryotwari*, other government, alienated). But these reports appeared too late to see the process of increase in coverage and in any case can shed no light on lands which were within villages already reporting.

How the problems have been dealt with

Bighas have been converted to acres on the basis of the best data available. The "total" series used throughout is "gross sown acres plus current fallows," because it is the series most consistently available. Data for years before the inclusion of alienated lands into the agricultural reporting system have been multiplied by some factor to produce consistent series. It would be nice to be able to say that these factors were derived in some highly scientific fashion. They were not: they are my best guesses after examining all the data.

TABLE D-1. Acreages Planted with Selected Crops — Gujarat (five-year averages in thousands of acres)

Quinquennium	Rice	Wheat	Jowar	Bajra	Total Foodgrains and Pulses	Cotton	Oilseeds	Gross Sown Area	Current Fallows	GSA and CF[a]	Double-Cropped	Net Cropped[b]
1856-1860	185	223	271	265	1,120	296	52	1,698	222	1,920	NA	NA
1861-1865	222	198	414	357	1,478	396	73	2,041	364	2,405	NA	NA
1866-1870	282	265	536	457	1,901	512	106	2,606	477	3,084	NA	NA
1871-1875	324	283	509	508	1,926	503	47	3,017	408	3,426	106	2,908
1876-1880	271	369	579	451	2,331	473	118	2,974	739	3,713	130	2,845
1881-1885	369	388	509	399	2,357	580	123	3,134	799	3,935	170	2,965
1886-1890	358	328	686	482	2,620	699	132	3,529	1,010	4,538	161	3,367
1891-1895	393	353	706	488	2,769	668	146	3,683	962	4,645	182	3,499
1896-1900	331	246	582	343	2,258	511	111	2,963	1,459	4,421	142	2,821
1901-1905	188	214	666	470	2,091	570	171	2,906	1,452	4,357	81	2,825
1906-1910	265	233	631	443	2,220	748	162	3,203	1,218	4,422	101	3,103
1911-1915	277	185	606	394	2,012	731	128	3,021	1,474	4,495	147	2,874
1916-1920[c]	241	203	740	422	2,134	923	108	3,969	889	4,857	196	3,773

[a]Sum of gross sown area and current fallows.

[b]Gross sown area less double-cropped acreage.

[c]Approximately 250,000 to 300,000 acres of the increase in gross sown area and decline in current fallows is attributable to a reclassification of grasslands from fallows to crops.

NA = not available.

SOURCE: See text of Appendix D.

TABLE D-2. Acreages Planted with Selected Crops – Deccan (five-year averages in thousands of acres)

Quinquennium	Rice	Wheat	Jowar	Bajra	Total Foodgrains and Pulses	Cotton	Oilseeds	Gross Sown Area	Current Fallows	GSA and CFa	Double-Cropped	Net Croppedb
1856-1860	133	815	4,139	2,939	8,902	341	594	NA	NA	11,424	NA	NA
1861-1865	250	1,016	4,702	3,329	10,201	606	718	NA	NA	13,923	NA	NA
1866-1870	274	1,095	4,713	4,776	11,738	696	648	NA	NA	16,048	NA	NA
1871-1875	152	722	4,233	3,870	9,894	660	285	12,298	1,563	13,860	93	12,205
1876-1880	167	627	3,241	4,080	9,590	683	749	11,262	1,742	13,004	128	11,135
1881-1885	218	950	3,754	3,719	10,491	990	976	12,695	1,887	14,583	169	12,529
1886-1890	201	1,181	4,330	3,609	11,240	973	1,120	13,609	2,156	15,764	273	13,335
1891-1895	220	1,055	4,242	3,712	11,344	1,197	1,127	13,968	2,023	15,991	325	13,644
1896-1900	217	672	4,107	3,257	10,135	1,091	1,009	12,517	3,583	16,101	363	12,154
1901-1905	203	642	3,707	3,765	10,220	1,345	957	12,782	3,393	16,175	368	12,415
1906-1910	228	548	3,451	4,003	10,350	1,611	877	13,121	3,344	16,463	308	12,812
1911-1915	243	664	3,485	3,909	10,255	1,791	746	13,396	3,268	16,663	405	12,991
1916-1920	276	741	4,388	3,214	10,468	1,602	510	14,082	3,033	17,115	436	13,644

aSum of gross sown area and current fallows.

bGross sown area less double-cropped acreage.

NA = not available.

SOURCE: See text of Appendix D.

TABLE D-3. Acreages Planted with Selected Crops – Karnatak (five-year averages in thousands of acres)

Quinquennium	Rice	Wheat	Jowar	Bajra	Total Foodgrains and Pulses	Cotton	Oilseeds	Gross Sown Area	Current Fallows	GSA and CFa	Double-Cropped	Net Croppedb
1856-1860	183	295	1,614	164	2,702	455	214	NA	NA	4,066	NA	NA
1861-1865	245	426	2,928	437	4,439	991	166	NA	NA	7,074	NA	NA
1866-1870	243	296	2,818	450	4,051	885	84	NA	NA	6,461	NA	NA
1871-1875	236	430	2,980	442	4,371	859	136	6,129	494	6,622	39	6,091
1876-1880	237	206	2,420	406	3,999	659	169	4,952	1,650	6,602	117	4,837
1881-1885	249	470	2,787	347	4,691	1,003	310	6,137	931	7,067	135	6,000
1886-1890	269	549	2,712	443	4,996	985	361	6,499	935	7,435	83	6,417
1891-1895	276	507	2,815	455	5,063	946	364	6,550	1,067	7,616	75	6,473
1896-1900	283	462	2,622	380	4,711	810	328	6,011	1,698	7,709	89	5,919
1901-1905	271	462	2,628	616	4,961	1,125	310	6,498	1,226	7,723	81	6,416
1906-1910	260	429	2,438	582	4,688	1,301	284	6,442	1,324	7,766	77	6,365
1911-1915	263	437	2,455	561	4,620	1,500	203	6,601	1,192	7,793	64	6,538
1916-1920	265	566	2,596	360	4,667	1,451	158	6,784	1,068	7,851	64	6,720

aSum of gross sown area and current fallows.

bGross sown area less double-cropped acreage.

NA = not available.

SOURCE: See text of Appendix D.

TABLE D-4. Acreages Planted with Selected Crops – Totals for Gujarat, Deccan, and Karnatak (five-year averages in thousands of acres)

Quinquennium	Rice	Wheat	Jowar	Bajra	Total Foodgrains and Pulses	Cotton	Oilseeds	Gross Sown Area	Current Fallows	GSA and CFa	Double-Cropped	Net Croppedb
1856-1860	501	1,333	6,024	3,368	12,724	1,092	860	NA	NA	17,410	NA	NA
1861-1865	717	1,640	8,044	4,123	16,118	1,993	957	NA	NA	23,402	NA	NA
1866-1870	799	1,656	8,067	5,683	17,690	2,093	738	NA	NA	25,593	NA	NA
1871-1875	712	1,435	7,722	4,820	16,191	2,022	468	21,444	2,465	23,909	238	21,204
1876-1880	675	1,202	6,240	4,937	15,920	1,815	1,036	19,188	4,131	23,319	375	18,817
1881-1885	836	1,808	7,050	4,465	17,539	2,573	1,409	21,966	3,617	25,583	474	21,494
1886-1890	828	2,058	7,728	4,534	18,856	2,657	1,613	23,637	4,100	27,737	517	23,119
1891-1895	889	1,915	7,763	4,655	19,176	2,811	1,637	24,201	4,052	28,253	582	23,616
1896-1900	831	1,380	7,311	3,980	17,104	2,412	1,448	21,491	6,740	28,231	594	20,894
1901-1905	662	1,318	7,001	4,851	17,272	3,040	1,438	22,186	6,071	28,257	530	21,656
1906-1910	753	1,210	6,520	5,028	17,258	3,660	1,323	22,766	5,886	28,652	486	22,280
1911-1915	783	1,286	6,546	4,864	16,887	4,022	1,077	23,018	5,934	28,952	625	22,394
1916-1920	782	1,510	7,724	3,996	17,269	3,976	776	24,835	4,990	29,824	425	24,407

aSum of gross sown area and current fallows.
bGross sown area less double-cropped acreage.

NA = not available.

SOURCE: See text of Appendix D.

Bibliography

Government Documents

Bombay Presidency

Selections from the Records of the Bombay Government (abbreviated as SRGB)

Old Series

Report by Captain Wingate, Revenue Survey Commissioner, on the plan of survey and assessment most suitable to the province of Khandesh and also the instructions issued on the subject by government. No. 1, Bombay, 1852.

Report on the Village Communities of the Deccan with especial reference to the claims of the village officers in the Ahmednugger Collectorate to "Purbhara huks," or remuneration from their villages independent of what they receive from Government. By Mr. R. N. Gooddine, No. 4, Bombay, 1852. (*Gooddine's Report.*)

Report explanatory of the revised agreement introduced into the talukas of Badamee and Bagalkote in the Belgaum Collectorate. By Captain Wingate. No. 5, Bombay, 1853.

Report on the revenue survey settlements of the Hoobullee, Nuwulgoond, Kode, and Dharwar Talookas of the Dharwar Collectorate. By Captain G. Wingate. No. 12, Bombay, 1853.

New Series (N.S.)

Papers relative to the introduction of the revised rates of assessment into eight talookas and two pettas of the Khandesh Collectorate. N.S. No. 93, Bombay, 1865.

Papers relative to the introduction of revised rates of assessment into parts of the Uthnee Talooka, the Tasgaum and Sumpgaum Talookas, and Part of the Padshapoor Talooka all of the Belgaum Collectorate with an appendix bringing up the revenue history of these districts to 1864-65. N.S. No. 94, Bombay, 1865.

Papers relating to the revisions of assessment in six talookas of the Ahmednugger Collectorate. N.S. No. 123, Bombay, 1871.

Papers relating to the revision of the rates of assessment on the expiration of the first settlement in the Old Kod Taluka of the Dharwar Collectorate. N.S. No. 160, Bombay, 1883.

Papers relating to the revision of the rates of assessment on the expiration of the first settlement in the old Miskakota Mahalkaris Division of the Old Hubli (now Kalghatgi) Taluka of the Dharwar Collectorate. N.S. No. 162, Bombay, 1883.

Papers relating to the revision of the rates of assessment on the expiration of the first settlement in the Shevgaon Taluka of the Ahmednagar Collectorate. N.S. No. 167, Bombay, 1885.

Papers relating to the revisions of the rates of assessment on the expiration of the first settlement of 140 villages of the Sampgaon Taluka of the Belgaum Collectorate. N.S. No. 172, Bombay, 1885.

Papers relating to the revision of the rates of assessment on the expiration of the first settlement in the Nagar Taluka of the Ahmednagar Collectorate. N.S. No. 175, Bombay, 1886.

Papers relating to the revision of the rates of assessment on the expiration of the first settlement on 126 villages in the Old Bagalkot Taluka of the Bijapur Collectorate. N.S. No. 176, Bombay, 1886.

Papers relating to the revision survey settlement of 149 villages of the Old Badami Taluka of the Bijapur Collectorate. N.S. No. 179, Bombay, 1886.

Papers relating to the revision of the rates of assessment on the expiration of the first settlement in the Old Athni Taluka of the Belgaum Collectorate. N.S. No. 181, Bombay, 1886.

Papers relating to the revision survey settlement of 7 villages of the Ron Taluka of the Dharwar district and 8 villages of the Badami Taluka, Bijapur District. N.S. No. 213, Bombay, 1887.

Papers relating to the revision survey settlement of 275½ government villages of the Amalner Taluka of the Khandesh Collectorate. N.S. No. 229, Bombay, 1889.

Papers relating to the revision survey settlement of 277 villages of the Erandol Taluka of the Khandesh Collectorate. N.S. No. 239, Bombay, 1890.

Papers relating to the revision survey settlement of 72 government villages of the Man Taluka of the Satara Collectorate. N.S. No. 240, Bombay, 1890.

Papers relating to the revision survey of 55 government villages of the Khatav Taluka of the Satara Collectorate. N.S. No. 241, Bombay, 1891.

Papers relating to the revision survey settlement of the Nevasa Taluka of the Ahmednagar Collectorate. N.S. No. 260, Bombay, 1892.

Papers relating to the second revision survey settlement of the Navalgund and Ron Talukas of the Dharwar Collectorate. N.S. No. 472, Bombay, 1908.

Papers relating to the second revision settlement of the Kod Taluka of the Dharwar Collectorate. N.S. No. 515, Bombay, 1912.

Papers relating to the second revision settlement of the Athni Taluka of the Belgaum Collectorate. N.S. No. 552, Bombay, 1917.

Papers relating to the second revision settlement of the Sampgaon Taluka of the Belgaum Collectorate. N.S. No. 553, Bombay, 1917.

Papers relating to the second revision settlement of the Badami Taluka of the Bijapur Collectorate. N.S. No. 560, Bombay, 1919.

Papers relating to the second revision settlement of the Bagalkot Taluka including Bilgi Petta of the Bijapur Collectorate. N.S. No. 564, Bombay, 1920.

Papers relating to the second revision settlement of the Shevgaon Taluka including the Pathardi Mahal of the Ahmednagar Collectorate. N.S. No. 569, Bombay, 1920.

Papers relating to the second revision survey of the Nagar Taluka of the Ahmednagar Collectorate. N.S. No. 575, Bombay, 1920.

Papers relating to the second revision settlement of the Amalner and Parol Talukas of the East Khandesh District. N.S. No. 585, Bombay, 1921.

Papers relating to the second revision settlement of the Erandol Taluka of the East Khandesh District. N.S. No. 595, Bombay, 1923.

Papers relating to the second revision settlement of the Khatav Taluka of the Satara District. N.S. No. 622, Bombay, 1928.

Papers relating to the second revision survey of the Man Taluka of the Satara District. N.S. No. 634, Bombay, 1929.

Irrigation Series

A paper on irrigation in the Deccan and Southern Maratha Country. By Colonel Playfair, R.E., Superintending Engineer for Irrigation. No. 5, Bombay, 1866.

Serials

Annual Report of the Director of Agriculture.
Annual Report of the Sanitary Commissioner for the Government of Bombay. Title changed, 1926, to *Annual Report of the Director of Public Health for the Government of Bombay.*
Quarterly Returns of Railborne Trade of Bombay Presidency.
Season and Crop Reports.

Miscellaneous

Gazetteer of the Bombay Presidency. 22 vols. and supplements. 1879.
Official Correspondence on the System of Revenue Survey and Assessment Best Adapted for, and more or less completely carried into effect in the Collectorates of Poona, Sholapur, Ahmednugger, Belgaon, and Dharwar, in the Bombay Presidency with an appendix consisting of a prior correspondence, in which the plan of operation then in force, which did not materially differ from that above, is discussed with reference to that followed in the North-West Provinces. (Joint Report.) Bombay: Education Society's Press, 1850. Revised ed., 1859.
A Report Exhibiting a View of the Fiscal Judicial System of Administration introduced into the conquered territory above the Ghauts under the Authority of the Commissioner of the Dekhan. By William Chaplin of the Madras Civil Service, Commissioner of the Dekhan. (*Chaplin's Report.*) Bombay: Government Press, 1824. Reprinted, 1838.
A Statement and remarks relating to the expenses of irrigation from wells in the Deccan, Khandesh, &c. By Meadows Taylor [Philip Meadows]. Bombay: Education Society's Press, 1856.
Statistical Atlas of Bombay Presidency. 2nd. ed. Bombay: Government Central Press, 1906.
Statistical Report on the Pergunnahs of Padshapoor, Belgam, Kalaniddee and Chandgurh, Khanapoor, Bagalkot and Badamy, and Hoondgoond in the Southern Mahratta Country. By the late Thomas Marshall. (*Marshall's Report.*) Bombay, 1822.
The Bombay Survey and Settlement Manual. 2 vols. and supplement. By R. G. Gordon. Bombay: Government Central Press, vols. 1. and 2, 1917; supplement, 1922.

The Survey and Settlement Manual. 3 vols. Bombay: Government Central Press, vol. 1, 1882; vols. 2 and 3, 1902.

Department of Land Revenue and Agriculture, *Dates of Sowing and Harvesting Important Crops in the Bombay Presidency.* Bombay: Government Central Press, 1904.

Meteorological Office, *Rainfall of the Bombay Presidency for Years Previous to 1891.* 6 vols. Bombay: Government Central Press, 1910-1922.

Unpublished documents

Famine Relief Code, 1885.
Famine Relief Code, 1896.
Famine Relief Code, 1900.
"Mortality from the Famine of 1877 in the Bombay Presidency." Minute by the Governor of Bombay, dated 20 August 1878. In *Proceedings of the Public Works Department.* L/PWD/3/580. India Office Library.
"Note on the Census Taken in January 1878 of Certain Talukas Within the Area Affected by Famine in 1876 and 1877." In *Proceedings of the Public Works Department.* L/PWD/3/580.
Report on the History of the Late Famine in the Southern Division, 1891-1892.
Report on the Famine in Bombay Presidency, 1899-1902.
Report on the Famine in Bombay Presidency, 1905-1906.
Report on the Famine in Bombay Presidency, 1911-1912.
Report on the Famine in Bombay Presidency, 1912-1913.
Review of the Famine Administration in Bombay Presidency, 1918-1919.
Revenue Proceedings, Famine, 1897-1919. India Office Library.

Madras Presidency

Review of the Madras Famine, 1876-78. Madras: Government Press, 1881.

India

Commissioner of the Census, *Census of India.* 1872, 1881, 1891, 1901, 1911, 1921, 1931.

Famine Commission, *Report of the Indian Famine Commission, 1898.* 7 vols. Simla: Government Printing Office, 1898.

India Meteorological Department, *Monthly and Annual Rainfall and Number of Rainy Days, period 1901-1950.* Nasik: Government of India Press, 1965-1970.

Revenue and Agriculture Department, *Papers connected with the Bombay Revenue and Settlement System.* Calcutta: Office of the Superintendent of Government Printing, 1883.

Sanitary Commissioner, *Annual Report of the Sanitary Commissioner with the Government of India.*

Great Britain

Parliament. *Parliamentary Papers*, 1901. Cmnd. 876. "Report of the Indian Famine Commission, 1901, and Papers Relating thereto."

United States

U.S. Congress, Senate. *U.S. and World Food Situation, Hearings before the Subcommittee on Agricultural Production, Marketing, and Stabilization of Prices and Subcommittee on Foreign Agricultural Policy of the Committee on Agriculture and Forestry.* 93rd Cong., 1st sess., 1973.

Books and Articles

Baier, Stephen. "Economic History and Economic Development: Drought and the Sahelian Economies of Niger." *African Economic History* 1 (no. 1, 1976):1-16.

———. "Long-Term Structural Change in the Economy of Central Niger." In *West African Culture Dynamics*, pp. 587-602. Edited by B. K. Swarz and R. E. Dummet. The Hague: Mouton, 1980.

Baier, Stephen, and Lovejoy, Paul E. "The Tuareg of the Central Sudan: Gradations of Servility at the Desert Edge (Niger and Nigeria)." In *Slavery in Africa*, pp. 391-411. Edited by Suzanne Miers and Igor Kopytoff. Madison: University of Wisconsin Press, 1977.

Ballhatchet, Kenneth. *Social Policy and Social Change in Western India, 1817-1830*. London: Oxford University Press, 1957.

Bennett, M. K. "Famine," In *International Encyclopedia of the Social Sciences*, vol. 5, pp. 322-326. Edited by David L. Sills. [New York:] Macmillan & Free Press, 1968.

Bhatia, B. M. *Famines in India 1860-1965: A Study in Some Aspects of the Economic History of India*. 2nd ed. New York: Asia Publishing House, 1967.

Boserup, Ester. *The Conditions of Agricultural Growth*. Chicago: Aldine, 1965.

Bryson, Reid A. and Murray, Thomas J. *Climates of Hunger*. Madison: University of Wisconsin Press, 1977.

Caldwell, John C. *The Sahelian Drought and Its Demographic Implications*. Washington, D.C.: Overseas Liaison Committee, American Council on Education, 1975.

Catanach, I. J. *Rural Credit in Western India, 1875-1930*. Berkeley and Los Angeles: University of California Press, 1970.

Choksey, R. D. *Economic Life in the Bombay Gujarat 1880-1939*. Bombay: Asia Publishing House, 1968.

Clayton, H. Helm. *World Weather Records*, Smithsonian Miscellaneous Collections, no. 79. Washington, D.C.: Smithsonian Institution, 1944.

Das, P. K. *The Monsoon*. 2nd ed. New York: St. Martins Press, 1972.

Davis, Kingsley. *The Population of India and Pakistan*. Princeton: Princeton University Press, 1951.

Dewey, Clive J. "The Government of India's 'New Industrial Policy' 1900-1925: Formation and Failure." In *Economy and Society: Essays in Indian Economic and Social History*, pp. 215-257. Edited by K. N. Chaudhuri and Clive J. Dewey. Delhi: Oxford University Press, 1979.

Dutt, Romesh. *The Economic History of India:* Vol. 1, *Under Early British Rule;* Vol. 2, *In the Victorian Age*. First Indian edition, with a critical introduction by Prof. D. R. Gadgil. Delhi: Publications Division, Ministry of Information and Broadcasting, Government of India, 1960 (original publication, London: Kegan Paul, Trench, Trübner, 1902-1904).

Easterlin, Richard A. "An Economic Framework for Fertility Analysis." *Studies in Family Planning* 6 (March 1975):54-63.

Elvin, Mark. *The Pattern of the Chinese Past*. Stanford: Stanford University Press, 1973.

Fenoaltea, Stefano. "Authority, Efficiency, and Agricultural Organization in Medieval England and Beyond: A Hypothesis." *Journal of Economic History* 35 (June 1975):693-718.

———. "Fenoaltea on Open Fields: A Reply." *Explorations in Economic History* 14 (October 1977):405-410.

———. "The Rise and Fall of a Theoretical Model: the Manorial System." *Journal of Economic History* 35 (December 1975):386-409.

———. "Risk, Transaction Costs, and the Organization of Medieval Agriculture." *Explorations in Economic History* 13 (April 1976):129-151.

Frisch, Rose. "Population, Food Intake, and Fertility." *Science* 199 (January 6, 1978):22-29.

Fukazawa, H. "Land and Peasants in the Eighteenth Century Maratha Kingdom." *Hitotsubashi Journal of Economics* 6 (June 1965):32-61.

———. "A Note on the Corvée System (*Vethbegar*) in the 18th Century Maratha Kingdom." *Hitotsubashi Journal of Economics* 11 (February 1971):1-10.

———. "Rural Servants in the 18th Century Maharashtrian Village—Demiurgic or Jajmani System?" *Hitotsubashi Journal of Economics* 12 (February 1972):14-40.

Gadgil, D. R. *The Industrial Evolution of India in Recent Times 1860-1939.* 5th ed. Bombay: Oxford University Press, 1971.

Gopalan, C., and Naidu, A. Nadamuni. "Nutrition and Fertility." *Lancet* 2 (November 18, 1972):1077-1078.

Gordon, Stewart N. "Recovery from Adversity in Eighteenth Century India: Rethinking 'Villages,' 'Peasants,' and Politics in Pre-Modern Kingdoms." *Peasant Studies* 8 (Fall 1979):61-82.

———. "The Slow Conquest: Administrative Integration of Malwa into the Maratha Empire, 1720-1760." *Modern Asian Studies* 11 (February 1977):1-40.

Greenough, Paul R. "Indian Famines and Peasant Victims: The Case of Bengal in 1943-44." *Modern Asian Studies* 14 (April 1980):205-235.

———. "The Ultimate Insurance Mechanism: Patterned Domestic Break-Up during the Bengal Famine, 1943-44." Paper presented at a Workshop on the Effects of Risk and Uncertainty on Economic and Social Processes in South Asia. University of Pennsylvania, 1977.

Habib, Irfan. *The Agrarian System of Mughal India (1556-1707).* New York: Asia Publishing House, 1963.

————. "Colonization of the Indian Economy, 1757-1900." *Social Scientist* 3 (March 1975):23-53.

Harnetty, Peter. "Cotton Exports and Indian Agriculture, 1861-1870." *Economic History Review* (series 2) 24 (August 1971):414-429.

Heston, Alan. "A Further Critique of Historical Yields Per Acre in India." *Indian Economic and Social History Review* 15 (April-June 1978):187-210.

————. "Official Yields Per Acre in India, 1886-1947: Some Questions of Interpretation." *Indian Economic and Social History Review* 10 (December 1973):303-332.

Ho, Ping-ti. "Early Ripening Rice in Chinese History." *Economic History Review* (series 2) 9 (no. 2, 1956):200-218.

————. *Studies on the Population of China, 1368-1953.* Cambridge: Harvard University Press, 1959.

Hoffman, Richard C. "Medieval Origins of the Common Fields." In *European Peasants and Their Markets: Essays in Agrarian Economic History*, pp. 23-71. Edited by William N. Parker and Eric L. Jones. Princeton: Princeton University Press, 1975.

Hsiao, Kung Chuan. *Rural China: Imperial Control in the Nineteenth Century.* Seattle: University of Washington Press, 1960.

Hurd, John II. "Railways and the Expansion of Markets in India, 1861-1921." *Explorations in Economic History* 12 (July 1975): 263-288.

Inden, Ronald. "Ritual, Authority, and Cyclic Time in Hindu Kingship." Mimeo. June 1976.

Jodha, N. S. "Effectiveness of Farmers' Adjustments to Risk." Paper presented at a Workshop on the Effects of Risk and Uncertainty on Economic and Social Processes in South Asia. University of Pennsylvania, 1977.

————. "Famine and Famine Policies: Some Empirical Evidence." *Economic and Political Weekly* 10 (October 11, 1975):1609-1623.

Jones, E. L. *The Development of English Agriculture 1815-1873.* London: Macmillan, 1968.

Kahan, Arcadius. "Natural Calamities and Their Effect Upon the Food Supply in Russia (an Introduction to a Catalogue)." *Jahrbucher für Geschichte Ost-europas* Neue Folge 16 (September 1968):353-377.

Kessinger, Tom G. *Vilyatpur, 1848-1968: Social and Economic Change in a North Indian Village.* Berkeley and Los Angeles: University of California Press, 1974.

Krishna, Raj. "Farm Supply Response in India-Pakistan: A Case Study of the Punjab Region." *Economic Journal* 63 (September 1963):477-487.

Kulkarni, A. R. "Village Life in the Deccan in the 17th Century." *Indian Economic and Social History Review* 4 (March 1967):38-52.

Kumar, Dharma. *Land and Caste in South India: Agricultural Labour in Madras Presidency during the Nineteenth Century.* Cambridge: Cambridge University Press, 1965.

Kumar, Ravinder. "The Rise of Rich Peasants in Western India." In *Soundings in Modern South Asian History*, pp. 25-58. Edited by D. A. Low. Berkeley and Los Angeles: University of California Press, 1968.

————. "Rural Life in Western India on the Eve of the British Conquest." *Indian Economic and Social History Review* 2 (July 1965):201-220.

————. *Western India in the Nineteenth Century: A Study in the Social History of Maharashtra.* London: Routledge and Kegan Paul, 1968.

Langer, William. "American Foods and Europe's Population Growth 1750-1850." *Journal of Social History* 8 (Winter 1975):51-60.

Lucas, H. S. "The Great European Famine of 1315, 1316, and 1317." *Speculum* 5 (October 1930):343-377.

Ludden, David. "Ecological Zones and the Cultural Economy of Irrigation in Southern Tamilnadu." *South Asia* (NS) 1 (March 1978):1-13.

————. "Patronage and Irrigation in Tamil Nadu: A Long Term View." *Indian Economic and Social History Review* 16 (July-September 1979):347-365.

Mandelbaum, David G. *Society in India,* 2 vols. Berkeley and Los Angeles: University of California Press, 1970.

Mann, H. H. *Rainfall and Famine: A Study of Rainfall in the Bombay Deccan, 1865-1938.* Bombay: Indian Society of Agricultural Economics, 1955.

————, and Kanitkar, N. V. *Land and Labour in a Deccan Village.* Bombay: Oxford University Press, 1921.

Mayer, A. C. *Caste and Kinship in Central India.* Berkeley and Los Angeles: University of California Press, 1970.

McAlpin, Michelle Burge. "The Effects of Markets on Rural Income Distribution in Nineteenth Century India." *Explorations in Economic History* 12 (July 1975):289-302.

———. "The Impact of Railroads on Agriculture in India, 1860-1900: A Case Study of Cotton Cultivation." Ph.D. dissertation, University of Wisconsin-Madison, 1973.

———. "The Impact of Trade on Agricultural Development: Bombay Presidency 1855-1920." *Explorations in Economic History* 17 (January 1980):26-47.

———. "Price Movements and Fluctuations in Economic Activity, 1860-1947." In *The Cambridge Economic History of India*, vol. 2, pp. 878-904. Edited by Dharma Kumar. Cambridge: Cambridge University Press, 1982

———. "Railroads, Cultivation Patterns, and Foodgrain Availability: India 1860-1900." *Indian Economic and Social History Review* 12 (January-March 1975):43-60.

———. "Railroads, Prices, and Peasant Rationality: India 1860-1900." *Journal of Economic History* 34 (September 1974):662-684.

McCloskey, Donald N. "The Enclosure of Open Fields: Preface to a Study of Its Impact on the Efficiency of English Agriculture in the Eighteenth Century." *Journal of Economic History* 32 (March 1972):15-35.

———. "English Open Fields as Behavior Towards Risk." In *Research in Economic History*, vol. 1, pp. 124-170. Edited by Paul Uselding. Greenwich, Conn.: JAI Press, 1976.

———. "Fenoaltea on Open Fields: A Comment." *Explorations in Economic History* 14 (October 1977):402-404.

McKeown, Thomas. *The Modern Rise of Population.* New York: Academic Press, 1976.

Moreland, W. H. *From Akbar to Aurangzeb: A Study in Indian Economic History.* Reprint ed. New Delhi: Oriental Books Reprint Corporation, 1972 (originally published in 1923).

———. *India at the Death of Akbar.* Delhi: Atma Ram & Sons, 1962.

Morris, Morris David. "Development of Modern Industry to 1947." In *The Cambridge Economic History of India*, vol. 2. Edited by Dharma Kumar. Cambridge: Cambridge University Press, 1982.

———. "Economic Change and Agriculture in Nineteenth Century India." *Indian Economic and Social History Review* 3 (June 1966):185-209.

———. *The Emergence of an Industrial Labor Force in India: A Study of the Bombay Cotton Mills, 1854-1947.* Berkeley and Los Angeles: University of California Press, 1965.

———. "What Is a Famine?" *Economic and Political Weekly* 9 (November 2, 1974):1855-1864.

Morris, Morris David, and Dudley, Clyde B. "Selected Railway Statistics for the Indian Subcontinent (India, Pakistan, and Bangla Desh) 1853-1946/47." *Artha Vijnana* 17 (September 1975):187-298.

———; Matsui, Toro; Chandra, Bipan; and Raychudhuri, T. *Indian Economy in the Nineteenth Century: A Symposium*. Delhi: Indian Economic and Social History Review, Delhi School of Economics, 1969.

Mukherjee, S. B. *The Age Distribution of the Indian Population*. Honolulu: East-West Center, 1976.

Narain, Dharm. *Impact of Price Movements on Areas under Selected Crops in India 1900-1939*. Cambridge: Cambridge University Press, 1965.

Pearson, Michael N. *Merchants and Rulers in Gujarat*. Berkeley and Los Angeles: University of California Press, 1976.

Post, John D. "Famine, Mortality, and Epidemic Disease in the Process of Modernization." *Economic History Review* (series 2) 39 (February 1976):14-37.

———. *The Last Great Subsistence Crisis in the Western World*. Baltimore: Johns Hopkins University Press, 1977.

Robbins, Richard G., Jr. *Famine in Russia, 1891-1892: The Imperial Government Responds to a Crisis*. New York: Columbia University Press, 1975.

Roumasset, James. *Rice and Risk*. Amsterdam: North-Holland, 1976.

Sanyal, Nalinaksha. *Development of Indian Railways*. Calcutta: University of Calcutta Press, 1930.

Schlesinger, Lee I. "Agriculture and Community in Maharashtra, India." In *Research in Economic Anthropology*, vol. 4, pp. 233-247. Edited by George Dalton. Greenwich, Conn.: JAI Press, 1981.

Sen, A. K. "Starvation and Exchange Entitlements: A General Approach and Its Applications to the Great Bengal Famine." *Cambridge Journal of Economics* 1 (March 1977):33-59.

Spate, O.H.K. *India and Pakistan, A General and Regional Geography*. 2nd ed. London: Methuen & Co., 1957.

Stokes, Eric. *The English Utilitarians and India*. Oxford: Clarendon Press, 1959.

Thirsk, Joan, ed. *The Agrarian History of England and Wales*. Vol. IV: 1500-1640. Cambridge: Cambridge University Press, 1967.

Tilly, Charles. "Food Supply and Public Order in Modern Europe." In *The Formation of National States in Western Europe*, pp.

380-455. Edited by Charles Tilly. Princeton: Princeton University Press, 1975.

Waldron, Ingrid. "Why Do Women Live Longer than Men?" *Social Science and Medicine* 10 (nos. 7-8, 1976):349-362.

Walford, Cornelius. "The Famines of the World: Past and Present." *Journal of the Royal Statistical Society* 41 (September 1878): 433-526; 42 (March 1879):79-265.

Whitcombe, Elizabeth. *Agrarian Conditions in Northern India, vol. 1: The United Provinces under British Rule, 1860-1900.* Berkeley and Los Angeles: University of California Press, 1972.

White, Theodore H., and Jacoby, Annalee. *Thunder Out of China.* New York: William Sloane, 1946.

Wilson, H. H. *A Glossary of Judicial and Revenue Terms.* 2nd ed. Delhi: Munshiram Manoharlal Oriental Publishers and Booksellers, 1968.

Wiser, William H. *The Hindu Jajmani System: A Socio-Economic System of Interrelating Members of a Hindu Village Community in Services.* Lucknow: Lucknow Publishing House, 1936.

Wittwer, S. H. "Food Production: Technology and the Resource Base." In *Food: Politics, Economics, Nutrition, and Research*, pp. 85-90. Edited by Philip H. Abelson. Washington, D.C.: American Association for the Advancement of Science, 1975.

Woodham-Smith, Cecil. *The Great Hunger: Ireland 1845-49.* New York: Harper and Row, 1962.

Index

Library of Congress Cataloging in Publication Data

McAlpin, Michelle Burge, 1945-
  Subject to famine.

  Bibliography: p.
  Includes index.
  1. India—Famines—History—19th century.   2. India—Famines—History—20th century.   I. Title.
  HC439.M39   1983   338'.1'9547   82-61376
  ISBN 0-691-05385-5